NANNY
KNOWS BEST

FROM MARY POPPINS TO SUPERNANNY

NANNY KNOWS BEST

THE HISTORY OF THE BRITISH NANNY

KATHERINE HOLDEN

This book is dedicated to my dearest aunt, Ursula Holden, who first inspired me to start researching and writing about nannies.

First published 2013

The History Press
The Mill, Brimscombe Port
Stroud, Gloucestershire, GL5 2QG
www.thehistorypress.co.uk

© Katherine Holden, 2013

The right of Katherine Holden to be identified as the Author
of this work has been asserted in accordance with the
Copyright, Designs and Patents Act 1988.

British Library Cataloguing in Publication Data.
A catalogue record for this book is available from the British Library.

ISBN 978 0 7524 6174 8

Typesetting and origination by The History Press
Printed in Great Britain

CONTENTS

AUTHOR'S NOTE

The roots of this book are long and dense. They can be traced in the first place to a desire to make sense of my own history and to understand why, as a single woman in my early sixties with no children of my own, I still had an abiding interest in other people's children. This interest began during my teenage years when I became involved in the care of babies and young children belonging to a succession of single mothers who came to live with my family as lodgers or mothers' helps. These young women were there to help my mother in the house, and the idea that they might have needed a nanny for their own children never entered anyone's head. The help I gave these incomers was inexpert, unpaid and intermittent: rocking a baby to sleep, bathing, dressing and changing nappies. In the absence of the mother and with no one else around to consult, I once asked a 2-year-old child how to fold its terry towelling nappy and where to place the safety pins! Yet it offered me a role as assistant to and occasionally temporary replacement for a mother, a position which became increasingly familiar as I grew up and my friends began to have children and I did not.

My frustrations about not having children came to a head in my late thirties when I took a class in feminist theory. After several weeks of a seemingly excessive focus on motherhood, I asked the tutor if we might focus on women who were not mothers. Her response was to encourage me to write an essay on single women, a subject she correctly predicted

7

I would soon take much further. Its final incarnation was a book, *The Shadow of Marriage: Single Women in England 1914–1960*, published seventeen years later, by which time my prospects of becoming a mother had vanished. As I interviewed women who had never married for this project I was struck by how often single women during the early and mid-twentieth centuries became involved with children, professionally and personally, and I began to see them as an invisible support system to families. I have since discovered that this point had been made in a much more generalised way by anthropologist Sarah Blaffer Hrdy, who believes that a species with young as dependent as human children could not have evolved without access to what she calls 'alloparents' – individuals other than the genetic parents who helped care for them.[1] In early and mid-twentieth century Britain, many of those individuals were single women.

It was not only nannies who interested me at that point, although a surprisingly high number of the single women I interviewed had been nannies or mothers' helps at some time in their lives. In doing this research, I encountered an army of other women who had spent their lives looking after children as aunts, midwives, matrons, teachers, foster and adoptive mothers, and social workers. Some of these women saw the job of supporting mothers to bring up children as hugely important, giving colour and meaning to their lives. Others ended up in these occupations by default because few other choices were available. But, however much or little they loved the work, all of them faced the challenge of looking after other people's children without the status and authority of being a mother.

The decision to narrow my focus to nannies, rather than including other child-related occupations, was made partly because not much has been written about them. But I also had a more personal reason: both my parents both came from colonial families and had been brought up by nannies. My mother, the eldest daughter of a missionary, had Indian nurses known as ayahs for the first eight years of her life. My father and his four sisters, children of a civil servant who worked abroad in Egypt, were cared for by nannies and, later, a nursery governess who took full charge when their mother was away.

My relatives recalled their experiences in different ways. My mother remembered that her younger sister Noreen had learned their ayah's language, Marathi, before she knew any English, and the older children had to translate so that their parents could understand her. Although Noreen left India at the age of 6 and never saw her ayah again, the bond between them was never entirely broken. Many years later, when my grandparents made a return visit to India, the ayah gave them bangles for Noreen's future children, a gift for the little girl she had loved and lost.

My father had no memory of his nanny, who left when he was 2 or 3 years old, but his older sister Ursula remembered being smacked by her and all the nanny's attention being focused on my father, 'the treasured boy'. My father characterised their governess, Miss Caryer, as a rather rigid, prudish spinster who insisted that they say 'rhubarb oranges' rather than 'blood oranges', while Ursula remembered her as calm and loving. Both siblings stressed the importance of the continuity she gave them through a childhood of agonising parental departures. Ursula deeply regretted that Miss Caryer had never known how much she owed her.

Although I never had a nanny, these stories fitted into an imagined world of middle-class children already familiar from my childhood reading: the warm comforting Nana in Noel Streatfield's *Ballet Shoes* who never left her charges, and the magical Mary Poppins who was always coming and going. But what struck me most about my aunts' and parents' tales was that the relationships they had with their nannies and governess were not recognised as important. These women were being paid to look after the children and had at some point to leave them. Any attachments that were formed were inevitably affected by the contracts (whether or not these were written down) that the carers held with my grandparents. I could see the potential for tension in these arrangements in Ursula's adult writings. Haunted by the governess, nanny and servants who dominated her young life, her 1980s novel *Tin Toys* replays the petty struggles and rivalries in her childhood household, observed from the perspective of an 8-year-old child:

> Nurse's complexion went darker, she narrowed her dark-lidded eyes. She felt her position and Maggie knew it. Nurse should be running the house not Gov who wasn't a relation and very old. Nurse despised Maggie for being a servant and lowly born. For her part Maggie pitied Nurse, an aunt by marriage without status or love. No relative would get such treatment in her country. No wonder Nurse was so sulky.[2]

I wondered about the longer-term legacy of this kind of upbringing, not just for Ursula, my parents and their contemporaries but also my own generation's post-Second World War childhood when traditional nannies were much rarer. One clue seemed to lie in my father's belief in the importance of infant attachment, unknown in his own parents' time: the idea that a child needs one secure and permanent mother or mother figure during the first few years of life. This theory was developed by John Bowlby, with whom my father worked as a psychiatrist and psychoanalyst at the Tavistock Clinic in London during the 1960s. Bowlby and most other analysts of his generation had been brought up by nannies and, though direct connections with their own pasts were rarely made, it seemed to me that their focus on a child's relationship with the mother, to the exclusion of others in the family, must be linked partly to their own experiences. The ideas of Bowlby and the equally well-known paediatrician Donald Winnicott about the importance of mothers were widely publicised after the Second World War. Were their theories, which they applied to all classes of mothers, rooted in their own upbringing by what sociologist Cameron Macdonald has called shadow mothers? These were women who devoted their lives to caring for children, but who always took second place to the mother and who might all too easily leave.[3]

For a short period I too became a shadow mother. In 1971, at the age of 19, I took a job as a mother's help caring for two young children in a large house in North London. When I met my employer Gill again many years later I discovered she had been brought up by a trained nanny in the early 1940s, at the time when Bowlby was first developing his theories. Gill had disliked her nanny, who had left the family when she was 3 or 4 years old, but her strongest memory was of a profound shock when the woman who had looked after her since birth suddenly disappeared. Gill's childhood experiences had led her to a rather different pattern of nanny employment with her own children. Determined that she should remain at the centre of her children's lives, Gill tried to ensure her children would not grow too attached to their carers, and selected young women who would not stay too long. She also worked from home and made sure her helpers did things her way.

I was in my gap year between school and university and did not want to get closely involved with Gill and her family. Although I had a six-month contract, I only intended to stay for three months, not wanting to miss a family holiday. Despite Gill's good intentions, her childcare system could not protect her children entirely from pain. Most of the day-to-day care of the children was undertaken by her helpers. If they woke in the night, I would soothe them, and it was I, not their mother, who usually greeted them when they woke in the morning. Three months was long enough for Gill's 1-year-old daughter to become attached to me; I found out afterwards that she had been quite disturbed for a while after I left. I knew why she was upset (after all, I'd been brought up with Bowlby's *Childcare and the Growth of Love*) but, rather than empathising with the child's distress, I felt pleased that she appeared to have loved me as much as her mother and saw it as a marker of my success as a mother's help.

My experience with Gill's family also gave me an insight into the day-to-day routines of a nanny's work. These were dictated partly by the physical layout of the house. Before the Second World War, nannies traditionally occupied an uncomfortable middle ground between family and servant, but even in the more egalitarian 1970s, household space could be segregated. The house I worked in was over four floors with a family kitchen in the basement, which in former times would have been the preserve of servants. I had meals and mixed with the family there, but spent little time on the middle floors. With their elegant furniture, the drawing room and dining room on the ground floor were the domain of Gill and her husband. Here Gill worked and entertained, while the floor above contained their bedroom and a spare room for guests. I had my own bedroom, a day off each week and time off in the afternoons, but I still often felt lonely, spending much of my time with the children in the garden or in their rooms next to mine on the top floor. And while the physical work of childcare was much lighter in the 1970s than earlier in the century, I experienced the boredom and fatigue of day-to-day childcare, carrying the baby up and down long flights of stairs and pushing a pram up those long Hampstead hills. Unlike many pre-Second World War nannies, my background was similar to that of my employers, but this did not make the boundaries between us easier to manage. Gill made efforts to include me and her other helpers in evening meals and conversation, but she often longed for time alone with her husband.

Remembering my time as a mother's help and hearing my relatives' memories of their nannies spurred me to look more closely at the dynamics of nanny employment. And what seemed most important to explore were the differing needs and interests of mother, nanny, and child, and the often unspoken conflicts that might help to explain the silence that surrounds this kind of work. There is a pervasive view in our society that a mother should be everything to her child. Coupled with the mother's power to hire and fire help, this belief made it hard for Gill to assign an equal but different status to her child's relationship with a paid carer, or recognise its importance. I wanted to know how mothers as well as nannies and children managed these relationships, how they felt about them, and whose interests took priority.

The powerful but often unacknowledged feelings I encountered lie at the heart of this book. Nannies were both insiders and outsiders in families, and the odd and ambivalent position they occupied had an effect on many people's lives. Those affected stretched far beyond my own family. They included women of all classes and many different cultures and ethnicities, and families of very different shapes, sizes, and backgrounds in twentieth-century Britain. By listening to the voices of children, nannies and mothers whose lives were intertwined in this way in the past, I hope that more light will be shed on the dilemmas families face in caring for children today.

ABBREVIATIONS

GMRO: Greater Manchester Record Office
HRO: Hertfordshire Record Office
IOWRO: Isle of Wight Record Office
LMA: London Metropolitan Archive
NCA: Norland College Archive, Bath
NCUMC: The National Council for the Unmarried Mother and her
  Child
PC: Princess Christian
SSUS: Sussex University Special Collections
WLAM: Wellcome Library, Archives and Manuscripts
WTS: Wellgarth Training School

1

INTRODUCTION
HIDDEN LIVES

Jimmy put the light out
When you go to bed.
Jimmy put the light out, or you'll get a head-
<u>Ache</u> that will remind you
That you shouldn't read in bed.

This piece of doggerel verse, addressed to my grandmother, who was nicknamed 'Jimmy',[1] was composed by a prominent politician sometime in 1914–15. It was written on the back of a printed thank-you card and discovered by my aunt among her mother's possessions after she died in the 1970s. As one of the very few documents she had kept from that period of her life, it was a tantalising find. Jimmy was an attractive young woman in her early twenties working as an under-nanny. She only stayed with the politician's family for six months and never said much about the job. Although she had done two years' training at the prestigious Norland College, this was her only post, and the explanation given to her daughters was that she didn't want to spend her time pushing prams.

Why, then, did she keep the card? It was probably attached to a book and kept as a reminder of the present she received from a famous man who may simply have known that she loved reading. Yet the language and tone of the verse suggests that nanny and father could have had closer contact. Going to bed and putting the light out were hardly appropriate suggestions

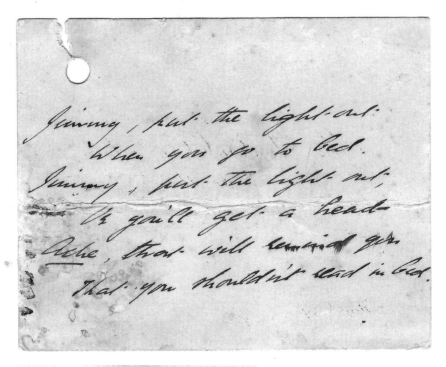

Jimmy, put the light out
When you go to bed.
Jimmy, put the light out,
Or you'll get a head-
Ache, that will remind you
That you shouldn't read in bed.

'Jimmy put the light out'.

'Jimmy': my grandmother, Belle Jameson, in 1918.

for a man in his position to make to a young lady of her background who was also his employee. The underlining of the word ache on the card might have simply been adding emphasis in a rhyme, but might also suggest that he was missing her or believed she was missing him. Could it be that an illicit flirtation, if not a full-blown affair, had taken place? It was customary for husbands and wives of this class to have separate bedrooms. The fact that this man knew that his nanny read late into the night indicates that he may have visited her room on the floor above, easily accessible yet conveniently out of his wife's view.

It was not uncommon for upper- and middle-class men to have sexual liaisons with servants, who were usually dismissed if they were found out or became pregnant.[2] But, as the daughter of a Northern Irish protestant minister, my grandmother would not have thought of herself as a servant. The shame of discovery would have been too much to bear, and she might have fled before things went too far. Intrigued by the card, I visited the politician's family archive to see if I could find out more. Letters written to him by his wife gave glimpses of my grandmother playing happily on the beach with his son, giving no indication that anything was wrong. But her sudden disappearance from the household not long afterwards suggests the wife may have discovered or suspected something was amiss but chose not to reveal it, at least in writing.

What makes this story so compelling is the fact that my grandmother kept the card throughout her life and did not show it to anyone. Whether or not my interpretation is entirely correct, her behaviour shows that any attraction between her and her employer (whether mutual or not, and even if only at the level of fantasy) was forbidden; it could never have been openly admitted by either party. The card, therefore, is a small but important clue to the hidden lives of nannies and to the powerful but often unacknowledged feelings of love and loss that lie at the heart of this book.

The fact that love and loss are so significant in a book about the history of a particular type of childcare needs further explanation. We can begin to see why this is the case by thinking about the wider resonances of my grandmother's story, particularly for upper- and middle-class families. The story is about class: her love of reading was a sign of her education; it gave her employer an easy opportunity to breach the barriers between them and exploit her feelings. It is also about family secrets, marital betrayal and, possibly, unrequited love. And it is about work which could be tiring and demeaning (pushing prams) but also rewarding (playing with a child on the beach). Above all, it is about relationships that provoke strong emotional responses yet have never been part of the main family story in Britain, being deemed much less important than those between husband and wife or mother and child.

Nannies' apparent lack of importance in families may be one reason why, despite the ubiquity of figures like Supernanny and Mary Poppins, few histories of nannies have been written. The last major study, Jonathan Gathorne Hardy's *The Rise and Fall of the British Nanny*, was first published more than forty years ago. As both an elegy for the golden days of nannies and an exposure of nanny abuse, Gathorne Hardy's findings are compelling, but warrant further investigation and updating. His story is also part of my own. My initial purpose in writing this book was to find out why nannies have so often been glorified and demonised, even though we know so little about them, and to discover what lies behind their remarkable longevity in the British imagination.

The period I write about, from the end of Queen Victoria's reign in 1901 to the early 1980s, is separated from our own by more than thirty years, and the personal and domestic service traditions in which nanny employment was embedded seem today, in some ways, like a distant memory. Yet there is much in this book that will resonate with families today. The triangular relationship of mother, nanny and child at the centre of the book is still with us, and much of what I will reveal has relevance for hard-pressed mothers seeking the best kind of care for their children. For example, the relief mothers may feel about delegating the care of their children so that they can get on with their own lives is often mixed with sadness and guilt for leaving their offspring, worry that the carer will not be good enough, and anger and blame if things go wrong.

That these feelings are not unique to the present becomes clear when we read Joan Kennard's thoughts about her nannies in letters to her parents written more than a century ago. As an army officer's wife, her loyalties and expectations of childcare were not the same as ours today. She did no paid work, and some of her views about raising children will appear unreasonable, even shocking, by today's standards. Yet, as we shall see in Chapter 2, the dilemmas she faced about what kind of nanny would be right for her family, worries about her children's health and wellbeing, anger at the apparent neglect of one child, and the conflicts between her roles as a mother and wife are familiar to many mothers today.

DIFFERENT VOICES

We know about Joan Kennard because her parents preserved her letters and deposited them in a family archive. It is rare to find such unguarded and forthright views written by nannies themselves. Correspondence from nannies held in other family collections tells a rather different story. Lady Desborough's nanny Harriet's letters (located in the Desborough family archive) give a fascinating picture of her day-to-day responsibilities as well as showing her deep love for the children. Yet the accounts she gave of her charges rarely say anything negative and often feel unreal. To understand why this was so, it is important to think about the conditions of service and relationships that shaped the correspondence and others like it. Where did power lie, and who was dependent upon whom?

A unique feature of this book is the space it gives to these different voices, offering multiple perspectives on similar events and employment scenarios. As well as looking at letters and diaries, I have interviewed and corresponded with nearly fifty mothers, nannies and people brought up by nannies, all of whom were born between the early 1900s and the 1990s.[3] All but one of the participants was born in England, Scotland or Wales, but the locations where they lived and worked are not confined to the United Kingdom; they include British families who employed foreign nannies and au pairs, and British nannies working for foreign families. There is often more than one viewpoint on the same set of dynamics, either nanny and child or more than one sibling from the same family; in one case the views of mother, child and nanny have been brought together. I have mixed these oral histories with autobiographies and memoirs, mostly of early twentieth-century childhoods. Putting these sources together allows deeper reflection on the dynamics of the nanny–mother–child relationship. They give us a more interesting view of the rather one-sided stories of perfection or evil told by children and of accounts by mothers and nannies that show themselves in the best light or as the wronged party. Many of these stories are by necessity anonymous, given the sensitivity of information they reveal, with names and identifying details changed.

Children often betrayed the strongest feelings, perhaps because they were the least powerful and least heard voices in the triangle. We encounter a full range of emotions: adoration, sadness, hatred and sometimes abuse. For example, letters written by Lady Desborough's son reveal how much he missed his nanny and his use of her as an intermediary between himself and his mother. This is important because it shows things that could not be said to each party as well as what could. But such insights are rare. And because most accounts of nannies by their charges are written with hindsight, usually after they had grown up, they also give little sense of the ordinariness of nursery life, with only the most traumatic events or idealised views preserved in memory.

One such account, published in *Nursery World* magazine in 1926 entitled '"Nannie": a tribute to all real nannies and to one in particular by ONE OF HER BABIES', is nothing short of elegiac. 'Devoted to her mistress, adoring her babies – true to the servants'; this nanny 'knew nothing of disappointed old age'. 'Tucked away in a chair in the corner … with an assured home and security of a pension in the future should she need it', she remained part of the family and even in death became 'a guardian angel to her children's children'.[4] But did such paragons of perfection really exist, and were they really so fortunate? Or do stories like this conceal more brutal realities, like those that will be revealed in the letters Harriet sent Lady Desborough in the last few months of her life when she was confined to an institution against her will? Such sources call romanticised accounts of old retainers into question.

The view that most nannies were looked after in old age by the families they cared for hides a more complicated picture. While some employers and/or former charges worked hard to ensure their nannies were well cared for, it was not always an easy task, and some nannies continued working into extreme old age. Connections between nannies' different families are important to explore, including their blood relations and those they worked for, which often included more than one family. What was the relationship between them during and after employment, and who took responsibility for a nanny in old age and death? The locations of nannies' graves and inscriptions written on them tell us a lot about their ambivalent position as both insiders and outsiders in families, and suggest the importance of finding out more about their lives beyond the job.

ATTACHMENT AND LOSS

Views of nannies as either all good or all bad were often given by children who had multiple or serial carers. 'Good' nannies were rarely viewed as unkind or hurtful, nor could 'bad' nannies ever be kind or loving. Sibling jealousies and favouritism by nannies intensified these feelings, and when a hated carer suddenly disappeared children could be burdened with guilt, believing that their bad feelings must have destroyed her. I was told one story by a woman who, as a child, had been given no clear explanation of why her governess had died during an operation, and wondered if she had jumped out of the window because she hated looking after them. Children's feelings when 'bad' nannies left the family were also quite ambivalent. My aunt Ursula at the age of 5 was dismayed to see her 'bad' nanny crying in the nursery just before her imminent departure. She assumed that her adored baby brother was the cause and did not relate the tears to herself. Yet Ursula could not entirely let go of the person upon whom she had been dependent from a very early age; so she kept her nanny's gift of an expensive Italian doll for twenty years, until after her own children were born.

Losing a much loved carer was even more difficult. Children coped in a variety of ways, some of which were more successful than others. Anger with the person they had lost was common, as was punishing the replacement nanny. In order to understand why a child behaved in one way or another, we have to go inside that particular triangle and observe its dynamics. When Ursula's much loved governess, Miss Caryer, was leaving to go to a new post, the child was told by her mother to stay away. But Ursula glimpsed her governess's 'red, twisted face averted from the taxi window' and felt a 'hot unease'. She likened this feeling to the time she had carelessly injured a rabbit that had to be put to sleep,

The Holden children with their nanny, *c.* 1925.

thinking it was her fault that the governess was upset. Feeling unable to confide in her mother or fully acknowledge her loss, she reacted by retaliating cruelly. In a letter to Miss Caryer she emphasised her freedom by describing her newly polished nails, an adornment her governess would never have allowed.[5]

Timothy, a 93-year-old man who told me his story from a care home, had a different strategy for coping with loss. Memories of his ayah in Thailand, whom he adored, were focused primarily on the love this young girl felt for his family. Prominent highlights of his tale were her youth and beauty, her attachment to his sick baby brother, her desperation not to be sent back to an abusive husband, and the horror of her returning the next day with some of her hair pulled out. Timothy stressed his ayah's devotion as she had watched over him, making sure he did not drown in the family pond (my aunt Noreen told a similar story about her ayah rescuing her from drowning), and he told of her sadness when one of the more senior ayahs was chosen to return to England with the family. We can never know how accurate his memories were or whether the ayah saw things in the same way. But the tears Timothy shed when he spoke about her had probably as much to do with his sadness both in the past and in the present, in the care home where he now feels abandoned. Removed from his ayah's care to a boarding school at the age of 7, where emotions could not easily be expressed, he had survived by attributing some of his own feelings of loss to her.

Losing the person who had been the primary carer, particularly for a child under the age of 5, was an event which the psychiatrist John Bowlby, writing in the 1950s, believed could 'be as significant as losing a mother'.[6] Yet the adverse effects of nannies' relationships with children must not be overstated. In the many cases where care was successfully shared between mother and nanny, where nannies stayed throughout childhood or where a nanny's departure was handled well, children thrived under their care, and the help and friendship nannies offered

The Holden family, *c.* 1936. The woman second from left is my grandfather's old nurse, who was looked after by the family. The governess, Miss Caryer (fourth from left), is in the least prominent position at the back.

mothers was highly valued. The fact that the effects of maternal loss were only widely recognised after the Second World War, when Bowlby's work became well known, is also of some significance. His theories were misused to blame mothers for leaving their children, and the feelings of guilt this provoked probably increased their reluctance to admit that a nanny's relationship with a child was of real importance.

The fears lying behind this refusal to recognise the nanny–child relationship probably arose from a deep but often unspoken rivalry about who the child loved the most, a problem for mother and nanny alike. Cameron Macdonald illustrated this in her book *Shadow Mothers*, which explores the relationships between mothers and nannies in contemporary America. At the age of 16, Macdonald had taken a summer job as a nanny. Initially, the family all seemed to love her and were keen to have her as a regular babysitter. But when the youngest child hurt herself and refused to be consoled by her mother, only wanting her nanny, the family promptly paid her wages and never saw her again. This abrupt parting left Macdonald with feelings of guilt and shame, realising that by getting too close to the child she had crossed an invisible line.[7]

The nanny's side of the line was particularly clearly explained in a 1956 article titled 'Mother and/or Nanny' in the magazine *Nursery World* by psychologist Phyllis Hostler, who was a regular contributor. Responding to concerns frequently aired in the letters columns over the previous three decades, she tried to help parents and nannies resolve their difficulties and make things easier for the child. Hostler recognised the emotional problems for the nanny on her departure, and in the above article she argued that:

It is always difficult to believe when we have served well and faithfully, that any other will do or be as much loved. One of the hardest things a nurse can be called upon to face, is to hand over her charge to another, wholly and undivided.[8]

Opposite: Illustrations for the article 'Mother and/or Nanny' in *Nursery World* by Phyllis Hostler, December 1956. *Reproduced courtesy of* Nursery World

Mother has the product

"The child has become to one a doll, to sit sweet and clean on one's knee for half-an-hour when visitors come, to enchant briefly with pretty ways or astoundingly clever remarks."

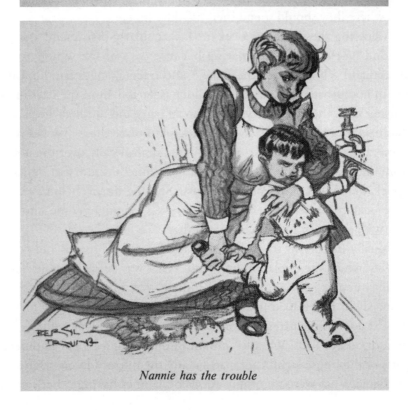

Nannie has the trouble

CHANGING DEBATES AND CONDITIONS

Nursery World magazine offered a useful forum for parents and nannies to express concerns of this kind, and their views can be traced in the correspondence columns over a fifty-year period. These were by no means confined to nannies' comings and goings. Mothers wondered if it was better for a nanny to be trained or untrained and whether or not she should be a 'lady'; they explained the implications in each case and debated whether a nanny should be treated like a servant, family member or friend. They discussed what kind of work nannies should do, objected to being told that nannies knew more than they did, and hated being represented as 'interfering mothers'. They also gave their views on whether it was better if a nanny was a mother's helper or in sole charge. Nannies joined in the discussion about whether being trained at college or learning on the job was best, what role a mother should play in her child's upbringing, what hours they should work, what 'time off' meant, and where they should spend their off-duty time.

Following these debates over time, particularly before and after the Second World War, is fascinating because we can see which aspects altered and which stayed the same. I also trace changes and continuities in home-based childcare over a longer period, from the days of wet nursing until the post-war years when au pairs and mothers' helps were the main source of help. It has been useful to place these changes in the context of childcare advice, which shifted dramatically over the period, from the days of Truby King in the early twentieth century to Benjamin Spock, the most famous post-war guru. Shifting norms help to explain why a nanny trained under one childcare regime might come into conflict with a mother influenced by another.

Equally important to consider are the household spaces and conditions in which these relationships arose. What was different about having a nanny in a large or a small house, if there were lots of children or only one or two? Did it matter if the nursery was in a separate wing or floor, or next door to the parent's bedrooms, or if the nanny slept with the children or on her own? Was the amount of time nannies spent in different parts of the house significant, particularly the nursery, living rooms and kitchens? What were the implications of nannies having other servants to wait upon them, if they were the only paid helper in the house, and if they did housework or prepared food as well as childcare? How different was it if the child was breast- or bottle-fed, and if the mother did some of the childcare herself or delegated it all to the nanny?

Many of these things altered over the twentieth century as class barriers became less stable and family sizes declined. More jobs became available for women of all classes, appliances such as washing machines and electric irons became common in middle-class homes, and domestic service went into terminal decline. However, while these factors had an impact on the number and type of nannies being employed, they did not, as Gathorne Hardy argued, largely disappear after 1939. Post-war middle- and upper-class women still often looked for live-in help with their children, even though many of them were not called nannies and their employment conditions had changed.

WHAT'S IN A NAME?

The fact that there were so many names for this kind of work can be confusing. Nannies, mothers' helps, lady helps, nurses, lady nurses, children's nurses, nursemaids, nursery maids, nurse/generals, nurse/housekeepers, nursery governesses, babysitters (more common in America) and au pairs were all common. Some names were markers of class – the terms 'maid' and 'lady' disappeared in the second half of the twentieth century – and some indicated whether or not housework or teaching would be part of the job. Yet matching an occupational name to a role is not straightforward, as there was too much overlap. Most of the time I use the generic term 'nanny', partly for convenience but also because of the difficulties in distinguishing one kind of post from another.

Names for home-based childcare workers were so varied because their jobs not only crossed class boundaries but also took the workers into maternal territory. While it was useful for mothers, delegating childcare was not always easy or comfortable, and knowing what to call the women who did this work could be difficult. Names were particularly tricky when mother and worker were of a similar class, as was the case with Amelia (born 1905), daughter of a corn merchant whose business failed in the 1920s. She explained that she didn't really have a job title but was simply known as 'Miss Wilson'. She had no qualifications and would not have described herself as a nurse or a nanny because of their associations with domestic service. Although she likened herself to a governess, the work was not educational but rather involved taking the children out for walks, reading to them and putting them to bed. Most significantly, she explained how convenient her presence was for the children (as indeed it was for their mother) because, as she put it, 'the mother had other things to do.'[9]

For Amelia, the benefits of the job were mainly financial. It involved emotional as well as physical labour, not just in relation to the children but also by providing their mother with 'reassurance and non-intrusive' childcare. To do this, Amelia had to set boundaries on her own feelings for her charges.[10] Her fondness for them was based on their dependence upon her, but she also knew that she must not get too attached. The convenience for mothers lay in the time away from their children women like Amelia gave them. They did the work that mothers had either rejected as beneath them or delegated to another in order to do tasks they could not do with their children around. We can link this delegation of the care and protection of children to a meaning of the word 'nanny' in common usage since the 1960s. The *Oxford English Dictionary* defines it as 'a person, institution, etc., considered to be unduly protective or interfering'. To attribute these qualities to a nanny suggests the difficulty many British people have with feelings of dependency, and it has been widely employed to encourage us to stand on our own two feet.

It is not coincidental that the term 'nanny state', coined by the Conservative politician Ian Macleod in 1965, was used to deride governmental interference in affairs deemed to be personal and properly beyond the jurisdiction of the state. The nanny was the woman who had the most power in that generation of middle- and upper-class male politicians' personal lives when they were children and at their most vulnerable. By deriding nannies, these men were by extension denying any continuing dependence on the labour of women or of working-class people. In this way the fantasy of the self-made man, who achieved success as a result of his efforts alone, was – and still is – maintained. At the same time the important role of the state in protecting weak and vulnerable members of society, just as their nannies had protected them as babies, is dismissed as worthless. It is noticeable also that the term 'nanny state' was widely used by Margaret Thatcher to deride Labour party policies. This is particularly ironic, as she had depended on a nanny to bring up her own children, and at that time Labour was perceived as representing the interests of the class from which most nannies originated.

The use of the term 'nanny' to mock dependency suggests how deeply embedded nannies are in our national imagination, despite the fact that most of us have no direct experience of their care. It is not coincidental in this respect that the fictional nanny Mary Poppins was one of the earliest figures to be associated with the idea of a nanny state, and that she appeared in the 2012 Olympic ceremony protecting children in the National Health Service from harm as she chased away the evil Voldemort from the Harry Potter stories.[11] The nanny we all know best is not a real nanny at all. She is a fantasy figure that many of us would love to have looking after us but whose overweening and sometimes frightening power we also fear. Even if we have never read the books or seen the film, most of us know her. I explore the significance of Mary Poppins and her kind in Chapter 7. But as we progress through this history of nannies and their relationships with mothers and children, it is well to remember how much our beliefs about them are shaped by fantasy nannies in our minds.

2

LIVING INSIDE THE
MOTHER-NANNY-CHILD
TRIANGLE

James came to me and I was crying and I said, 'I don't know what to do.'

He said, 'Pat can help you.'

I said, 'She won't, she won't be able to do it.'

He said, 'Why won't she be able to do it?' ... and I was in tears. It makes me cry to think of it ... I couldn't bear it, I thought she'd be repelled and James said, 'She won't, she won't, I'm going to go and talk to her' ... and I can remember to this day, my thrill.

I heard this voice saying, 'Tell her not to be so bloody stupid.' It was just wonderful and I felt this ... this wonderful sense of relief.[1]

When Beth's daughter Emily was born in the late 1970s with a serious medical condition, the family needed a nanny more than ever before. An artist whose husband was often away from home, Beth had employed a series of live-in nannies since her first child David had been a few months old, but it had never been an easy relationship. Beth needed to be in control and she did not want her nannies to be in sole charge or get too close to her family. So she lodged the nanny in the basement, as far away as possible from the family bedrooms. She hated having strangers in the house and thought that was the reason none of them stayed very long.

The crunch came for Beth after Emily was born. Desperate to find time to work, she had retreated to bed, refusing to believe her current nanny, Pat, could possibly help care for her sick child. Beth had finally let go because she could not cope with her sick baby alone and still be an artist. Her previous nannies had helped her achieve both roles but had remained outsiders in the family, and Beth remembered few of their names. But because Pat had been able to take charge of Emily when Beth was at her most vulnerable and at risk of having to stop working, she became Beth's saviour and was never forgotten.

Beth's reluctance to give up control over her child, and eventual relinquishment of Emily's care, illustrate the complex dynamics of the nanny–mother–child triangle. A nanny's job involves emotional and physical work so central to a mother's identity that giving them up to another person can never be simple. The feelings Beth and many other mothers experienced include guilt about wanting to have time to themselves rather than always being available to their children, anger at not being able to be superwomen, and fear of trusting people outside the family to take care of their most beloved family members.[2] No wonder finding a nanny Beth could rely on seemed like a miracle.

Beth's nanny Pat had a rather different perspective. She had looked after David before Emily was born, but left to go back to her native Australia, returning to the family just before Emily's birth. With little experience of childcare, she had taken the job mainly as a way of travelling. Like Beth's other nannies, Pat did not feel part of the family and was often lonely. But she had also enjoyed the work and felt comfortable doing it, and it had helped her gain confidence. Pat's memories were focused on the tension and stress the family had suffered after Emily's birth and how they had affected David. She described how having a succession of different people caring for him, especially at the time of his little sister's illness, had made him 'wary'. Pat's wisdom about the older child's feelings was matched by tenderness for the younger one, creating a strong bond:

I worried about her more – she was just so tiny and had so many problems. I remember carrying her around the house with her little head in the palm of my hand and her body resting along my arm.

Her feet came to my elbow. She was carried around like that against my body as I felt she was safe there. [3]

Nannies like Pat had many reasons for doing the work, including learning new skills, earning money, meeting people, and experiencing other cultures. But on the job they had to negotiate a tricky path as both insiders and outsiders in the family. While it could be a lonely position, it was also a site of intimacy where powerful feelings of love and attachment often arose on both sides. As outsiders in the family, some nannies recognised children's feelings and needs in ways that mothers, immersed in their own struggles to survive the exigencies of family life and preserve their own individual identities, might not.

David's memory of that time echoes Pat's account. He knew that it was very stressful but he 'didn't really know the ins and outs of why'. He became fond of Pat but found a later nanny much more difficult. Watching under-cooked eggs being forced into his baby sister's mouth as she screamed in distress, he immediately told his mother, who promptly sacked the nanny. Yet it still left a scar, giving him a lasting aversion to eggs. As he grew older David became aware that class and sexual taboos could be crossed if he got too close to his nannies. Another nanny's room was out of bounds when her boyfriend was there, and when David did go in he became aware that her preference for Danielle Steel books was different from his mother's taste. The distancing process was strengthened by some uncomfortable feelings of sexual arousal when the nanny took him into her bed after a nightmare. David saw this as clear evidence that she was not a mother figure.

Children's experiences of the nanny–mother–child triangle were as varied and complicated as those of their nannies and mothers. While sensitive nannies like Pat understood children's vulnerability, others did not. Although David was secure enough to tell his mother that a nanny was being cruel, some children felt powerless to speak out about abuse. Having a stranger inside the house could also be disturbing for older children, arousing new and forbidden feelings which took them beyond the family/ friend/servant territory that nannies normally inhabited.

Attachment and loss, love and lust, control and vulnerability, professionalism and detachment – all are present in Beth, Pat and David's stories. Nannies might be doing a mother's job, but being in sole charge of children was very different from working under a mother's authority and close supervision. The question of what was the most important part of a nanny's job arises in these testimonies. In addition to providing physical care, she had to manage emotions; she was employed to care *about* as well as to care *for* children. A strong bond between nanny and child was one of the major job satisfactions. Yet allowing this bond to become too strong could cause pain both for the nanny and the family she worked for. Nannies and mothers were mutually dependent on one another, but this was not always obvious or acknowledged, and physical and emotional exploitation was always a danger. The point at which love strayed into sexual attraction could be a slippery boundary, the 'elephant in the room' in nanny employment.

To explore these concerns, I look first through the lens of memory at the reasons why so many children split nannies into either angelic or demonic figures. These splits can be connected to the ways households were organised and to the work nannies did, particularly giving food and caring for the body. The intimacy of these interactions helps to explain why feelings were often so intense, as do practices such as sharing bedrooms and the changes children went through as they grew older and separated from their nannies. Two central themes, adoration and loss, are both shaped by the time and attention children received from their nannies and mothers. Finally, I consider the different ways that mothers and nannies created relationships with one another. To what extent did each party feel dependent or exploited? How far were nannies perceived to be servants, workers or family members? Why and when did they become the mother's friend or foe?

An understanding of household dynamics is essential: what places nannies, children and parents occupied both in and outside the house, where they slept and ate meals, when and where the different parties spent time together. Spatial divisions mirrored social hierarchies, which affected every member of the house, generating powerful feelings of belonging and exclusion. In big houses, nannies might be queen of the nursery, lording it over nursery maids, yet were largely separated both from the kitchen quarters and from the drawing room, where their charges were welcome only at strictly limited times. Servants and children might be on friendly terms but would usually be made aware by parents and nannies of the gap in status between them. In the grandest houses children had intimate contact with nannies and nursery maids but rarely encountered lower servants, barred from entering their working and sleeping quarters and discouraged from speaking to them.

In smaller establishments where work was shared with the mother, including cooking and household chores, nannies often ate in the kitchen with the children and mixed with the family in their living space. Yet this proximity did not always bring families and nannies closer. Class divisions were less clear, but unspoken hierarchies were still present. With more childcare done by mothers, intimacy between nannies and children was reduced in intensity and, particularly later in the twentieth century, they were less likely to share bedrooms. Despite this merging of parental and nursery territory, nannies had more personal space of their own away from their charges, a room where children could go only if invited and where nannies could retreat in off-duty hours.

CHILDHOOD MEMORIES

Detailed descriptions of the use of household space, common in pre-Second World War childhood memoirs, are often polarised, either warm and secure or bleak and miserable. Lesley Lewis, daughter of a lawyer born in 1909, gives us a vivid picture of her nurseries in the two large country houses where she lived as a child in Essex. They were presided over by a benevolent nanny, and Lesley seldom ventured to the front of the house until she was older, except by invitation. She recalled nostalgically her nursery toys, bright fires, lamps carefully trimmed, fireside chairs and hearth rugs where she lounged or sprawled reading to herself. For children with frequent changes of carer, memories of this kind meant security and were often recalled vividly later in life. Nannies and nursery maids might come and go, but the nursery never changed; its toy cupboard, piano, rocking horse, lino-clad floor, wooden table covered with an oil cloth, and polished fire guard made it a cheerful place. Lavinia Pearson, who came from an immensely wealthy family that had 'everything that money can buy', described a marvellous, purpose-built nursery in their country mansion during the interwar years. It had its own phone, pantry, special low basins and lavatories, and a high bath so that the nanny did not have to bend. But Lavinia's account contrasted this picture with the reaction of her 'horrid' nanny to her new workspace. Looking around disdainfully, the nanny made only one remark to her employer: 'I notice there is no mantelpiece. Where am I supposed to put the nursery clock?'[4]

Abusive behaviour and frequent changes of carer had long-lasting effects on children, casting deep shadows over their earliest memories. One of Lavinia's nannies beat her with a hairbrush and burnt her hands on the teapot, leaving her with an abiding childhood recollection of anxiety and 'awareness of impending doom'.[5] One of a long stream of nannies and nursemaids who cared for Viola Bankes, a daughter of the aristocracy living at Kingston Lacy in Dorset in the early 1900s, became the focus for reminiscences which read almost like a Victorian melodrama. Nurse Stanley was a stereotypical spinster: 'her dark gimlet eyes, set close together above her long pointed nose offered no hope of affection'. She beat Viola and her sister, gave them frequent purgatives, nearly starved their brother Ralph to death, and was eventually sent away by Viola's mother to a care home, where 'guilt and remorse, coupled with epilepsy, drove her out of her mind'.[6] Mary Butler, whose mother died when she was a baby, had equally unhappy memories. Daughter of a draper's buyer, she had thirteen different housekeepers looking after her, most of whom drank and never played with her. The first one was particularly nasty, beating her for the slightest offence, and so painful and humiliating was this memory that in retelling it more than eighty years later Mary could still feel the pain. She was also regularly punished by being shut in a wardrobe, leaving her with a lasting aversion to mothballs,[7] much like David's lifelong hatred of runny eggs.

These stories stand in stark contrast to an account given by Felicity, who grew up during the interwar period in a large country house owned by her grandmother. She felt totally secure in her nursery with a nanny who was always fair. She was 'the one stable, immutable, fact of our childhood' and, until Felicity married, was the most beloved person in her life. The clean, fresh fragrance of her nanny's clothes signified love and security to the child, reassuring her that Nanny was not a servant but one of the family and much more of a mother than her real middle-class one.

It is important to understand the origins of these accounts, while not denying their subjective truth. The roots of the nannies' behaviour lay partly in family dynamics and their conditions of employment, but their charges were usually only able to reflect on these things much later in life. Felicity recognised that she loved her nanny, not just because she was utterly consistent and stayed for fifty years, but also because Felicity's parents were unhappy together and 'Nanny and the nursery was a refuge from quite a lot of quarrelling'. Mary had thought carefully about her

Felicity's nanny later in life. She remained in touch with the family, and Felicity's sister cared for her in her last illness.

Ralph recovering after being starved by his nanny. He is with his mother Henrietta Bankes. *Courtesy of Bankes Collection, Kingston Lacy House, National Trust*

childhood and understood 'how wretched and lonely her housekeepers' lives must have been'. While Felicity's nanny had given her whole attention to her charges, Mary's first housekeeper had been a widow with a daughter of her own to support, and depended on the family for work. Having to care for a little girl who took precedence over her own child may partly explain her cruelty. This woman could never have been a replacement for Mary's mother, as the child's affections were reserved for her father alone. Mary refused to go to sleep until her father had come home; she remembered him racing up the stairs and gathering her into his arms, so that 'the horrors of the day just faded away'.[8]

Viola Bankes' hatred of her nanny was intensified by class differences. Nurse Stanley had 'coarse attitudes' and a Cockney accent, showing her London working-class origins. She had epilepsy, a frightening and stigmatising condition for which at the time there was no effective treatment; if the family had known about her condition, she could have been dismissed and been unable to get another job. Her vulnerability and dependency on the family for employment, which Viola eventually recognised, explained why the youngest child had been deliberately starved. The nurse exploited her employer's ignorance about children in order to be kept on: 'The weaker he became, so she [Nurse Stanley] must have thought, the more my poor mother would depend on her.'[99]

The psychic dimensions of these stories are important to explore. Perhaps because the wish to have a fantasy carer who will always be available to give us their total love and attention is so common, the role of nanny carries a particularly heavy emotional load. Childhood memoirs seldom describe nannies as ordinary, fallible human beings, but often describe them either as angels who could do no wrong or demons who hated or persecuted children. Viola's memoir exhibits this tendency. She had a difficult relationship with a mother who was so distant from her children that she never told them their father had died. Unable to confide in her mother, Viola reacted not just by demonising her nanny, Nurse Stanley, but also by idealising her nursemaid Alice, portraying her as a martyr of the nanny/nursemaid system.

In contrast to the ugly Cockney nanny, Alice was pretty and country-bred. Viola recalled waking early in the morning, watching her black the grate and lay the fire in the huge stone fireplace and gazing into the flames. She explained how her nursemaid would have already risen at 4.30 a.m. in her cold, cheerless room under the roof and made fires in two or three other cold bedrooms before dressing the children. The life of a nursery maid was much harder than that of a nanny, and from the perspective of the 1980s (when she wrote her book), Viola wondered whether Alice had been happy working in such spartan conditions. Constantly scolded by Nurse Stanley, she was regularly threatened with dismissal without a reference for being too slow. The story had a tragic ending: not long after, Alice died 'uncomplainingly' of neglected appendicitis.[10] The working conditions described may not have been atypical for nursemaids at the time, but Viola's memories of Alice were probably shaped by her own feelings of loss, making the loved one appear more perfect than she could ever have been in real life.

NANNIES' WORK

These happy and unhappy childhood memories must be set in the context of the work that nannies and nursemaids did earlier in the twentieth century. Susan Field's memories of her low-paid job as an Edwardian nursery maid echo Viola's description of Alice's life, although Susan worked in a much smaller household caring for a minister's family. By the 1970s, when she told her tale, the exploitative features of early twentieth-century domestic service had been publicised in the media.[11] So it is not altogether surprising that Susan gave full voice to the frustrations and difficulties she had suffered as a 13-year-old with four unruly children to care for. There was no older nanny in charge, and only a cook-general to do the cooking and housework. Susan, who (like Alice) slept in a cold garret, found the work endless: taking the children out for walks, washing them, feeding them, and putting them to bed in their nursery on the third floor. She was also blamed when the children were tired and cried, or if they made too much noise playing games in the nursery and disturbed their father writing his sermons. Like Viola, these children had a distant mother, which must have intensified the children's attachment to Susan. She believed they took more notice of her than their parents, running after her on her day off. This upset their mother, with whom Susan generally had little contact.[12]

Susan's strongest grievance was the inadequate diet. Rice soup to start her day with a small portion of meat and a few vegetables to follow was not sufficient for a growing girl doing such heavy and demanding work, making her look like 'a scarecrow'. Servants often had better food in service jobs than in their own homes, which made it all the more upsetting. Susan saw it as a sign of her employers' meanness, which she related to their Scottish origins.[13] She was not alone in thinking food important. The subject features strongly in many nanny stories and is often at the centre of the nanny–mother–child relationship.

Mealtimes are recurring themes in pre-Second World War memoirs and reminiscences. Food symbolised the love, or lack of it, that children received from their nannies and parents, and tensions and battles were common. Managing food and supervising mealtimes were perceived as important aspects of a nanny's work. To be a success it was essential that her charges learned the table manners appropriate to their class and grew up strong and healthy, but neither of these things were easily achieved.

In houses where other help was kept to do the cooking, nannies' main jobs were to make up bottles, to feed babies and young children, and to supervise older children's meals. Preparing a baby's food correctly was particularly important when mothers could not or would not breastfeed. In Lesley Lewis's house a special table was put aside for this purpose, with an oil-topped cloth and a spirit lamp for warming the milk, while a cane nursing chair was reserved by the fire for the nanny to feed and attend the baby.[14] Failure to feed a baby properly could easily result in death. Infant diarrhoea was a major killer at the start of the twentieth century, often caused by poor sanitation and contaminated water as well as indigestible milk mixtures. This was especially risky when working abroad in hot countries. A Norland nanny writing from India explained the dangers of looking after a baby abroad in a letter to the college newsletter in 1909: every drop of water and milk had to be boiled, strained and filtered and it must not be put in any vessel except the 'precious darling's own'. There were often no fires on which to boil kettles or burn rubbish and, if there were fires, they were usually large and unprotected.[15]

Bottle-feeding was usually a nanny's job, but some mothers liked to participate in or supervise this task, often checking feeds against the baby's weight and fretting if things went wrong. The politician Austen Chamberlain's wife Ivy was beside herself when her eldest child failed to thrive and wrote to her husband who was away from home:

> I [am] worried he has only gained 4 oz in the fortnight when he ought to have gained 16 oz. Nurse is very distressed and thinks it is a reflection on her, I think. He has been very fretful and hasn't had a smile for anyone. I think he hasn't found his bottle satisfying as he has demanded them every 2 hours, so we are giving him Horlicks malted milk and nurse is going to weigh him on Wednesday and if he hasn't gained we must try something else.[16]

Mothers had long been advised that it was safer to breastfeed babies, but in the twentieth century the psychoanalyst Melanie Klein made a baby's relationship with the breast central to mental health. Nini Herman, a German Jew who came to England in the late 1930s and had been in psychoanalysis, later confronted her elderly mother on this subject. The hard evidence produced to show that her mother had cared about her was confined mainly to details of her weight and the amount of feed she had taken, as recorded by the nanny. For Nini this was insufficient proof. Not being breastfed involved a fundamental separation, and Nini stressed the part her nanny had played in giving her food, as she wrote:

> The rustle and papery starch of Nanny up against my cheek. And a swimming circle over me. Was it the face or the breast? Or the bottle in my nanny's hand when after several horrid days, Mother abandoned the struggle and put my life in nanny's charge?[17]

Nursery fare was often dull and bland, as anything rich or spicy was regarded as dangerous. Manners were strictly enforced, and 'nanny law' was particularly prominent at mealtimes. Sir Hugh Casson and Joyce Grenfell memorialised the etiquette of their childhood meals in a book of nanny wisdom entitled *Nanny Says*. These sayings stressed the importance of good table manners and posture: 'sit up straight at the table so there's room for a cat at the back and a mouse at the front', 'no elbows on the table until you are an aunt'. Above all, they focused on ensuring that children ate what they were given – 'make a nice clean plate' – and did not waste food: 'think of the poor starving children who'd be grateful for that nice plain bread and butter'.[18]

Nannies often claimed that their charges always ate what they were given, but Lavinia Pearson's memoir suggests otherwise. She could not always eat the large plate of food put before her: 'Nannies knew in those days that the more you could persuade a child to eat the stronger it would grow,' and she was grateful to her mother for not being 'caught up in the nice clean plate syndrome'.[19] Some children would have been glad to have been given so much food by their nannies. John Bowlby's brother Tony, a doctor's son in the early twentieth century, remembered sharing an egg with John – one had the white, the other the yolk. Nurse Stanley was dismissed from Kingston Lacy because she gave the treasured heir Ralph nothing but the juice of one pound of raw beef.[20] In all these cases, nannies' position as food gatekeeper was the source of their power, but sometimes left the children in their charge frustrated and miserable.

In other cases, nannies sided with children who rebelled against parents' or doctors' nutritional demands. When Joan Kennard's consumptive son Dennys lost weight after a bout of bronchitis his doctor advocated the 'stuffing' system. His mother thought it a great success as he gained 4.5 pounds in four months, but nanny and child were less convinced of its merits. Joan's letter to her parents shows the power some mothers exerted over their children's feeding regimes:

> It takes hours, sometimes he refuses to swallow! I am very sorry for him. Nurse Freeman said Symes [the nanny] would not see the importance and would be inclined to give in to D, so I sent for Dr Rich and he made her see alright! I have superintended everything since nurse left and so far all well.[21]

Lesley Lewis found she had to be much better behaved in the dining room with her parents than in 'the relaxed atmosphere of nursery' where the nanny was not so strict. The children were outspoken and finicky about the nursery food they did not like and battled with their nanny, messing about with food until it grew cold and became even more unattractive.[22]

Children commonly had Sunday lunch with their parents, often supervised by nannies. As they grew older, they graduated to having other meals in the dining room alone with their parents, leaving the younger ones behind in the nursery, although they usually waited until they were in their teens before being allowed to stay up for dinner. Kensington nanny Vera emphasised the gulf between herself and the father at Sunday lunch; she sat at the far end of the table with the children, referring to his 'posh' language when he told his young daughter, struggling to get a pea on her fork: 'It's quite permissible to use a spoon'. Sympathising with the child and pointing out how inappropriate these words were to his daughter, Vera said [to me in the interview], 'You and I would have said "use your spoon, love"'. Although she had accepted them at the time, speaking with hindsight from her home village in South Wales at the age of 93, she made her employer's pretensions seem absurd.

Feuds between nursery and kitchen staff were common: Lavinia's nanny was constantly at war with the cook, and the children were subjected to slanging matches between them.[23] If food was sent up on a lift known as a dumb waiter (as was the case in many of the larger houses) it was easier to ignore one another, although sparks might still fly if the food was cold. Hostility between the nursery and kitchen was also a permanent fixture in the Leigh family in the interwar years. They lived in a large, highly stratified household in the Home Counties with an extensive staff, including nannies, nursery maids and a governess. Maids flatly refused to bring up trays of food to the nursery, leaving them on a slab at the bottom of the stairs and blowing a whistle to signal the nanny or nursemaid to collect them. Household disputes of this kind had much to do with nannies' uncertain status midway between servant and family. Nursery governesses who gave themselves pretensions provoked particular hostility. So disliked was the Leigh nursery governess that the maids refused to have anything to do with the nursery. Cleaning the nursery had to be contracted out to a girl from the village, well known for having a series of illegitimate babies, or in her absence to the laundress, who was also a single mother. As social outcasts who might not easily have found other jobs, these women were more willing to do the dirty work eschewed by other servants.

Later in the century, as social distinctions became less rigid and ideas about children's food more relaxed, cooking and meals became more casual affairs. Before the Second World War, Felicity's nanny had little to do with food preparation and children's meals were served in the nursery. But when the servants were dismissed during the war, she took over the cooking and the whole family ate together in the dining room. Jane Robinson came from an upper-middle-class military family and had been brought up in a large house with servants and a nanny in the 1940s. However, when she went on to employ help for her own children in the late 1960s, they lived 'hugger-mugger' in a tiny cottage, sharing cooking and meals with her Colombian au pair.

Nannies were more likely to eat with the family after the Second World War, even in houses where they were not expected to do the cooking. In 1947, when my aunt Noreen was employed as a mother's help for two little girls, she had been treated as more of a family member than a nanny and always had meals with the family. But not being in charge of food had its own difficulties. At the height of rationing Noreen remembered feeling hungry because the food the cook sent in was so limited. A small mound of mashed potato sitting in the middle of the dish wasn't nearly enough to feed three adults and two children, so she supplemented her diet with dried bananas sent by her aunt. Noreen's account echoes nursemaid Susan's complaint forty years earlier. Continuing divisions between servants and family even in the immediate post-war years are suggested in her final comment: 'I bet the cook and her maids down below gorged themselves jolly well.'[24]

PARADING PRAMS AND CLOTHES

The other significant physical tasks undertaken by nannies were looking after children's clothes, bathing them, dressing and undressing them, supervising rests and bedtimes, and taking them for walks each day. Two long walks a day were a customary part of the routine, deemed essential because of the high value attached to fresh air and exercise, which was drummed into nannies during their training. But the attraction of the long walks most nannies took with children every day can also be related to the prestige attached to the large shiny prams they pushed. This was one of the perks of a good job, a status symbol which became increasingly important in the interwar years and beyond. By the 1930s, utilitarian deep-bodied prams became unfashionable, replaced by smarter models with high wheels and shallow bodies where the baby could be easily viewed and have plenty of air.[25] These new kinds of prams were shown off by Kensington nannies in the late 1930s; it was a great thrill when policemen stopped the traffic for the daily pram parade. Pictures of luxury prams, such as Pedigree and Silver Cross, were common in advertisements in women's magazines, with one 1950s advert featuring a glamorous young mother in a flowing dress and high heels being admired by a uniformed guard.[26]

Prams were also a showcase for children's clothes, which it was the nanny's job to manage. Ensuring their charges were smartly and warmly dressed was an essential and important duty. Failing to ensure that children

Norland Nannies parading prams. *Courtesy of Norland College, Bath*

were wearing the right clothes could even become a sackable offence, as Joan Kennard's letters attest. When her son caught cold, she did not hide her bitter feelings against her nurse and complained to her father:

> Imagine letting a delicate child of 5 get hot and not being there to put his coat on herself. She had no other charge except him and how can one trust any child of that age to do that sort of thing. I consider it criminal negligence on her part, though of course unintentional.[27]

Managing children's clothes was a far greater labour than simply ensuring children were wearing the right garments at the right times. Before the advent of washing machines, which did not become common in middle- and upper-class homes in Britain until the 1950s, doing laundry could take all day. Nannies might or might not have been directly involved in washing, starching and ironing children's clothes, depending on whether or not a nursery maid or other help was kept. But the objections so many nannies made to doing housework after the collapse of domestic service during the Second World War can be related partly to this time-consuming work.

Although some mothers decided what clothes their children should wear, it was the nanny's job to make sure her charges were turned out nicely and did their parents credit. Most nannies in the first half of the twentieth century were expected to mend and also make children's clothes, with needlework a highly prized skill, often mentioned in job advertisements. This included fine embroidery on girls' dresses and even on undergarments, and was usually done in the evenings after the children went to bed.

As well as making clothes, nannies could be involved in choosing materials and patterns, liaising with dressmakers, asking mothers to make purchases when they were in town, and ordering clothes on approval from department stores. Getting material and clothing on approval was a system that wealthy families hung on to as long as they could, although it became rarer later in the twentieth century. An under-nanny in the 1960s was impressed by the five sets of tartan trews (traditional Scottish trousers) sent to her employer's house on approval by Marks & Spencer. But in 1916, when Harriet Plummer, nanny at Taplow Court in Buckinghamshire, wrote to her employer, the glittering society hostess Lady Ettie Desborough, it was the normal way of doing things. Harriet explained how she had ordered and approved all the materials for her youngest charge Imogen's dresses and sent measurements to Handley Seymour, a dressmaker to the court and aristocracy, famous for designing the wedding dress of Queen Elizabeth's mother, Elizabeth of York.[28] She also checked the price and shade of stockings and heel height of the slippers sent by the store, returned the slippers, and asked for more to be sent on approval.[29] Pleasure and gratitude towards Lady Desborough shine through Harriet's letters. Daughter of a local gamekeeper, she was dependent on her employer for work but also proud of the skills she had learned and the faith that was placed in her. The mutual dependency between these two women offered Harriet a job with responsibility and access to illustrious circles she could only have dreamed of as a child.

Dressing children to look their best took time and effort, particularly in winter and in best clothes. For the first half of the twentieth century, central heating was uncommon even in the bigger houses, and generally inadequate, and the smaller upstairs fireplaces where nurseries were located gave out limited heat. Windows were usually left open and

A Norland student's sewing sample. *Courtesy of Norland College, Bath*

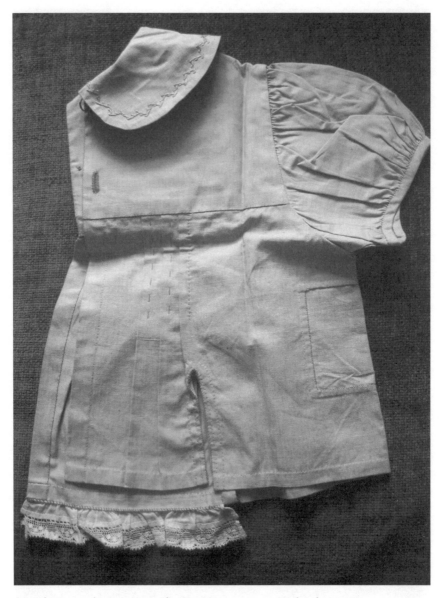

A student nurse's sewing sample. Nannies were expected to be expert needlewomen. *Courtesy of Nicola Harland*

babies put to rest outside in their prams even in the coldest weather. To keep them warm enough, children wore many layers of clothes with buttons, suspenders, drawstrings and laces taking the place of the zips, elastic and Velcro commonly used today. Lavinia Pearson remembered taking hours to get dressed in the winter, and both she and Lesley Lewis described the underwear they wore. This started with combinations, with long arms that had to be folded back under a party dress, and over them a sleeveless liberty cotton bodice to which suspenders could be attached. Lesley also wore prickly white cotton drawers with frilled and banded legs, a waist-length flannel petticoat embroidered with scallops by her nanny, and finally a stiff white cotton petticoat tied around the neck by a narrow tape.[30] As everything fastened at the back, it was hard for her to dress herself, and in a household with several children, dressing could be a long, tedious process for nannies.

A Norland nurse writing to the college magazine in 1926 had many complaints about children's clothes. While accepting the importance of warm underwear, she had no time for the scratchiness of woollies, was concerned about the suffering of children wearing 'irritable and tight garments', and stressed the importance of giving them 'liberty of movement'.[31] Tight clothing was perceived to be so great a problem that an advertisement in *Nursery World* for Viyella (a shrink-resistant fabric of mixed cotton and wool) coined the term 'clothes repression', a syndrome supposedly diagnosed by a child guidance specialist that made children bad-tempered.[32] Lavinia recalled great rejoicing when she was allowed to graduate from combinations to a vest, but still had to wear two pairs of knickers in case she caught cold. Tights and leggings were unknown, so she wore shiny leather gaiters fastened down the side with a button hook, a long-winded process that could be painful when the hook nipped bare flesh.[33]

Formal standards of dress meant that some children had to change, not just when they got dirty but also before seeing their parents in the afternoon. Lavinia described how she and her sisters were changed by their nanny into three sets of completely different clothes, including black patent leather shoes with silver buckles. Children were not always happy to dress up for parents, particularly when clothes were starched. Lesley believed her brother, who had to change from his everyday striped sailor

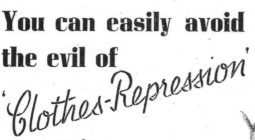

You can easily avoid the evil of 'Clothes-Repression'

says the

CHILD GUIDANCE SPECIALIST

BOBBY used to have the most terrible tantrums. 'His bad moods are beyond me', said his mother and took him to consult a child guidance specialist.

'Goodness!' said the Specialist when she examined him. '*Feel his blouse and undervest round the neck — and at the armholes. Tight as a string! His clothes have shrunk and "felted"—badly. He's desperately uncomfortable; it must be a struggle getting these things over his head. The boy's* a victim of what we call "Clothes Repression", and he'll grow up really bad-tempered, unless...'

'Well', said Mother 'if *you* know of any way to prevent children's clothes, always in and out of the tub, from shrinking!'

'But I do', said the Specialist. '*Make them of Viyella*'.

Bobby's tantrums are now a thing of the past.

*   *   *

Viyella washes without shrinking, and without losing any of its dainty appearance and pretty colours. It does not irritate, or keep the air away from the skin. It is always warm enough, but never too warm. Children are comfortable and happy in Viyella.

You'll be glad you dressed him in

'Viyella' REGD.

GOOD-BYE TO CLOTHES REPRESSION

WILLIAM HOLLINS & CO. LTD., VIYELLA HOUSE, NOTTINGHAM

A   VIYELLA   HOUSE   PRODUCT

Clothes repression: an advert for Viyella underwear in *Nursery World* in 1936. *Courtesy of* Nursery World

Parents and children in their best clothes in the Edwardian era. *Copyright Chippix, Shutterstock*

blouse to a stiff white one, suffered even more from starch than she did in her embroidered broderie anglaise dress worn with elegantly tapered thin-soled bronze shoes.[34] The Bowlby brothers in the 1910s wore silk shirts and velvet knickers. So important was the dressing-up ritual that when Tony Bowlby once came down in a blue jersey and serge shorts, he was chased back upstairs by his father who gave him a few cuffs on the bottom because he'd been rude to his mother by appearing in dirty clothes.[35] Although it was an everyday occurrence, the children's hour was special enough to need best clothes; it had a distancing effect, making children guests in their parents' rooms.

Nannies also changed clothes during the day, often wearing different outfits in the afternoon. Children were acutely aware of these uniforms, which provoked powerful memories. For more than half a century, Nini Hermann could bear nothing that was blue because it reminded her of her lost nanny's dress.[36] Felicity's memory of snuggling up to her nanny's 'marvellous white apron' exuded a sense of security, while Viola Bankes described her nasty Nurse Stanley's white apron as 'stiff as a card', beneath which were visible a black skirt, thick black stockings and

65

Party Wear

Nannies who choose the "Shenley" for Christmas will find it delightfully cool to wear at parties. The poplin has a soft silky finish, and is always much admired as it looks fresh and new however much it is worn and washed.

In all the most popular uniform colours **15/6**

STOCK SIZES:— Bust.. 32 32 34 34 36 36 38 ins.
Length 44 46 44 48 46 48 48 ins.

Garrould's

E. & R. GARROULD, LTD.

Party wear shown in *Nursery World* (1938). Clothes manufacturers sold a wide range of nanny uniforms, including special outfits for children's parties. *Courtesy of* Nursery World

Tim, his mother Ursula and his nanny Agnes wearing smart clothes, *c*. 1945.
Courtesy of Tim D'Arch Smith

flat black laced shoes. Tim, who grew up in 1930s and 1940s London, remembered three different nannies:

> There was the overall, you know, when she was working … and then there would be the night nanny with the teeth out, you know, and the hair down and a dressing-gown and long flannelette night-gown … [There] was the smart nanny, a nice dress with a coat and a hat and smart shoes, sensible shoes, thick stockings [when she went out].

INTIMACY: BODIES AND EMOTIONS

Tim's memory of his nanny's nightgown can be explained by the fact that they shared a bedroom. He was an only child, but this practice was also common in larger families where the head nanny often slept with the baby, and nursery maids either shared a room with the other maids or with older children. Lesley Lewis, Lavinia Pearson and Sadie Leigh all slept with their nannies and younger sisters in night nurseries, while older children were promoted to their own bedrooms. Sadie felt safer sleeping with her nanny and became nervous when she moved in with an older sister in a more distant room. Lavinia was enormously relieved that she did not have to sleep alone; the open door into the nursery where she could hear the voice of her nanny gossiping with the servants was a comfort.[37]

Nannies might insist that children turned their faces away when they were getting dressed, but close proximity at night strengthened children's attachment to their nannies by giving them intimate access to their bodies. Sexual arousal by a nanny was more likely when rooms or beds were shared, as we saw with David. But even where this was not the case, young boys bathed and dressed by their nannies could become aware of their physical attraction. In the 1970s and 1980s psychoanalytic theory was brought to bear on these kinds of feelings. It was believed that being brought up by a nanny could have implications for boys' future sexual preferences, caused by the psychic split they experienced between a distant idealised mother who did little of the hands-on care and the nanny from a lower social class who wielded power and physical control. Following Freud's self-analysis, it was suggested that because nannies took the place of the mothers in giving both love and bodily care, a boy's Oedipal fantasies, normally directed at his mother, would be transposed onto his nanny.[38] This was the reason Gathorne Hardy argued in *The Rise and Fall of the British Nanny* that many upper-class English men 'found it easier to regard working-class women as objects of their sexual fantasies than women from their own class.'[39]

Yet, most often, children remembered not sexual feelings but maternal love. Many children who shared their nannies' rooms had powerful nostalgic feelings about the care they received and saw their nannies as a haven of security. Psychoanalysts have identified the necessity for boys to detach themselves from mothers or mother figures in order to affirm their masculinity. For upper- and middle-class boys, this process was often enforced through being sent to boarding school.[40] Although this mechanism was effective, it could not entirely erase boys' continuing feelings of dependency. Boys could not admit to loving nannies in public, but did so in letters sent home. Later in life, the nannies from whom they had been parted were often remembered as paragons of perfection, as was the case for Tim and his nanny.

After the Second World War, sharing a bedroom with a nanny was much less common. As a 1945 article in *The Lady* pointed out, smaller houses meant children's quarters were 'being crowded out' and 'one room must serve for day and night nursery'.[41] But it was also part of a longer trend towards valuing personal space more highly. Children no longer shared beds, and nannies were in a better bargaining position to demand a room of their own. When Doreen, a farmer's daughter, worked as a nanny/housekeeper in the 1960s she had her own room and there was no nursery. The three children played at one end of the drawing room and each had a separate bedroom. Not being in such close proximity to the children day and night made a difference. Doreen cared about them deeply and, after their mother committed suicide, was determined to stay in touch. However, while there was mutual affection, the relationship Doreen described with them had a less physical quality than is suggested in many pre-Second World War nanny and child interviews and memoirs.

The containment of younger children in the pre-war nursery, while older ones were with governesses and/or parents, often created powerful divisions in the family. Different age cohorts of children were given collective names that marked the divide. Those still in the nursery, labelled 'babies' or 'little ones', could feel left out and unimportant. Tony Bowlby's elder sisters had been upset when they were ejected from the nursery into the care of a governess, but Evelyn, the youngest child, left there with a brother with mild learning difficulties, could not understand why they wanted to stay. She described her household as 'living in separate flats and which didn't overlap much', with servants on the top floor, the nursery area with nanny and younger children on the next floor, and her parents' and elder sisters' bedrooms on the floor below.[42]

Moving away from Nanny was a necessary part of growing older but was not always an easy transition. A move to a room of one's own nearer the parents' bedrooms could be seen as a welcome advancement and might be envied by younger siblings, but was difficult for a child who had never been alone before. Lavinia Pearson did not envy her elder sister Veronica who had to sleep in her own room at the end of a long passage. Veronica's terror of foxes in her chimney frequently sent her running along to the nursery for help. She got little sympathy from her nanny, but was rather reprimanded and taken straight back to bed.

For older children, spending more time with parents or involved a rejection of childhood values. Nannies who had been relied upon, obeyed and often adored when children were younger no longer seemed such heroic figures. It was at this point that class differences became more apparent. Psychologist T.H. Pear, writing in the mid-1950s, suggested that being trained and disciplined by a working-class woman who was not his mother might be beneficial for adult men making decisions:

> [...] for at least he may be free from any haunting doubt whether his mother would approve his action, and by that time he will probably regard 'Nanny' as incapable of judging the rightness of his conduct, even if she could understand the issues involved, which he would consider unlikely.[43]

Yet the reality for most mid-twentieth children was more complicated. Growing away from Nanny often did mean rejecting her values, at least for a time. Marion, a child in the 1950s, had adored her nanny, Jean, and was never close to her mother, but she recognised on her return from boarding school that Jean was no longer on the same intellectual level and could not understand her worries. Yet, rather than rejecting her, Marion enlisted her nanny as an ally. Jean became more like a sister, accepting her smoking and hippy clothes and concealing her knowledge of Marion's boyfriends from her mother. Other children strengthened bonds with their mothers as they grew older. Gillian had the same nanny from birth, recruited by her grandmother during the Second World War to support a sometimes unstable mother. As a teenager, Gillian thought her mother was more like a sister, inviting confidences and giving her cigarettes, while her nanny remained strait-laced and disapproving, worrying about her being seen with more than one boyfriend. Tim felt that his relationship with his mother improved when he started to smoke and drink in his teens and they became more like 'brother and sister'. Although both Gillian and Tim teased their nannies, they continued to love and rely upon them, and 'nanny law' held a powerful position in Tim's psyche throughout his life.

MOTHER TIME AND NANNY TIME: ADORATION, DEPRIVATION AND LOSS

Children's memories of mothers and nannies were shaped by how much time, attention and love they received from each, the extent to which each was involved in hands-on care, and the length and timing of a nanny's period of service. In the bigger houses before the Second World War, children's contact with mothers was generally limited to outings, nursery visits (often at bath- or bedtime), and the late afternoon when children spent an hour or so alone with parents, usually in the drawing room. Children's recollections of this time could be very positive if attention was concentrated completely on them. Lavinia Pearson remembered her mother hardly ever taking the time to go upstairs to say goodnight but, in the drawing or garden room, 'a magic land set apart from the humdrum reality of the nursery', she was unfailingly kind.[44] Charlotte (born in 1905), the eldest of seven children of a Anglican vicar living in Nottinghamshire, recalled regularly playing games and dancing while her mother played the piano, leading visitors to think they were at a party.

In other families, especially larger ones, time spent with parents was scarce or marked by tension. While Charlotte was given extra story time after her younger siblings were sent off to bed at fifteen-minute intervals, other children received less attention. Lady Margaret Egerton and her six brothers and sisters went into the drawing room under sufferance. Her parents did not read to the children as they sat in a row on the sofa; as soon as they were allowed to leave, the seven youngsters shot back 'like scalded cats' to the nursery wing where they were back 'in heaven'.[45] Some children saw their parents as remote strangers and longed to spend more time with them, but experiences varied greatly among siblings. While in the early 1900s Tony Bowlby remembered being adored, cuddled and read to by his mother, his younger sister Evelyn never recalled her mother paying her much attention or having a book read to her in which she took any interest, as the story was always chosen by her elder brothers.

The children's hour was still in place in some upper-middle-class families after the Second World War, although the more formal conventions associated with it had been loosened. In her job with the Robinsons, a military family, Ada remembered that her employer banged on the ceiling when she had had enough of the children, signalling it was time for the nanny to take them off to bed. Just as dressing for dinner was no longer routine, children were allowed to wear their normal daytime clothes when they saw their parents and felt less constrained in adult territory. While they might be sent back to the nursery if they were messing around when guests were present, at other times the Robinson children made dens in the living room and whizzed into the kitchen on a tea trolley. Yet Ada was still the Robinsons' principal carer, and the middle child Matilda was left with long-lasting feelings of sadness that she had spent so little time with her mother. Being sent to boarding school not long afterwards compounded her feelings of loss. Neither she nor her sister developed close relationships with their mother until they were grown women.

By the 1960s and 1970s, working mothers with nannies were much less likely to separate themselves so completely from their children. Living in a townhouse in the 1970s, Beth had attempted to paint with her son in the same room when he was a small baby, and even after she employed nannies she had encouraged her children to interrupt her work and visit her whenever they needed to, a liberty few parents would have considered in the early part of the century. Differences of this kind had a major influence on mother–child relationships. David remembered his mother as always being around:

> You know, she'll be in her study and at that age I'd probably rock in going, 'Mum, Mum, look at this' or 'I've just built this' and she'd go, 'Oh, that's lovely darling, well done' and be brilliantly enthusiastic.

In the early twentieth century, most mothers from wealthy families were less readily available. They loved their children and, like Beth in the

1970s, were devastated when they became seriously ill. At the start of the twentieth century, infectious diseases such as tuberculosis and diphtheria were still endemic and could be life-threatening. Mothers sometimes kept diaries or notebooks with considerable detail on children's illnesses, diets and weight gain or loss. However, they did not expect to give hands-on care or know how to relate to children as easily as nannies. Having been brought up themselves in a similar way, they did not expect things to be otherwise. This may explain why in 1910 Joan Kennard left the elder boy with his nanny and grandparents immediately after the younger one died of appendicitis at the age of 2½. She had never spent much time with either child and found it easier to grieve apart from her surviving son rather than keeping him with her, a choice most mothers today would find incomprehensible.

Mothers expected a lot of their nannies and blamed them if they did not keep the children safe and healthy, but they showed less understanding of emotional attachments. Joan sacked the nanny she had left looking after her elder child, Dennys, when he caught a cold. Considered delicate, the boy had recently experienced another change of nannies after having been confined to a sanatorium with tuberculosis. But Joan's main concern was that one child's death and the other's poor health meant that she would no longer be able to go abroad for the winter. Her position as an army wife and companion to her husband had always taken precedence over her maternal role.

The Bowlby children's mother May also prioritised her position as a wife over her duty as a mother. When her eldest daughter was a young baby, she left her with nannies for six months in order to join her husband when he was wounded during the Boer War. John Bowlby's influential theory of maternal deprivation was inspired partly by his response to his mother's inability to give him the attention he desired as a child.[46] In company with other mid-twentieth-century psychoanalysts with similar upbringings, John focused far more attention on mother–child attachment than he had experienced in his own childhood.

Another factor which fed into the maternal deprivation story was nanny loss. John's nursemaid had departed when he was 4, and his wife Ursula's nanny have left when she was 5. These kinds of experiences could be devastating for children and often led to the creation of idealised memories. Ursula's main recollection of her nanny was sitting by the fire in her starched white apron, ready to play with her, tell fairy stories and comfort her tears away; she never entirely recovered from her loss.[47] The departure of Nellie, one of the Selwyn sisters who worked for the Bloomsbury group of families, was equally upsetting to one of her former charges, Nicholas Henderson, who loved her more than any other woman in his life. He remembered the Selwyns as 'paragons of perfection' who had been 'the central focus of our lives'.[48] Other children reacted to such losses with anger as well as sadness. When Ada left the Robinsons, the effect of her departure was so traumatic that the middle child Matilda 'went ballistic', screaming and kicking the new nanny. Rather than idealising her time with her nanny, however, Matilda's few memories of her young childhood were suffused with the hurts she had suffered.

In the 1980s, historian Ronald Fraser explored the complexities of having a distant mother and a nanny who left him at a young age. He did this by revisiting his childhood home, a manor house in Amersham, interviewing his old nanny and other servants who still lived in the neighbourhood, and recording their memories of his childhood. Through this reminiscence work, with the help of a psychoanalyst, Fraser identified an unbearable split in his psyche which must have been common to many other children with similar upbringings. He described two manors in his memory under different roofs. The old one was at the rear, where he lived with the servants and his nanny, and was completely separate from the imposing new manor at the front; he ventured into this semi-alien territory with caution. Fraser characterised his mother, who inhabited this territory, as 'the distant star, the cold moon', and he could not forgive her for not being the kind of parent he wanted: 'an island in the sea from which a child can set sail on its own, always sure there is a refuge to return to'.[49]

Fraser spent nearly all his time as a young child with his German nanny Ilse in the nurseries, or walking and playing outdoors in parks and gardens. Ilse exercised considerable power since she had relatively little interference from her employers; she allowed them little contact with Ronald and sometimes ordered Fraser's mother out of the nursery. Being isolated in her nursery kingdom made her emotionally over-dependent on her relationship with her charge, whom she described as filling her life. Fraser, in turn, became more reliant on Ilse than he later thought desirable, making it all the more difficult when he had to give up sleeping with her after his younger brother Colin was born.

Ilse understood how difficult this event must have been, just as Beth's nanny Pat had recognised David's feelings when his little sister was getting all the attention. In the interview Fraser did with her she explained, 'It was the only time you were really ill. Perhaps you felt a bit excluded. You suffered, I know, when you couldn't sleep in my bedroom any longer because I had to have Colin with me.'[50] Fraser saw Ilse's preoccupation with his brother and his own removal from her room as a second rejection, since his mother had been unable to breastfeed him and spent so little time with him. The final straw came when Ilse was sent home to Germany at the start of the Second World War, leaving him with unbearable feelings of loss.

Class and racial differences made children's feelings about losing nannies even more complicated. A psychoanalytic case study casts light on the racial dynamics of nannying in a former British colony, which made it particularly exploitative. In a recurring dream told to his analyst, a white South African man was watching a black Xhosa boy happily herding cattle in a place he remembered from his childhood. The man was not present in the dream and could not talk to the boy, but only observe him. The dreamer's childhood circumstances cast light on this dream. Indoctrinated with racist values at school during the apartheid era, he had for years distanced himself from his Xhosa nanny. This woman had looked after him and loved him like a mother, while his own mother had behaved more like a competitive child. But it was not until many years later that he finally understood the dream and acknowledged his nanny's love and his emotional dependence upon her as a young child. When he met his nanny again, the dreamer was able for the first time to recognise his black self. He discovered that, after his birth, while she was attending to his mother, the nanny had buried his umbilical cord in her paternal home, linking him to her ancestors and thereby making him Xhosa. This was a bond between them that he could now reclaim.[51]

MANAGING BOUNDARIES:
DEPENDENCY AND EXPLOITATION

Nannies were often critical of mothers' inability or disinclination to care for their own offspring. Tensions and conflicts between nannies and mothers frequently centred on differing childcare standards, and the slippery boundary between dependency and exploitation was never far away. Susan, the Edwardian nursemaid, complained that her mistress never got up to tend her children in the night. Even highly valued nannies noted maternal deficiencies. Ada, who stayed with the Robinson family for five years, cherished the trust that was placed in her and regarded Mrs Robinson as 'like a mother' to her. Yet she had other feelings that were more difficult to express, displaying little confidence in her employer on the rare occasions when Mrs Robinson took sole charge of the children. Not only did she allow the baby Nigel to burn his hand on a white-hot poker, but later, when left alone for a few minutes with the children on a train, she did not prevent the eldest boy from slamming his little brother's finger in a door. A nanny who was dependent on her employer for work could not easily rebuke her for neglecting a child, particularly when she had formed such a deep attachment to the family. But on this occasion Ada did not try to hide her views:

> I was cross because I'd been up a while and I can't remember the words but, 'I've looked after them all night, and you sleep by for nothing … I give you the babies for two minutes and look what happens'. And his finger, his nail, never grew back again. And of course when we got to London, I was pushed in a taxi, sent to the hospital on my own – I didn't even know London – to take him to have his finger X-rayed.

Ada's conflicting feelings about her employer suggest both the complexities of nanny–mother relationships and that class hierarchies were becoming less stable as deference to employers waned after the Second World War. Much depended on a nanny's own family background. Vera, a trained nanny in a large house in the 1930s, did not mix with the servants but, since she was a miner's daughter, the gap in status between

Children having a picnic with their nannies and a chauffeur, *c.* 1935. This was an 'upstairs, downstairs' household with a large staff. The children only saw their parents at certain times and had extended holidays with the nannies. *Courtesy of Diana Hounsome*

herself and the family meant that she had no expectations of sharing any time with them either; she was mostly on her own with the children. The gulf between their social worlds can be gauged by Vera's excitement when a maid offered to mind the children so that she could go downstairs to look at the table laid for a grand dinner; she thought the flowers, silver and cutlery 'magnificent'.

By the 1920s, values and expectations were beginning to change, particularly where the nanny's background was closer to that of the employer. In an early issue of *Nursery World*, an article by the founder of the Association of Nursery Nurse Colleges urged mothers to negotiate the gap between them by being kinder to their nurses. She pointed out that this was a professional relationship in which nurse and mother must work together in complete co-operation in order to create an atmosphere of peace and harmony. Stressing the heavy responsibilities of the job, the long hours, and the love and care nursery nurses gave to the children, she called on mothers to 'consider the nurse, to make her work easy and her nursery a happy home'.[52]

Jessie Dawber, principal of the Princess Christian College for nursery nurses, addressed younger employers, exposing the difficulties for a woman who might be a similar age and have similar tastes to them and yet be relegated to a lonely life in two rooms with only children for company. She suggested breaking down boundaries by talking about subjects other than children and occasionally inviting the nurse into the drawing room or for dinner. She pointed out that lending her a book or magazine and drawing her a little into the family circle would pay dividends in appreciation and increased energy. Yet Dawber was still anxious to assure her readers that she was not advocating that 'the nurse should be "one of the family"; that is a mistake'.[53]

Correspondence columns of *Nursery World* and college magazines offered a forum for employers and nannies to debate these questions throughout the twentieth century and open a window on the tensions of the period. In 1909 in the *Norland Quarterly*, Cicely Colls pointed out how hard it was for nannies to adapt to mothers' differing standards. They often had to move from a well-ordered household where children were expected to be spotless to another where noise and dirt prevailed, as well as suffering the frustrations of not being allowed to use their own initiative.[54] A trained nanny with seventeen years' experience, writing to *Nursery World* in 1925, argued that the problems lay mainly with mothers. 'With a baby, an experienced Nurse once she is used to that baby, knows exactly what to do for him and why he is crying. Were it her own baby her task would be lessened, but so often Mother worries when baby cries and thinks there is something wrong with him. If a mother has a really good competent nurse would it not be better if she left the baby entirely to nurse.'[55]

Several weeks later, Joan Bateson stated the employer's perspective. In 'A Mother's Advice to Nurses: An Answer in Effect to "Those interfering Mothers"', she pointed out how often mothers kept their mouths shut to avoid conflict. She posed the problem in relation to rather idealised memories of her own self-sacrificing old-fashioned nanny who dedicated her life to children and 'never took one minute off, day or night'. This was the regime under which she believed most employers had been brought up. While there were now opportunities for them to develop friendships with new young lady nurses (which would never

have arisen in the past), Bateson also recognised the problems of negotiating a relationship in which class divisions and social differences were
becoming less important and less clear:

> What should we call her? … Where ought she to feed? Will she
> hate your friends, or will she want to know them? If you are smok-
> ing, do you offer her a cigarette? Is she in fact like ourselves inside,
> or has she some relationship to the starched miracle of our own
> childhood?[56]

Yet some nannies did not want to be friends with their employers.
A nanny writing to *Nursery World* that same year resented being obliged
to go down to dinner after spending the whole day with the children to
sit and sew or talk with her employers. Longing for 'a moment alone',
she felt she 'could scream' but was afraid to leave in case she could not
get such nice people to work for again.[57]

All these examples illustrate the fundamental clash between employment and personal relationships as nannies and mothers had to manage
increasingly blurred boundaries. Nannies were no longer simply in
an intermediate position between family and servant, but might now
also be viewed as professional workers or family friends. Boundaries
between mother and nanny became even less clear-cut after the Second
World War, particularly in houses where the nanny was the only live-in
member of staff. Post-war nannies often struggled to describe a working
relationship in which they felt both included and excluded. As Flora, a
Norland nanny in the 1960s, explained, 'You couldn't be in the house
and not be around, so you were part of the family in that way, but you
had your role which was not a member of the family, if you appreciate
the difference.'

Much depended on how willing employers were to recognise a nanny's professional status and treat her accordingly, as another Norlander's
story shows. In her first probationary post in the early 1950s, Alison
had eaten breakfast and lunch with the family in the dining room but
had not been given the freedom to bring up the child in the way she
believed was best. She soon became deeply frustrated at being obliged
to struggle up the stairs with a heavy pram, rather than leaving the baby

to sleep outside. She also felt demeaned when bringing the child down to the drawing room by her employers' insistence that she should sit on the floor rather than the sofa, and decided to leave before the end of her probationary year. Her second post was a marked improvement. Here she was given sole charge of the child by her employers, who had complete confidence in her abilities. Yet, when she was invited to share her evening meal with them, she was uncomfortable. Feeling that she would be intruding on the couple's personal space, she made an agreement that she would take her food to her room. This was both to allow husband and wife to be alone together and because she preferred time to herself listening to the radio.

Alison's account suggests both the advantages and disadvantages for parents of employing a childcare expert and the difficulties when standards of care were radically different. Walter and Pamela, an academic couple, found the trained nanny they chose in the 1970s determined to be in charge and much stricter with their daughter than they thought necessary. Pamela recalled:

> So she was telling us what to do; we weren't telling her what to do. So she told us what colour she wanted the children's room painted. She got us a cleaning lady; she wasn't having any of this dirt and she made it perfectly clear to us she wasn't putting up with this and she wasn't putting up with that. And she was incredibly big, she was as tall as Walter and heftily built, so we were scared of her and she jolly well ruled the roost.[58]

Tensions often arose between mothers and nannies whose tastes differed, and one of the ways nannies could assert their own authority over both the children and their mother was in the choice of clothes. Mothers remembering these conflicts explained how they had suppressed their annoyance. Pamela's nanny had dressed their daughter in coats with velvet collars and buckled shoes to keep up with the Kensington nannies and, to keep the peace, Pamela decided 'well, let's go along with it, [her daughter] Ruthie's not going to remember wearing these dreadful things'. Beth knew that she had to contain her feelings – which she realised were unjust – towards one of her nannies because 'she dressed girly, she dressed in pink and white. She liked to do Emily's hair in little bunches and there was something very prissy about her.'

Another common difficulty between mothers and nannies that recurred throughout the century was the jealousy that arose when children and nannies became too deeply attached and mothers felt excluded. Sophia Leigh's nanny, Norma, had worked for the Leigh family since the 1920s. Explaining that they had made an agreement when she was younger, Norma had persuaded Sophia – slightly against her better judgement – to re-employ her in the 1940s to care for the next generation of children. Although Sophia had liked Norma, the arrangement had not worked out. The two women became rivals for the youngest child's affection, and when the toddler had innocently claimed to be Norma's little girl her mother was not at all happy.[59]

Sophia's discomfort with Norma also stemmed from some uncomfortable feelings relating to their respective backgrounds; she did not altogether approve of Norma's view that she should be treated as if she were on the same social level as the Leigh family.[60] But Sophia could not easily reject a nanny who had been loyal to the family for so many years. The difficulty here was not simply that Norma was laying claim to the affections of a second generation of Leigh children. She had also failed to let go of her first set of children and remained an authority figure, reprimanding them even as adult women. The younger Leigh children continued to be grateful to Norma for offering them love and stability in a childhood fractured by parental incompatibility and later by divorce. Still, it was probably fortunate that, after many years' service to the Leighs, Norma was called upon to look after her own brother's three motherless boys and finally departed.

Tensions in negotiating the boundary between dependency and exploitation, which so many of the preceding examples reveal, often revolved around the question of 'time off'. An early twentieth-century domestic service survey showed that not all mistresses saw time off as necessary, particularly when there were children in the house. A number of them thought that a maid 'became part of her employer's family, and like other feminine members of a family she must expect to share its life and needs'. This subject was much debated by employers and nannies. A letter from an employer to the *Norland Quarterly* not only shows how little time mothers expected nannies to have to themselves – her original proposal was twelve hours a month, exclusive of church-going and evening hours after 8 p.m. – but also wonders what time off should actually mean:

Is it time off when the nurse goes out of the house after 8 p.m. when the children are all in bed, or should she start out at 7 p.m. is it only time off for the one hour from 7–8 p.m.? Suppose the Nurse was to argue that her evening hours, however disposed of, were anyhow not to count as 'times off', what is to prevent her going out every night at 8 p.m.? No body of employers would agree to that, for wherever there are young children there has to be one pair [of] ears open to possible sounds from the night nursery at all times.[61]

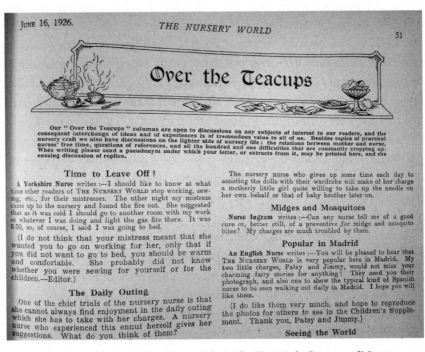

Nursery World correspondence column: 'Over the Teacups'. *Courtesy of* Nursery World

Many nannies would have taken issue with this viewpoint. They frequently pointed out how reluctant mothers were to give them any off-duty time and that this had been a recurring issue in otherwise happy posts. Off-duty hours became more generous as the century progressed; one day off a week and one weekend a month were more common by the 1970s. Yet a basic difficulty remained. The nanny and mother shared a home and family life, which made counting working hours appear unnecessary and even, at times, inappropriate. But they were also participants in an economic contract which had to be fulfilled, even if it was not written down.

Nannies who were entrusted with sole charge of a household did not worry so much about having 'free' time. Letters written by nannies in this position show the pleasures and responsibilities of being in charge, including recruiting and paying other servants, and they routinely emphasise how good and happy the children were in their parents' absence. Any frustrations or problems felt by nannies in this position could not be admitted if they wanted to preserve their employers' trust. But in ensuring that the children's attention remained on the absent parent, they also downplayed the importance of their own relationship, much as Cameron Macdonald believes nannies in America do today.[62] Elfie, nanny to the upper-middle-class Beamish family in East Sussex in the 1920s, wrote to her charges' parents:

> I have wished so often that you could peep at us especially when I draw!!! A boat sailing to Mum – all sorts of nice things are in the hold for you and Dad only I haven't time to enumerate them.... but it has just helped them think of and *for* you and to *do* something for you.[63]

Letters from Elfie and another nanny preserved in the Beamish family archive are full of anecdotes describing the children's activities in minute detail. They annotated the children's pictures and letters as they were learning to write, urging the parents to respond and make special reference to their drawings. Elfie appears from this evidence to have been the perfect shadow mother, completely in tune with the family she trusted and loved and with no outside interests of her own.

Where nannies stayed with families for long periods, time off became increasingly irrelevant and friendships could develop between mother and nanny which, though unequal, were mutually beneficial. Jeannie's employer was a Czechoslovakian Jew who had lost most of her relatives in the Holocaust and frequently flew into rages. Offering devotion and practical support, Jeannie soon became indispensable. Her charge Marion explained in retrospect that although her mother lorded it over her nanny 'and she was Mrs H and Jeannie was Jeannie', Jeannie was a very important companion and confidante. Being needed in this way was equally important for Jeannie, as she had lacked a stable home life as a child and regarded Marion's family as her own.

Dependencies of this kind did not always work in the nanny's favour in the longer term, particularly in cases where strong emotions came to the surface. In Nicholas's much smaller middle-class family, his mother held on to her help Gertie long after the children had stopped needing her services. Nicholas's mother had very little income after her husband died and relied on Gertie to help her run a small business making homemade cakes and sweets and raising chickens and ducks. When she was no longer needed, Gertie was asked to go. Nicholas recalled that she 'was terribly upset, tears and tears and tears and "how could you do this to me? I felt I was now with a family". You know, "instead of having my own family, I've got a family. I belong"'. The sad irony here is that, however much Gertie wanted to become part of Nicholas's family, as a 'plain', uneducated spinster from a much lower social class, she was destined to be an outsider.

Friendships between mother and nanny were sometimes jeopardised by sexual attraction between nanny and father. In one anonymous case a mother's discovery that her nanny was getting too close to her husband led to the nanny's immediate dismissal and separation from her much loved charges. The nanny remained deeply unhappy about the situation many years later. Yet not all mothers felt able to take this kind of initiative. Nicholas's mother had chosen not to dismiss her sick husband's nurse until after his death, even though it was clear that he was in love with her. This nurse, unlike their mother's help Gertie, was young and attractive, much loved by the children and a great help in the house. As a young boy in the 1920s Nicholas understood why his father had fallen for her reddish-gold hair, white cotton stockings and very short skirt, but in retrospect he wondered why his mother had accepted her, thinking the situation must have been 'a little fraught'.

The interdependency of mothers, nannies and children is apparent in all of these stories, but its effects in different households varied markedly. In jobs where childcare standards differed, where nannies' work was unappreciated, and where hours were long and time off limited, nannies felt exploited. This situation led to tensions, disputes and changes of job, which could be very difficult for all parties, and could even lead to abuse, particularly in households where mothers rarely saw their children. But where relationships were more harmonious, nannies were offered security and were regarded as much loved family members or friends by mothers as well as children. In places where they were highly valued and given responsibility, nannies accepted the long hours and often subordinated their own needs by prioritising the parent–child bond. In some cases, they protected children from parental discord.

It is impossible to know how often children were abused by 'bad' nannies or how perfect the 'good' ones really were, but nannies became the object of powerful projections, whether they were loved and lost or blamed for a host of childhood ills. The feelings that are articulated in this chapter cannot be separated from the social and economic conditions in which they were embedded. Chapter 3 gives another perspective on these interconnections as we explore where nannies came from, what kind of households they lived in, and the changing domestic service relationships and theories about childcare that influenced their work.

3

CONTINUITY AND CHANGE OVER TIME

Faith, I can tell her age unto an hour … Come Lammas-eve at night shall she be 14.

'Tis since the earthquake now 11 years; And she was wean'd, I never shall forget it, Of all the days of the year upon that day….

Thou wast the prettiest babe that e'er I nursed: An I might live to see thee married once, I have my wish.

Were not I thine only nurse, I would say thou hadst suck'd wisdom from thy teat.

(William Shakespeare, *Romeo and Juliet*, Act 1, Scene 3, *c.* 1595)

These lines, delivered by the nurse who plays such an important part in Romeo and Juliet's courtship, remind us that the employment of women as nannies goes back much further in history than the twentieth century. Juliet's nurse had a better memory of her age than her mother, remembered the day she was weaned, and longed to see her married. But she had a much closer association with her charge. That she was Juliet's *only* nurse attests to the fact that it was she, rather than Juliet's mother, who breastfed the child. She even suggests the possibility that Juliet might have inherited wisdom through her milk, though she modestly denies it. The nurse's role in the play continues well beyond infancy. As a family go-between, she was caught up with the lovers and with Juliet's parents and their daughter in a vortex of powerful emotions,

'Yet I cannot choose but laugh', *The Illustrated Shakespeare* (1847). This Victorian image of Juliet's nurse reproduces a common stereotype, showing her as old, ugly and foolish.

including adoration, fear, anger and contempt. While she was dismissed by Juliet's father as 'a mumbling fool', she is a central character in this tragic tale of romance and revenge between families.

To understand why the nurse came to be in this position and what connections she has with our twentieth-century nannies, we need to know more about her occupation. I start by tracing the history of professional wet and dry nurses of earlier centuries (a subject usually considered only in relation to the history of childhood), looking at continuity and change over time. As it would be impossible to cover the entire range of childcare arrangements, I focus on women who were paid to do childcare in the parental home. Charting nannies' working conditions across classes is useful because it helps to explain the variety of relationships within the mother–nanny–child triangle and why some aspects of its dynamics remain in play today.

WET NURSING

Mothers have delegated the feeding and care of infants to other women throughout most of recorded history, and baby nursing practices have been similar between societies and over many centuries. Why was this so? One answer lies in the practice of breastfeeding, which before the twentieth-century development of nutritious alternatives to human milk and an understanding of the principles of food hygiene, was the best way of ensuring their survival. The fact that another lactating woman could provide the same kind of nourishment as the baby's mother is highly significant. Although doctors and childcare experts often urged mothers to feed their own babies,[1] their advice was not always heeded. Whether or not they were physically able to breastfeed, women employing wet nurses could more easily engage in economically productive and social activities while still retaining the status and authority of a mother.

Evidence of wet nurses appears as far back as 3000 BC in ancient civilisations and can be found in Egypt, Mesopotamia, India, China and Japan. Nursing other women's children was an important source of household income for married women, who usually looked after nurslings in their own homes and kept them until they were weaned before returning them to their parents.[2] In wealthy households, however, wet nurses nearly always lived-in, becoming the equivalent of a nanny,[3] and were often highly regarded as status symbols. In ancient Greece they supervised other servants and, like Juliet's nurse, remained with girls they had nursed into adulthood. Nurses sometimes even stayed with their charges after they had married, accompanying them into the new household as a high-class servant/companion. This practice was also found among the aristocracy in eighteenth- and nineteenth-century England.[4]

There is ample evidence that nurses loved their babies; close, life-long ties between nurse and child existed in all periods and societies.

Memorials to wet nurses in ancient Greece and Rome pictured them nursing the child, and epitaphs put up by their former charges displayed gratitude, grief and deep mourning.[5] In eighteenth- and nineteenth-century Britain, feelings of loss when a nurse left or died can often be found in memoirs. One memoirist was never able to speak of her nurse's memory 'without considerable emotion', and another described 'pacing with sorrowing steps the now deserted apartment' where she had once rehearsed her nurse's 'lessons of wisdom'.[6] Still, it was only the richer families who could hold on to nurses long enough to produce such memories. Most households could only afford to keep them until the baby was weaned, usually at around a year but, as Shakespeare suggests, it could be as long as two or three years.

Mothers were advised to look for wet nurses who were healthy and who had the right size and shape of breasts, good-quality milk which would nourish the child, and the right temperament. It was supposed that children would inherit the physical and mental characteristics of their nurses because milk was thought to be a form of the mother's blood; indeed, if suckled by an animal, a human baby might develop bestial qualities.[7] An English manual *The Complete Serving Maid* (1729) reproduced this idea in its advice to mothers on how to choose a nurse, showing that it was still in currency in the early eighteenth century.[8] Some mothers kept a close eye on their nurses' behaviour and diet. Frances Bankes, wife of a major landowning MP, Henry Bankes of Kingston Lacy in Dorset, in the late eighteenth century, kept a diary in which she recorded the doctor's instructions for the wet nurse's diet, which must contain 'the most innocent food possible' and 'only half the porter allow'd her that she usually drunk'.[9]

By the late eighteenth century, the use of wet nurses was being heavily criticised by preachers and doctors on the grounds that a nurse would not look after the child as carefully as its mother and might transmit disease. The degeneracy of the aristocracy was thought to be the result of inferior milk from a dubious source, and the fact that one in five boys from the nobility died in infancy compared with one in seven nationally suggests that wet nursing did pose a greater risk to the child.[10] But mothers were slow to follow this advice and were probably more influenced by their own experiences with bad nurses than by the experts. Mothers

'The fashionable Mamma: or the convenience of modern dress', *c.* 1820. James Gillray's caricature criticises upper-class mothers' reluctance to breastfeed. An older child looking through the window is also being ignored. Maternal love is shown in a picture of a young mother on the wall suckling her baby. © *The Trustees of the British Museum*

'A drunken wet-nurse about to give the Prince of Wales (later Edward VII) a drop of alcohol as a horrified Queen Victoria and Prince Albert burst in on the scene' (Lithograph, *c.* 1842). *Courtesy of Wellcome Library, London*

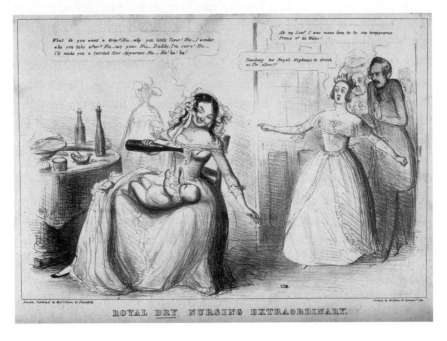

of the landowning classes were increasingly choosing to feed their own babies, but they still delegated much of their care to others. Servants had long been expected to include childcare as part of their work, but in larger households a more elaborate division of labour led to the employment of servants specialising in childcare as dry nurses or nursery maids for older children and babies who had been weaned.[11]

Controversy continued, particularly among men. For example, James Gillray's cartoon 'The fashionable mamma, or the convenience of modern dress' shows a nurse holding a child to the breast of a mother who shows no interest in it and is not even touching it. Good reasons were given for why delegating childcare was frowned upon. The philosopher Jean Jacques Rousseau warned that for a mother to give her child into the care of a nurse carried the risk of 'seeing her child love another as much and more than herself', while the social commentator William Cobbett deplored the sight of 'banished children' later being put into the arms of their mothers and screaming to 'get back to the arms of their nurse'.[12]

FROM WET TO DRY: CHILDREN'S NURSES IN THE NINETEENTH CENTURY

The move from wet to dry nurses was driven by both supply and demand. Wives could earn more reliable income from rural industries such as straw plaiting and lace-making, which allowed women to work at home. At the same time, declining infant mortality rates reduced the supply of 'respectable', lactating women without babies of their own to feed who were willing to be wet nurses. Through the first half of the nineteenth century, wet nursing continued to be regarded as safer than bringing a child up 'by hand' if the mother could not breastfeed. By then, however, wet nurses were no longer primarily married women, but could be young and unmarried women whose child had died or was being cared for elsewhere. In the absence of the right kind of wet nurse, dry nurses became more prevalent. Driven by a new interest in hygiene, coupled with a recognition that their children were not going to develop characteristics of the animal whose milk they drank, the upper classes were more willing to look for alternatives. Young babies could be fed cow's milk diluted with water by a nurse, a safer and more nutritious substitute for mother's milk than the traditional pap made from boiled wheat or barley.[13]

Employing a nurse whose sole task was childcare was usual in upper-class homes, but never normal among the middle classes. Smaller households usually contained one or two servants, either a cook and a nurse/general, or a cook/general. By the 1850s 750,000 women were employed as domestic servants and by the end of the century the total had risen to over 1,125,000.[14] But although many of them were involved in childcare, relatively few were named as nurses. A story written at the end of the nineteenth century by the popular children's author E. Nesbit shows how important this kind of servant could be. As the child narrator pointed out, 'A great deal of your comfort and happiness depends on having a good General'.[15]

The numbers of nursemaids and nannies rose steadily through the nineteenth century, but occupational titles such as 'domestic nurse' who might tend the sick or do childcare make it difficult to tell exactly how many of them there were. From 1881, nurses were not separated from other servants in the census employment tables. A generous estimate would probably be one in ten servants, but this does not include those servants who undertook childcare in addition to other duties. A survey of residential domestic servants employed in Lancaster in 1891 showed that three-quarters of servant-keeping households had only a single general servant. Although about half the households with servants in the town contained at least one child, very few employed nurses.[16]

A nursemaid working alone or with one other servant had a particularly hard life, often looking after several children with little help; if the mother had died, she might even be on her own.[17] She was expected to work from dawn until late into the evening and, especially if she were young, could be paid as little as a 'general' servant. Nurses' pay averaged under £15 a year in London at the end of the Victorian period (the equivalent of less than £1,000 today). The work was back-breaking: having a nursery on an upper floor meant that everything, including buckets of coal, water and slops as well as the children, had to be carried up and down stairs. It was little wonder that servants generally preferred places without children.[18]

Donald Black, a Scottish collier manager with his wife, children and their maidservant/nursemaid, *c.* 1900. *Courtesy of West Lothian Local History Library*

Lillian Burstall, nursemaid to a clerk in Edwardian London, had to care for three children including a baby. Although childhood ended early in working-class families, at 14 she was not much older than the middle-class children she looked after.[19] She stayed in this position for three years, but turnover among nurses in these kinds of households was generally high, contradicting the popular stereotype of the nanny who stayed with one family for years. Indeed, an 1899 survey estimated that nearly half of all nursemaids in London had held their current job for less than a year.[20] The diary of Elizabeth Lee, daughter of a draper living in Birkenhead in the 1880s and 1890s, records four different nurse girls employed by her mother in one year. Some of these girls were clearly at loggerheads with their mistress; one Welsh girl ran away after only a few days.[21] She was probably lonely living so far away from her own family in an English-speaking household.

In her history of domestic service in the eighteenth and early nineteenth centuries, Carolyn Steedman gives graphic descriptions of the hardships young girls suffered who were not strong enough physically or psychologically to carry out childcare work. Washing dirty, smelly bodies and stinking napkins (nappies) was bad enough, but nursemaids were often plagued by rude and disobedient children who would not accept their authority. During the long hot summer of 1800, the patience of two nursemaids snapped and they murdered the children in their care. Enraged by being called a 'dirty slut' by her mistress, Ann Meade gave her 18-month-old charge arsenic. Ann Vines killed a toddler whom she described as 'a nasty little creature' by dumping it in a copper full of boiling water after it had soiled itself.[22]

Specialisation in childcare became more common later in the nineteenth century. As an expanding and increasingly wealthy upper-middle class moved into bigger houses, they took on more staff, with wives supervising servants' labour rather than doing domestic work themselves. Mothers in these households had less to do with the day-to-day care of babies and older children. Nursemaids from humble backgrounds might be promoted within the house or recruited from another place, often recommended by their own or their employer's family or friends, to head nurse or nanny. Here they took sole charge of the children, often with younger nursemaids to help with the dirtier work.

Once they were ensconced in their own nursery and had less direct contact with employers, nannies were more likely to stay. An upper servant in London who stayed in a family for over five years was often there for nearly two decades.[23] Nannies, like housekeepers and butlers, remained in places where they were loved and needed, had close relationships with their employers, and were given decent salaries. The 1899 survey showed that just over a third of nurses[24] in London were over the age of 30 and received nearly twice the wages of those aged under 20. Older nannies were most likely to be employed in the big households. Those in their thirties might live in a house with six or more servants, while those in their teens or early twenties were more likely to be a nurse or nurse/housemaid in a household with only one or two servants.[25]

SPACE AND CLASS AT THE START OF THE TWENTIETH CENTURY

The Edwardian period was the peak of the specialised servant.[26] Large country houses often had wings containing day and night nurseries, with their own staircase, and five- or six-storied townhouses usually had a nursery floor. This physical separation meant that children and their nannies and nursemaids in the 'best' nurseries led very different, often more restricted and isolated lives, apart from both parents and servants. Until the last decades of the nineteenth century when the birth rate among the middle and upper classes began to fall, nurseries were quite crowded places, a world away from the gracious but often empty drawing and dining rooms below.[27] Although family size had declined by the early twentieth century, children were still not always allowed into the kitchen and could be deliberately kept apart from the servants, seeing them only in passing as they went about their work (some employers even required servants to turn round and face the wall to avoid seeing the children).[28]

The paradox here is that many nannies came from a similar background to the servants. Yet their job was to ensure that children did not pick up the habits and accents of the 'lower orders'. For a nanny in this situation, being described as 'in the best sense a lady' allowed her charges

A row of Victorian townhouses. In five-storey houses of this size and type, servants slept on the top floor, with nurseries usually located on the floor beneath. *Markabond/Shutterstock*

to bridge the gaps in social status.[29] But it also meant that, like governesses and companions, she could be in a quite a lonely middle position between the family and the servants.[30] Still, nannies' function as social gatekeepers was not always a success and some children did become very fond of household servants, particularly where they felt distant from and estranged from their parents.

During this era, class differences were observed minutely and mattered in ways that are hard to comprehend today and, as tensions arose, children became caught up in them. Because they were from a lower social class, servants spoke differently and smelled different and were expected to call their charges 'master' or 'miss'. But at the same time they might be set in positions of authority over the children, making it hard to know who was or should be in charge. Sometimes children were at the mercy of servants, particularly where the nursery and servants' quarters were in close proximity and away from parental eyes. But the tables could be turned, as children acted out their feelings in displays of arrogance and contempt.[31]

Talking about these conflicts could be difficult. The Leigh sisters were only able to articulate them many years later. Some of the sisters remembered feeling constrained and uncomfortable in situations where maids refused to bring meals to the nursery and when their father could not come into the nursery when the chauffeur's son was invited to tea. One sister had to 'do a lot of negotiating' and be 'very diplomatic ... in a completely honest way'. But she could not explain this to her mother whose philanthropic work often seemed more important than the children. Their father was a doctor and well-known explorer, frequently away from home, and their mother, who was a Poor Law Guardian and local magistrate, seemed equally distant.

This system allowed mothers to socialise with other members of their class and to 'do good' to those less fortunate than themselves, or participate in political activities such as women's suffrage. But little account was taken at the time of the views of their children or carers. Historian Brian Harrison explored a nanny's and child's perspective in the 1970s in interviews with suffragist Anna Munro's daughter Margaret and her nanny Dorothy Adams. Dorothy expressed admiration and gratitude to her mistress for inspiring and encouraging her to become politically active and speak on suffrage platforms, enabling her to go on to become a magistrate. But she also noted Anna's reluctance to participate in bringing up her own children or even to play with them. Dorothy saw the effects on the children who were inclined to hang back; Anna's absence caused her son Donald difficulty in saying goodbye to people, even as an adult. Margaret was more forthright. She expressed considerable resentment about her upbringing, feeling that that her mother had no interest in her and that any mothering she had came from Dorothy.[32]

Smaller middle-class homes created different dynamics. In the rapidly expanding suburbs of the late nineteenth and early twentieth centuries, terraced or semi-detached houses proliferated. Houses belonging to those in the lower-middle and professional classes were likely to have two or three reception rooms, three or four bedrooms, and a kitchen and scullery either at the back or in the basement. One – or, at most, two – live-in servants had to sleep in a box room or even the kitchen, although, to emulate grander households, bells might be installed to communicate between the kitchen and the other rooms.[33] A mother living in this kind of accommodation found it more difficult to separate herself so completely from the children. The children's bedroom might also accommodate a nursemaid or mother's help. But with her husband out at work all day and often involved in social or civic affairs in the evenings, a mother was more likely to share meals, housework and recreation time with servants and children. She sometimes took her midday meal in the nursery with them[34] and had full charge of the children when the maid or nursemaid was given a few hours off.

Yet tensions still arose in these more cramped situations. These were recalled by Nicholas, who grew up in a modest middle-class home in the 1920s. Their help, Gertie, became a particular problem when richer relatives came to stay:

> Uncle Harold couldn't stand Gertie because she was a dump. She had no education, she was rather pretentious and rather plain to look at and he just didn't like coming … 'Oh, Gertie. Is Miss Williams going to be there again?' you know. There was certainly a class thing.

Fear that a nanny or servants from a lower-class background might be a bad influence on the children they cared for has always troubled some parents, although it was seldom spoken about directly in my interviews. It appears most memorably in Henry James's enduringly popular ghost story *The Turn of the Screw*, in which a governess tries unsuccessfully to save two innocent children from being perverted by a former governess and valet who come back to haunt them. One of the signs of the servants' corruption was the crossing of personal boundaries: the fact that the valet wore his master's clothes showed he was not a 'gentleman' and marked him as evil.[35] My interviewees Beth and Valerie had similar concerns. In the 1970s Beth sacked a nanny for stealing her underwear, and at the start of the twenty-first century, Valerie used acts such as borrowing clothes and using the family towels and shower as evidence to get rid one of her nannies. They justified her fear that her nanny had become too intimate with her family and might therefore be abusive, not just to her own children but also to any future charges.

COLONIAL NANNIES

'Native' nannies working for white, mainly upper-middle-class families in the British colonies were believed to be equally suspect, but the safety of children was improved if not guaranteed by the fact that they usually lived apart from the family. In hot climates such as India, where a sizable British-born population lived and worked as missionaries, civil servants, or in the armed services, the most common type of accommodation for British families was a bungalow situated within a compound, with the kitchen and servants' quarters at the rear in huts separated from the house. This physical distancing served to underline racial differences and hierarchies, which were even more acutely felt than class distinctions in England.

Most British children were brought up by ayahs.[36] White British nannies were employed only by the wealthy few: not only were they in short supply, but their wages were beyond the reach of many families. The job of an ayah was not caste-specific, and the wages were comparable with or higher than those of other service jobs.[37] British families employing ayahs were often criticised in advice books which pointed out the dangers they represented to children's health because of the native's unsanitary 'low standards' and fondness for the 'wrong' kind of food. Ayahs also apparently jeopardised the children's moral values: 'Training in obedience, straightforwardness and self-control is not to be obtained from her'. The children might 'go native' if they became too fluent in Indian languages; they would not speak English fluently and might even develop a 'chichi' (Anglo-Indian) accent. They might also be corrupted, losing the 'naturalness of childhood' by listening to inappropriate Indian conversations on subjects such as 'the events of birth, marriage and death' or by being exposed to 'primitive emotions'. For Kate Platt, author of *The Home and Health in India and the Tropical Colonies* (1923), these things outweighed 'the atmosphere of love and devotion' with which ayahs surrounded their charges and their 'infinite patience'.[38]

How far British families in India took account of advice books is questionable. Correspondence from mothers is often ambivalent, alternately praising and blaming Indian servants. Some worried about leaving children exclusively with ayahs, believing they would spoil them and had 'little idea of training a child'. Anglo-Indian nannies (women of British and Indian descent born in the colony) could be equally suspect: the Godden family dismissed theirs when their children developed her accent. For those who could afford it, employing a nanny from Britain was the most effective way of stopping children from mixing with Indians.[39] During the 1930s, Yoma Crossfield's parents did not dare to criticise their British nanny, who not only enabled Mrs Crossfield to work with the Girl Guides but also kept Yoma safely distanced from Indian culture.[40]

Views changed after India had gained its independence from Britain. A 1951 story in the *Illustrated London News* suggests a shift in favour of Indian culture and values. Here a discontented white mother was warned not to leave her baby alone with a native nurse. But when the mother decided, rather irrationally, to buy a monkey, it was the ayah who became the disapproving party.[41] Accounts by parents about events after the Second World War tend to minimise conflict and praise 'native' servants for saving their children from such dangers as snakes and scorpions. For my aunt Lesley (born in 1928), a young child in India and an army wife in Singapore and Malaya in the early 1960s, having Malay and Chinese amahs (servants who did childcare) was an invaluable help. Although Chinese women were sometimes criticised by white military wives for picking up and carrying children for too long, they also were reputed to be 'wonderful' with babies, and British mothers felt quite safe and relaxed leaving their children with them.

Childhood memoirs tend either to deny racial distinctions between servants and family or acknowledge them from the perspective of the more enlightened late twentieth century. Iris Butler's memoir of her Indian childhood insists that no notion of superiority ever entered her head. Yet a letter from her mother dated 1910 gives a better idea of the young Iris's views. When attempting to get away from an ayah who was trying to undress her, the child had retorted, 'I hate being dragged about by these natives'. Children often expressed love for ayahs and other indigenous nannies, but the relationship depended on the children's 'own inclusion in a privileged and exploitative white society'.[42]

Young children found it confusing to be taught to despise the culture and values of a nanny upon whom they were physically and emotionally dependent. When at the age of 7 or so they were sent 'home' to a British

The children of a British civil servant with their ayah in India (*c.* 1906).

boarding school, it became even harder. Losing both nanny and mother at the same time, without the comfort of seeing either of them in the school holidays, was bad enough, as happened to the care-home resident Timothy (mentioned earlier) after he was sent home from Thailand. But, as Jane Gardam poignantly illustrated in her novel *Old Filth*, in an unfamiliar 'mother-land', in a foster home, or amidst the spartan conditions of a British boarding school, feelings of love and loss for a 'native' nanny could not easily be named.[43] Repression of these kinds of emotions had a long-lasting effect on some children, who now often describe themselves as boarding-school survivors.[44]

'THE SERVANT PROBLEM' SINCE THE FIRST WORLD WAR

In Britain, unlike in the colonies, it became more difficult to recruit nannies and other servants during and after the First World War. As men joined the armed services, many women gave up working in service altogether in order to take up better-paid and more essential jobs previously taken only by men. Class divisions no longer seemed so stable, and servants did not always 'know their place'.

The career of Amy Dike (1894–1993), who lived and worked in Bristol, was typical. She started work at the age of 15 in 1909 as a live-in under-nanny for the child of a chemist and was not allowed to mix socially with the other servants, although she found some companionship with the family's older daughters. In 1913 she moved up to a position as nanny, taking sole charge of two boys in a doctor's family. But she left in 1916, not only because she was being asked to take on housework as well as looking after the children, but also because women were now being recruited to work in the Post Office.[45] This option was much more attractive, and it had the added bonus of enabling her to mix more freely with men; she eventually gave up work to marry a postman. This pattern drastically reduced the servant labour force. While women were encouraged to go back into service after the First World War, they often refused, particularly where alternative employment was readily available in shops and factories in the south of England.

Amy's working life reflects wider changes for many professional-class mothers. At the beginning of the twenty-first century they often had a full staff, including a governess, nursery maid and nanny, and could take advantage of their leisure to socialise and do good works with other women of their class. A generation later, their daughters often had to manage with only one or two servants, later replaced by au pair girls. Faced with more housework, which by the interwar years was described in magazines like *Good Housekeeping* as a profession for women, married women's energies became focused in the home. This gave them more direct contact with their children's upbringing than their mothers ever had.[46]

After 1914 it became more common for nannies and children to share space with parents, even in the larger houses if they fell on hard times. A Staffordshire vicar, the Reverend Plant, had enough money before the First World War to employ a number of servants in his spacious, albeit crumbling, vicarage. By the time his two children were born, the cracks in the family lifestyle were beginning to show, a common experience among the clergy whose status as 'gentlemen' did not match the often meagre incomes provided by the church. Although the house had a baize door to separate the family from the servants, the family sitting-room was located off the back corridor. Mrs Plant participated actively in family life, never becoming 'a remote figure like some mothers who kept a nanny'. Her daughter Ruth recalled her mother sitting by her bed during the nanny's day off and, when her nanny returned, demanding that they should both stay with her until she went to sleep.[47]

Mothers and children became closer, not just because servants were fewer but also because families were getting smaller. More than a third of mothers born between 1850 and 1855 gave birth to seven or more live babies, although they had to face the risk that some of them would die. The 1911 census showed that middle-class couples like the Plants were tending to have only two or three children, while almost half the women born between 1900 and 1905 only had one or two.[48] Because infant death rates among the middle classes had also declined, many more of these children survived into adulthood.

Nannies often preferred families with one or two children as it was less work to look after them, but the fact that domestic help was in short supply in the 1920s also made it easy for nannies to move on. Some nannies and nursemaids chose short-term work, and many left to marry and have children of their own. However, women who grew up during and immediately after the First World War found that potential husbands were in short supply. The 1921 census showed that there were substantially more unmarried women than unmarried men in the population, and the shortage of men was widely publicised in the press. Half of all unmarried women in their late twenties at that time had still not married a decade later. Domestic service jobs made it particularly difficult for women to marry. With more surveillance by employers than in other jobs, opportunities to meet and mix with men were limited. There was also greater competition for men in London and south-east England, where most servants were employed, than in other parts of the country, especially north-east England, where sex ratios were almost balanced. This difference was in part due to the fact that so many women had migrated to the south in search of work, most often in domestic service.[49]

Women who would or could not marry were being encouraged by doctors and psychologists at this time to sublimate their maternal instincts through work with children, and some regarded nannying as a long-term career and a substitute for having families of their own. A survey of Norland nurses in 1935 showed that only 25 per cent married. Brenda Ashford, who trained in the 1930s, described an unspoken assumption at Norland during that time 'that personal fulfilment could be found by serving your family and being the very best nurse you could possibly be', and that becoming a nanny was 'a little like giving yourself to the Lord'.[50] Training seems to have been particularly important here. A sample of the 1931 census shows that only one in twenty servants specialised in residential childcare. However, the likelihood of holding a specialist childcare job at a later age was greater if you were trained. More than half the untrained nurses or nursery maids in the sample were under 25, and very few were over 35. But there were many more nursery governesses and trained nannies, and more than half of them were over 35.[51]

Still, the number of families with the resources to employ any kind of nanny over the longer term was limited and, as living out became more common, mothers were required to give more care to their children. The stock market crash in 1929 and economic depression of the 1930s made the situation even more difficult. One child in the 1930s remembered a queue of desperate, lonely women stretching round the block in answer to an advert for a job which promised 5s more than the going rate for nannies, but high wages did not guarantee that nannies would stay. The child in this case had eleven nannies in eleven years whom she named individually in her prayers, even though many had been dishonest, cruel or uncaring and only two had stayed in touch with her afterwards.[52]

Tensions between the nanny and the mother and poor employment conditions in the household contributed to a high turnover, but even nannies who had given good service often had no choice but to leave. In an article in *Good Housekeeping* in the mid-1930s, the comfortless, transitory life of a middle-aged spinster nursery governess was pitied and mocked by her employer. Forced to depart when the children went to school, after giving 'six years of as passionate devotion as [her] mild frame can house', Miss Jenkins had to go off with her 'neat trunk' and begin all over again.[53] As untrained nannies grew older, finding new jobs became harder. Although some mothers sought women with experience, others preferred younger women who either were recently trained in the latest childcare methods or could be taught to do things their way.

GIVING ADVICE TO NANNIES AND MOTHERS: CHILD PSYCHOLOGY

Tensions between mothers and nannies often centred on baby care methods, which in the interwar period began to be affected by new trends in child psychology. Until the Second World War, the New Zealand childcare expert Truby King and the American behaviourist John Watson dominated the field, influencing nanny training and parental advice manuals in Britain. They generally advocated keeping a physical and emotional distance between mother or nurse and child and following a rigid routine. Regular times were allocated for feeding and all other activities. Babies were kept quiet and under-stimulated, with the expectation that they would sleep for twenty hours each day.[54] This kind of advice suited many British nannies, who found it easier to keep discipline if children did not have much contact with their mothers. Nurses were taught to let babies cry. One nursery nurse training manual advocated completely separating a nervous infant from its mother for twenty-four hours in order to solve breastfeeding problems, and sedating it before feeding in the worst cases. The baby was left alone, tucked up firmly to sleep by an open window, and fed mother's milk with a spoon at three- or four-hourly intervals. The following day, the mother was told not to hold the baby too tightly during feeds, and the nurse was to take the child away from her again immediately afterwards.[55]

Lying behind these regimes was the idea that too much affection and attention would spoil children, either by making them overly dependent or too demanding, a view which Freud endorsed in the early part of the century. Both nursery and boarding-school regimes were designed to cultivate a 'stiff upper lip'.[56] In response to the question, 'Do you believe that petting a child is bad for it?', an advice column in *Modern Woman* magazine (1929) stressed that mothers' and nurses' aim should be to prevent the child from becoming too attached to them. Fondling children would have the opposite effect: 'The adult who is always recounting his ills and looking for sympathy is the outcome of too much coddling in childhood. That is why psychologists say too much mother love is harmful.'[57]

This kind of advice was promoted in mothercraft manuals by Truby King and his followers, which became best-sellers in the interwar years. By the 1930s their views began to be challenged by psychoanalytic theories which saw a close bond between mother and child as crucial for child and adult health and wellbeing. Significantly, the principal psychoanalysts who developed and publicised these theories had themselves experienced the effects of early separation from their mothers and often also from nannies.

Susan Isaacs, an analyst who observed young children closely in a nursery setting and wrote a number of books on child development, was one of the first to disseminate views of this kind to a popular market. She encouraged mothers and nurses to relate closely to their children and engage with their feelings.[58] Her interest in this subject was probably initiated by her own childhood: Isaacs' mother died when she was only 6 years old, and she had an unhappy relationship with her stepmother.

An early edition of *Nursery World*. The image promotes the idea of mother and nanny working harmoniously in the nursery. *Courtesy of* Nursery World

During the 1930s the magazine *Nursery World* employed Isaacs (under the pseudonym Ursula Wise) to give advice to nurses and mothers, and in 1948 she published a book, *The Troubles of Children and Parents*, containing a collection of the letters received and advice given over the previous decades.[59]

Nursery World was started in 1925 with the main aim of giving advice to mothers and nannies. Its readers hotly debated Isaacs' views and those of other childcare experts in the correspondence columns. One anonymous contributor to these columns was Ursula Bowlby, wife of John Bowlby. She kept a diary recording her experiences as a mother, and co-authored a book with John giving advice to mothers, entitled *Happy Infancy*.[60] *Nursery World* often published letters from nannies complaining about mothers' behaviour; but Ursula was determined to assert her authority as a mother over nurses who had never had children themselves, and urged mothers to trust their own feelings and instincts. She stressed that she was her own 'head nurse' and described the suffering mothers went through when told that they should not pick up their babies when they cried. Like many other mothers of her class and gen-eration, Ursula chose to use the services of a local girl from a 'respectable background' when her babies were young and later employed au pairs, believing that they would be more likely to respect her views and do as they were told.[61]

Ursula's views on baby care were rooted in her idealisation of her own mother, her upbringing by governesses and nannies, her feelings and experiences as a young mother at home and in a hospital, and the availa-bility of domestic help to assist her with childcare. But perhaps the most important influence was her strong interest in and engagement with her husband's research. From the 1940s onwards, John Bowlby actively pro-moted the idea that children would suffer maternal deprivation if they did not experience a close, continuous relationship with their mother or a mother substitute. This theory, which he based on research with monkeys and studies of evacuated children during the Second World War, became hugely influential after the war, particularly following the publication of his best-selling *Child Care and the Growth of Love* in 1953.

Sigmund Freud's theories on the ways in which a child's early years determine its adult personality inspired many of his followers to focus on the interactions between mother and child. Freud's own childhood is of some significance in this respect. Like some other men of his class, he associated his working-class nanny with disturbing sexual experiences as a very young child. These experiences resulted in a psychic 'split' in his unconscious mind between his 'bad' eroticised nurse mother figure and his 'good' birth mother, whom he idealised as pure and asexual. As a result, Freud seemed unable to fully recognise the significance of mother–infant attachments until after his own mother's death in 1930.[62]

Freud's daughter Anna, like other analysts of her generation, had a much stronger interest in mothers and mother–child bonds. She regarded her relationship with her nanny as 'the oldest and the most genuine of her childhood'.[63] But her love for her nurse could not make up for the distance she felt from her mother, whom she felt had neglected her. Anna was worried about the damage a governess or nanny might inflict on a child, particularly if she was trying to compensate for her own lack of mothering. Anna Freud remained concerned with mother–child bonds throughout her working life. Her pioneering study of children in residential nurseries during the Second World War, *Infants without Families* (1944), led her to argue forcefully for the importance of continuity of care for children and to maintain that professional childcare workers should not see themselves as taking the place of a mother.[64] Although Anna never published books for a popular audience, her lectures were advertised in a report of her findings in *Nursery World* in 1943. This report argued that it was not the bombs that disturbed children but being separated from mothers and moved from billet to billet 'so that they could never find one grown-up person to whom they could securely turn'.[65] Both of the Freuds' ideas were promoted in books aimed at parents in the 1940s and 1950s, including Margaret Ribble's *Rights of Infants* (1943) and Edith Buxbaum's *Your Child Makes Sense* (1949).[66]

During that same period, the influential paediatrician Donald Winnicott (whose childhood had featured a distant, depressed mother and multiple carers, including both a nanny and a governess) was urging women to attune themselves to the developing needs and desires of their children in order to become 'good enough' mothers. It was not until after the Second World War years that the psychological costs of the nanny system were more widely recognised and the idea that middle-class mothers should remain with their children and not leave them with paid carers gained wider currency. The main driver of this change, however, was not psychology or psychoanalysis but wider changes in British society precipitated by the war.

DOMESTIC RELATIONS SINCE THE SECOND WORLD WAR

While the First World War exacerbated the servant problem, the Second World War destroyed residential domestic service beyond repair. In 1942, single women under 40 were conscripted into the war effort. Although some nannies managed to gain exemption, this was on a case by case basis, according to the size, composition and number of children in the household, and most had to leave their jobs.[67] Only a few older, long-serving nannies in big houses managed to hang on. When country houses were requisitioned by the military services, they could often accompany their employers to alternative accommodation, while other servants were dismissed.[68] Many working mothers used the wartime day nurseries which employed some women who had previously been nannies; but middle-class mothers with young children, most of whom still did not do paid work outside the household, had to get used to managing alone or with much less help. In the 1920s and 1930s Ursula Bowlby's mother had a large staff to help her care for her family, but only one of her seven daughters, all of whom married, employed a nanny; the others either did all the childcare themselves or used general servants, mothers' helps and au pairs. Ursula's sister Barbara regarded having two women looking after one child when a war was on as ridiculous. She dismissed her helper, who joined the Women's Auxiliary Air Force (WAAF), and remembered the joy of having her baby to herself.

By the time the war was over in 1945, few women wanted to return to domestic service and those who did rejected the term 'servant', preferring to be called 'domestic worker'.[69] Women were now more likely to take clerical or shop jobs, or to work in light industry or the new National Health Service (NHS). Public servant and social reformer Violet Markham and trade union leader Florence Hancock assessed the reasons for this decline in a report on the organisation of private domestic employment in 1945. They pointed out that, before the Second World War, service was commonly denigrated as low-skilled, non-unionised, menial work. They also blamed popular songs, music halls and cartoons for ridiculing servants and representing them as 'drunken, dishonest and incompetent'. While the report pointed out the strains and ill-health suffered by the upper and middle classes as a result of too little help, little was said about childcare, with training suggestions for domestic workers focusing on cooking and housewifery. Children were only mentioned in relation to mothers' leisure time: babysitting swaps with neighbours and getting young girls to 'sit' with children would allow women time off in the evening with their husbands. Daily care of children was now seen to be firmly in the hands of the mother.[70]

Historians have differing views on how far the war reinforced women's traditional role as wife and mother or transformed her into a 'modern woman'. Yet after the war, the pleasures of motherhood and the home were celebrated on all fronts and supported by state policies. Women were offered a family allowance for each child, and most state-sponsored nurseries were shut down, making paid work difficult for mothers of young children and of older ones outside school hours. Still, not all conservative commentators were entirely opposed to help with childcare. Dorothy Patterson, founder of the Council of Seven Beliefs for the Guardianship of Family Life, rejected the idea of working mothers, but she did suggest that single women should be making 'a valuable contribution to the future of the nation by caring for the young' as a 'second line of defence' behind the mother. This might allow the energy of mothers 'temperamentally unsuited to the rearing of children' to be 'diverted into other channels' although she did not say exactly what those channels might be.[71]

Most upper- and many middle-class women continued to obtain some help with childcare, though the helper was no longer in sole charge. It was the status of these women that changed, not the kind of work they did, although the increasing adoption of household appliances such as vacuum cleaners and washing machines made it easier. Rather than having a nurse or nanny, post-war mothers were more likely to look for mothers' helps, some of whom were single mothers (either pregnant or with children) in need of homes. This situation continued into the 1960s, when the number of unmarried pregnancies peaked and single mothers were not yet entitled to adequate living allowances and housing benefit from the state.

Au pairs were also recruited from abroad. These young women, often from middle-class backgrounds, were supposed to do light domestic tasks and have adequate time off to study English in exchange for room and board and pocket money (£2 a week was suggested in the mid-1950s, compared with £3–5 offered in advertisements for nannies and mothers' helps at the same time). Although the practice was not officially backed by the government, the Home Office produced informational leaflets, and au pairs were offered support by organisations such as Friends of the Island (set up in Germany to foster better relations with Britain after the war), the British Vigilance Association, the Young Women's Christian Association (YWCA) and International Travellers' Aid.[72]

A 1950s mother, daughter and au pair. Au pairs did not usually wear uniform and were supposed to be one of the family. *Courtesy of Stephanie Spencer*

Leaflets describing the au pair scheme explained exactly what girls should expect and offered guidance to the host family. The most important point was that au pairs should not be treated as servants or maids, since they did not have work permits and were not covered by minimum wage legislation; rather, they were viewed as family members. A Home Office report in 1973 referred to their relationship not as one between employer and employee but between 'the girl and her hostess'. One leaflet described them as 'house daughters' and stressed that they should share fully in the life of the family and have time off to socialise with friends one full day a week and during the afternoons and evenings.[73]

How far this worked in practice is questionable. With middle-class women often claiming that they were managing a 'servantless home', au pairs became a hidden labour force. Described as 'not quite a guest and not quite a servant', they filled the place occupied before the war by servants, and could be seen as getting domestic labour on the cheap; a point that was made in a 1971 parliamentary debate. A survey of au pairs in Hendon in 1957 found their working conditions were similar to those of general servants, with two half-days off a week and £3 a week wages.[74] In the privacy of the home, au pairs could easily be exploited, and au pair schemes have been always been beset with complaints that families ignored the rules.[75] One au pair in the Hendon survey felt humiliated when her employer dressed her up in a uniform and called her 'Nanny',[76] but others may have assumed they were in the same position as servants. Tensions are reflected in a story told by Stella, whose mother employed a series of au pairs to look after her in the 1950s. While most were happy to fit in with family routines, one au pair was not. Stella recalled her appearing on her first day in a uniform and remembered her father's discomfort:

> He shot back upstairs and shaved and sort of put his suit on before he went down and had breakfast, which was absolutely not what they'd been used to. But Marie [the au pair] very much saw that she was on duty in the morning and she was off in the afternoon.

Stella's mother saw this behaviour as 'cold' and was irritated by Marie's refusal to look after a child who had hurt herself on the grounds that she was 'off duty'.

Elizabeth Longford's book *All in the Family: Parenting the 1950s Way* (1954) illustrates the invisibility of post-war domestic help. Although Longford was a mother of eight, she put her energies into politics and good works, rather than domestic tasks. While she acknowledged her children and husband's part in helping her write the book, she did not mention her domestic helpers. We only discover them in a foreword written by her daughter in the 2008 edition, who referred to the succession of cooks and au pairs who were loved or tortured according to the children's view of their just deserts, and saluted the skills of 'these noble women'.[77]

More middle-class mothers did move into employment, particularly teaching, which coincided with school hours, or took up part-time and home-based work. But commentators in the 1950s and 1960s, who encouraged married women to work, still took the Bowlby line, supporting the view that children needed continuity of care. Sociologists Alva Myrdal and Viola Klein in *Women's Two Roles: Home and Work* advised mothers to take care of their own children until the age of 3 and only leave them for four to six hours thereafter.[78] But women who worked longer hours, often from financial necessity or because they were divorced, widowed or separated, needed more help looking after their children.[79] In the absence of day nurseries or of relatives willing to give care, live-in help was still often the best option, although it was not easy to find. The demand for childcare increased as divorce rates rose and more mothers were obliged to go out to work. After an immediate post-war high in 1946, divorce rates declined briefly[80] and then rose again rapidly from the mid-1960s.

Post-war mothers lacked easy access to nannies, but by the 1960s and 1970s they had a wider range of childcare options than was available before the war. Whether or not they were directly inspired by the Women's Liberation Movement, they looked outside the home and family for personal fulfilment and began to organise childcare for themselves. Rather than leaving their children at home with a carer, women created playgroups and babysitting circles where they and their children could socialise and develop new skills and interests.[81] Sarah, living in Glasgow in the 1970s, joined one such group with five other mothers unable to get their children into nurseries. They looked after one another's children for a morning in their own homes 'so that the other mums would have four mornings to themselves'. Mothers also lobbied for crèches to allow more women to work part-time and attend events. As more middle-class women went out to work or worked from home, they also used childminders who looked after several children in their own homes as a cheaper alternative to nannies. In the early 1970s this service became professionalised and subject to registration, making it more attractive to the middle classes.

Live-in mothers' helps and au pairs remained useful options in post-war Britain, enabling mothers to spend more time apart from their children, which was particularly important for women who felt trapped in the home.[82] Their presence was not merely a supply of cheap labour but also fulfilled mothers' desire for companionship and sociability. By the 1980s this became less necessary as many more mothers began to work full-time and the trained nanny, now with a state qualification, became popular once again.[83] Most trained carers worked in day nurseries, but mothers who felt that children would do better with home-based care often employed a nanny, now defined as a professional worker rather than as a servant or family friend. By the late 1970s, having multiple carers was no longer widely regarded as such a problem. John Bowlby's theories on maternal deprivation had been challenged and were less influential. Maternal separation, while it could be stressful, was no longer thought to be so damaging to children, and there was more interest in the importance of a child's relationship with people other than its mother.[84]

We have travelled a long way, both from the days of the wet nurse and from the turn of the twentieth century when nanny employment was at its height. Some things have come full circle, however. In times when wealthy women did not expect to do any childcare, nannies enabled them to have a life away from their children, to go outside the home to socialise and do publicly important work, even though it was often unpaid. While most upper-class women continued to employ nannies, mid-twentieth-century middle-class mothers had less freedom. Being expected to do more domestic work and to be everything to their children also made the help they did get less visible and seem less important. But by the end of the century, nannies came out of the shadows again, offering a professional service to working mothers.

Why these changes occurred becomes clearer as Chapter 4 looks in more depth at the training and recruitment of nannies and at their lives outside the job. We start by investigating how nannies learned to do their work. What difference did it make if they did or did not have professional training? How did training regimes differ across classes? Finally, what were the implications for babies and children who became part of their training?

4

NANNIES IN
TRAINING

There were other colleges, definitely other colleges but … I suppose
it was considered the best at that time, and amongst parents to have
a Norland nanny was prestigious … The mother liked me to wear
my uniform, particularly when I went to birthday parties in other
families, because her nanny would have had uniform on and some
of the others only had little girls from the village as nannies. Meow![1]

This story was told by Sarah, a nanny who trained at Norland College
in the 1960s. While it may appear primarily to be about rivalry and one-
upmanship between nannies and mothers, it obliquely refers to a central
question which most nannies and mothers faced at one time or another.
What kind of nanny was the best nanny? Was it better to have a trained
nanny who knew all the latest theories or a young untrained girl under
the authority of the mother?

In order to understand these alternatives, we must consider how
nannies learned to do their jobs, what they learned, and what they and
others thought about their training. While the majority of nannies today
have a nationally recognised childcare qualification, in the early and mid-
twentieth century there was huge variation in where, how and what
they were taught. Some nannies trained in private colleges, others in
state-supported domestic service and homecraft training centres, and yet
others learned on the job in children's homes or residential nurseries. But

even after the Second World War, when a national qualification became available, trained nannies were always in a minority. Although many working-class girls did some childcare practice at school, most nannies did not have any formal nursery training but rather drew on past experience, watched what others did, or simply worked it out for themselves. Some were taught domestic tasks by their own mothers and learned about childcare from looking after younger siblings or neighbours' children. Where care was shared between mother and nanny, they followed the mother's instructions. In the big houses where mothers were seldom directly involved, they started as nursery maids and were trained by the head nurse or older nanny.

As childcare became increasingly professionalised, formal training was more often seen as necessary. This was also part of a wider shift in the school curriculum for girls, giving domestic subjects taught at secondary level to less academic girls the status of a science, viewed as education rather than simply training.[2] Parents were told how much value a well-educated, trained nurse could offer their children compared with baby-tenders barely out of school, and untrained nursemaids were likened to the Dickens caricature of a nurse, 'Sairey Gamp'.[3] But colleges were also aware that parents might feel criticised and see a trained nurse as unapproachable and opinionated, so they were anxious to reassure them that 'a really good nursery college-trained nurse will put the children first and give them the same selfless love and devotion as the old-fashioned nanny'.[4]

Tensions between these two positions often arose because nannying was regarded both as a professional job needing a good level of education and thorough training, and as work that any woman would naturally be able to do. Norland College, the most prestigious school throughout the twentieth century, which is still going today, was a particular target. The following anecdote, reported in Norland College magazine in 1970, achieved the status of an urban myth and might have been repeated at any time in the century.

A young Norland trained nanny, new to the hierarchy of nannies in London, told a friend how she pushed her pram to the enclave behind the Albert Memorial in Kensington Gardens. The bench on which she sat was empty but after a while an older nanny appeared, pushing a pram on which was painted a small coronet. She sat down too and they eyed one another. Finally the older nanny turned to the younger one, coughed and said, 'Excuse me, nannie, but is your mummy a titled mummy?' 'Actually, no,' admitted the other one. 'You will excuse my mentioning it, nannie, but this bench is reserved for titled mummies' nannies, nannie,' was the reply.[5]

This tale speaks to a much bigger story of rivalry between 'on the job' nannies and college-trained nurses. This thread runs through this chapter as we look at the knowledge and skills acquired by nannies in different ways and by a variety of means, starting in childhood and ending with three of the best-known private colleges. These colleges are of particular interest because it was possible to compare the printed publicity and contemporary views of staff preserved in their archives with recollections and personal documents of nannies who studied there. But while college staff members' and students' views are given equal weight, babies and very young children who were the objects of training practice in homes, nurseries and hospitals had no voice at the time and their views have seldom since been heard.

CHILDCARE AT HOME AND IN SCHOOL

In the late nineteenth and early twentieth centuries, when large families were still normal among the working classes, most girls gained experience in childcare at home or in their immediate neighbourhood. Working-class and even middle-class girls were expected to look after younger siblings as a matter of course from quite a young age, and some also helped neighbours or relatives with their babies and young children.[6] Late nineteenth-century novelists and philanthropists described these girls as 'little mothers' and turned them into objects of pity in children's books and religious tracts.[7] Yet, while the work could be burdensome, girls were not simply taking over their mother's role. Rather, they saw it as 'a job which belonged to them' in which they could often take pride and pleasure,[8] and they sometimes pretended the babies were theirs. An 8-year-old watercress-seller interviewed by the journalist Henry Mayhew loved the baby she minded for her aunt from the age of 2 months because he laughed when she touched him under the chin and, although she was often tired from selling watercress, she still carried her little sister outside to play with other children.[9]

Because girls often missed school to do this work, regular childmind-ing increased their likelihood of going into nursery or domestic service rather than into jobs which required a higher standard of education.[10] The Education Report of 1899 for England and Wales found that girls as young as 5 or 6 were regularly paid to look after children, often pro-viding essential income for the family. Similar or higher proportions of older girls in two of the London schools surveyed were also minding babies, often in addition to other work. While younger children usually worked less than ten hours a week, those between the ages of 9 and 13 could be spending as much as thirty hours a week on paid work of this kind.[11] Later in the twentieth century, much smaller families and a higher school-leaving age (raised from 12 in 1899 to 14 in 1918, 15 in 1944, and 16 in 1972) made parents less tolerant of girls missing school. Although doing childcare was still an obligation for some girls, for others it could now be a choice or a way of earning extra pocket money.

A baby being bathed by a nanny, 1937. *Courtesy of Norland College*

Childcare was part of a package of skills like cleaning, sewing and laundry work which girls studied in schools through most of the century to prepare them for domestic service jobs and for their futures as wives and mothers. In 1910 a Board of Education circular on the Teaching and Management of Infant Care argued that older girls should be taught to look after children. At a higher grade school in Stepney girls learned about babies' sleeping routines, food, teeth ailments, formation of habits, playthings and intelligence. Pupils visited a nursery where they were shown how to bathe and undress babies, how to put them to bed and prepare their bottles.[12]

How effective this education was is doubtful. In her autobiography, Joyce Storey remembered similar skills being taught in a flat on the school grounds containing a tin bath and a pram. The girls had to bathe, change and rock a baby doll to sleep, but the doll was often upended and its head stuck in a potty.[13] Since many of the girls had already been looking after babies for many years, it would hardly be surprising if they resented being told how to do it at school. The emphasis for much of the century tended to be on bottle-feeding rather than breastfeeding, despite the fact that breast was always considered best by the medical establishment. Not only were teachers unable to show schoolgirls how to breast feed, but the marriage bar in teaching meant that few were mothers themselves and so had no direct knowledge of the practice.[14]

LEARNING ON THE JOB

Untrained nannies usually learned how to do their job by trial and error, helped, hindered or ignored by their employers, or by being shown what to do by the mother or other nannies. Experiences varied widely, but on-the-job training was most effective when nannies had good relationships with those in authority over them. Some younger nannies and nursemaids respected and were in awe of the grand or head nannies who showed them the ropes and supervised their work, while those in smaller households were grateful to their employers for teaching them how to cook and care for the children and for sharing the work with them. Others were simply left to fend for themselves.

Untrained working-class girls who had no choice but to go into service had the hardest time in positions where they were given little help by anyone. Ada, who later became nanny to the Robinson family, was the daughter of a farm manager who lived with her family in a tied cottage. She had enjoyed playing with dolls as a child, but her mother had never taught her to cook, so she was unprepared for the responsibilities she was given in her first post. As a mother's help at the age of 14 in 1942, she was expected to do 'anything and everything', including cooking, in a household with three children, of whom she was sometimes left in sole charge:

> You had to work because they just couldn't afford to have you living at home and not bringing anything in. So she [her mother] found me a job and I went with a family, but the oldest child was a year younger than me and I don't know, I felt as if she knew more than me. And then Mum said, 'Well you have to stay with them, there's nothing else for you to do at the moment.' So I had to stay.

Fiona (born in 1950), the daughter of schoolteachers who took a temporary job with an Israeli family as a 19-year-old in the 1960s, had little or no experience of looking after children or doing housework. She remembered cleaning the silver with wire wool pads, making cakes without a recipe, throwing saucepans at the children when they laughed at her attempts to do the washing up, and letting one of the children run into the road. In retrospect, Fiona found it hard to understand why the family put up with her. But she had chosen to go there in order to remain living abroad and was able to have fun with the children. As a post-war middle-class girl in her 'gap year' between school and college, she could also choose to leave her post, while Ada could not.

The longer-term prospects for untrained nannies seemed to depend on how much pride and confidence they acquired in the skills they learned on the job. Nursery maids working in the bigger houses before the Second World War could sometimes be promoted within the household. Emily, a farm labourer's daughter born in 1903 who went out to work at age 14, had a difficult time in her first post, with very low wages, heavy work and tiresome children. Her second job, as a nursery maid in a larger house, was a much better experience. The other staff mothered her, and because she was very anxious to stay there and to learn as much as she could, she worked her way up to under-nanny and eventually, at the age of 19, became a head nanny. Climbing this career ladder enabled her to assert her power; she claimed that she knew much more about children than their mothers did.

Bridget (born in 1906), a builder's daughter who worked as a daily nanny in a smaller house, never achieved that kind of confidence. As a youngest child Bridget had no experience of looking after siblings when she started work as a daily nanny in her early twenties, but she had learned cookery and laundry at school and been in other live-in service positions. At first being a nanny seemed easy, with no heavy work, and she enjoyed taking the children out to the park and making friends with another nanny. Her main problem was in her relationship with the mother, who Bridget believed was making the children wild. This was eventually the cause of Bridget's departure, because she could no longer control them. Lacking the belief in her skills that either childcare training or working under an experienced nanny might have given her, Bridget was left with a sense of failure.

STATE TRAINING CENTRES

For working-class girls like Bridget and Emily, attending a nanny training college was rarely an option. In the early decades of the twentieth century, similar skills were taught as preparation for domestic service in institutions for girls who were orphaned or considered 'friendless'. Instruction was also offered by domestic training schools set up by some local education authorities before the First World War; one in Birmingham was specifically for nursery maids.[15] The state became more actively involved in servant training in the interwar years when greater numbers of women were out of work. This situation pushed the Ministry of Labour into setting up homecraft training centres to encourage more girls to move from depressed areas to take jobs in domestic service and childcare. Although girls and women who trained in them were still a small fraction of the personal and domestic service workforce, these centres seem to have been increasingly popular following the stockmarket crash in 1929. Nearly 4,000 girls and women undertook the training between April 1929 and March 1930, and more than 90 per cent of them found jobs.[16]

Vera (born in 1917), daughter of a coal-miner from the Welsh valleys, was one of these young women. In the mid-1930s she saw an advertisement in her aunt's copy of *The Lady* for a training school near the Crystal Palace in London that prepared women for domestic service and nursery work. Vera described the school as being divided into sections, including cooks, under-cooks, house maids, kitchen maids and nannies, as well as the 'upper crust' who did secretarial work. Her decision to choose nursery work led to a post as nanny in a wealthy Kensington home, offering her a glimpse of a lifestyle undreamed of in childhood. The training gave her a status and level of responsibility she might have taken years to reach in this kind of household if she had gone straight into service after leaving school. In an otherwise quiet life spent working as a doctor's receptionist and looking after her parents, Vera nostalgically recalled this ten-year period as 'happy days' that she would never regret.

Childcare training became professionalised after the Second World War. In 1945 the new state-supported further education and technical colleges began to offer two-year training courses leading to the new National Nursery Examination Board (NNEB) certificate. These colleges were in competition with private training colleges, some of which closed while others struggled to survive in reduced circumstances. State-supported college courses also ran in parallel with domestic training centres which received government funding. Set up by the National Institute of House Workers (NIHW), which was founded in 1949, they were designed to persuade girls who had failed to get into college that domestic skills could lead to rewarding careers. The course included a three-month placement, either as a mother's help in a private residence or in an institutional setting.

Girls who chose to be mothers' helps usually worked with children, even if their main jobs were cooking and housework. Progress reports of girls doing the training show that those considered to have the right qualities, especially neatness, quietness, kindness, good manners and good personal grooming, were encouraged to work with children, and some did go on to become nannies or mothers' helps. The fact that this was not seen as a desirable choice for brighter students shows the low esteem in which childcare jobs were still held. One girl's determination to work with children was discouraged because she was a star student, particularly good at cooking and, her teachers hoped, destined for something better.[17]

A rare glimpse into the lives of these trainees comes through the eyes of Jenny, brought up in South Wales in the 1940s, whose memories capture a child's perspective on a student placement. Ellie was a coal-miner's daughter who trained to be a mother's help at Dan y Coed, a National Institute of House Workers Centre in Swansea. Jenny, then aged 9, remembered Ellie's arrival at her home on a placement in 1950 just before the birth of a new baby:

> She had blonde hair and wore grown-up clothes when not in uniform … I thought she was very sophisticated, though in fact she was barely six years older than me. On her half day off she went to the cinema with a fellow student who was similarly employed in a nearby household. They would then recount the film to me, sitting by the kitchen fire in the evening, causing me many sleepless nights remembering their account of the 'Five Fingered Beast' and other horror stories!

If Ellie had been trained at a prestigious nanny training college such as Norland or Princess Christian, she would have been cautioned against telling stories that would give children nightmares (a warning about this was given by the founder, Princess Christian, who was a daughter of Queen Victoria). But there were no lessons in child psychology given at Dan y Coed. At first Ellie's work involved helping with household cleaning and cooking; after Jenny's sister was born and Jenny's mother kept to her room for several weeks, Ellie more or less ran the house.

The new baby became the centre of attention, looked after by a rather unpleasant monthly nurse who was paid £35 in addition to her travel expenses. This nurse regarded Jenny as a nuisance, and Ellie (who, being on a placement, wasn't being paid anything) was ordered around and made to do 'some very unpleasant laundry'. Yet Ellie was an important presence for Jenny, who was being ignored by the rest of the family.

Ellie disappeared from the house not long afterwards to go back to Dan y Coed, and Jenny never found out what happened to her. The clarity of these memories suggests her significance at a time when Jenny was adjusting to no longer being the only child.[18]

RESIDENTIAL AND DAY NURSERY TRAINING

Nurseries and children's homes offered another important training route. During the Second World War most local authorities opened day nurseries in towns and cities in order to enable married women to join the war effort. Residential nurseries in the countryside had a similar objective, often located in large country houses and run by voluntary organisations such as the Red Cross or the Women's Royal Voluntary Service and taking in evacuated children. By training on the job in these institutions, women under 40 could avoid being sent to munitions factories or into the armed forces when they were called up to do war service, and could also gain a qualification in caring for children aged under 5. Even experienced nannies who may previously have been employed in similar houses were required to do two months' free training to cope with the different demands and routines in wartime nurseries. College-trained nurses were also offered extra medical training, enabling them to take senior posts in children's wards and hospitals.[19] Although some were happy to return to private employment after the war, others felt they had better working conditions and pay in the nurseries (annual salaries at non-residential nurseries started at £135 in 1943) and were reluctant to go back.[20]

For some nannies, these experiences opened their eyes to levels of poverty and deprivation for which their pre-war jobs had hardly prepared them. Norlander Brenda Ashford's jobs looking after evacuees in a country house and war nursery were both challenging and life-changing. She remembered feeling that her contribution 'was more powerful and needed more than ever before' and that the 'children of this dreadful war needed stability and love.'[21] How far children in residential nurseries got this stability is more questionable. Propaganda films made during the war stressed their benefits. The film *Heirs of Tomorrow* (1945) claimed they were 'providing the groundwork for an inspiring future' and 'moulding a generation of good citizens'; 'fresh air, a healthy environment, physical training, cultivation of character, sound education, adequate and whole-some food ... [were] every child's birthright'.[22] Nothing was said about the emotional effects of parental separation, but the blank, rather sad faces of some of the children saying prayers asking God to bless their mummies and daddies suggest the potentially damaging effects of insti-tutional care.

Further insights can be found in a study of two residential nurseries established at Dyrham Park, a country house in Gloucestershire, which employed trainee children's nurses who were mostly in their teens. The Pro Patria Nursery cared for children from an Islington day nurs-ery who had been evacuated there at the start of the war. Here nurses were encouraged to become attached to their charges, with the matron arranging for individual nurses to care for small groups of children, whom they remember with great warmth. The Anglo-American nurs-ery, which opened in 1941, took children from the severely bombed area of West Ham in London, together with the offspring of the unmarried domestic staff recruited from a home for unmarried mothers in Bristol. They were well cared for, but the model adopted (like much other resi-dential care at this time) was more similar to a hospital ward. Children were divided by age rather than into family groups, and nurses were discouraged, albeit not always successfully, from becoming too attached to individual children.

Parents were told not to visit children more than once a month, and many lacked the resources to make such a long journey. When visits were infrequent, some children barely recognised their parents when they arrived and clung to the nurses instead. These women had become their mother figures and at least one had longed to adopt a favourite child. Several former child residents still have vague, warm memories of their time in the nurseries, but going home was more difficult, and they often felt the odd one out. The Dyrham Park Anglo-American Nursery was held up in a post-war survey as one of the best-run nurseries. It provided an excellent training for nannies and nursery nurses and left its former staff with positive memories. But its legacy for the children is less certain; we do not know how well most of them got on.[23]

Staff and children at Dyrham Park residential nursery during the Second World War. *Courtesy of Jean Lloyd and the National Trust*

Most residential nurseries closed after the war, but some day nurseries remained open although their numbers were considerably reduced. Those that remained trained their nurses to obtain the NNEB qualification designed to be taken by girls of 15 or 16 over a two-year period. The certificate included practical work in a nursery with children under 5, who were studied at every stage of their development, as well as general and vocational subjects taken at a technical or further education (FE) college. The vocational subjects, for which there was a written exam, covered health and education, but considerable emphasis was placed on observation of children in the nurseries and their own homes. These observations were supposed to lead to discussions with tutors and matrons rather than formal lectures.[24] One former nurse at a day nursery in West London remembered being called into the matron's office to be questioned, and enjoyed the experience, but felt it was mainly a matter of ticking boxes to ensure that everything was covered.

An important advantage of the state-supported NNEB training was that girls received free meals while on duty and were paid annual salaries, which in 1956 ranged from £170 per annum for those aged 16 to £212 for those aged 18. Charities such as Barnardo's, which had residential nurseries, offered a similar level of remuneration for the same training, including board and keep and up to £90 a year. This policy made NNEB nursery training affordable for working-class girls and compared favourably with private colleges, which charged between £100 for an eighteen-month course and over £200 for twenty-one months at the most prestigious institutions.[25]

Mary (born in 1931) trained at a London day nursery. Her mother had died during the war after aborting another man's child, and her father had remarried and was running a pub where children were not welcome. Mary stressed her obedience to her parents' authority: 'Oh I mean, but you didn't argue. You see, I don't ever remember saying I wasn't going to do it.' Yet that did not stop her being less than compliant in the interview. Having been told by her father and stepmother to say 'yes' to everything:

> I had a particularly nice cardigan on that one of the aunts had knitted, with a Fair Isle insert into the cardigan … This medical officer said, 'Oh that's a nice cardigan you've got on,' she said 'Did you knit that?'
>
> And I said, 'Oh no, I wouldn't have the patience for that.'
>
> And she said, 'I'm afraid you're going to have lots of patience if you're going to be looking after children.' And when we got outside my stepmother was absolutely furious.
>
> She said, 'You really fell for that one, didn't you?'

Despite this faux pas, which could be read as an act of protest, Mary was accepted for training at the nursery. She had enjoyed the camaraderie there but continued to resist her father's plans for her future employment. After passing their NNEB examination many of the other girls looked for jobs in magazines like *The Lady*; one of the other nurses had been lucky enough to get a job as nanny to the sons of the Duchess of Gloucester. But Mary was different. With the support of the matron who ran the nursery, she was able to trump her father's low aspirations for her and get a place in a hospital to train as a general nurse.

THE NORLAND INSTITUTE AND PRINCESS CHRISTIAN COLLEGE

College training aimed to give parents and nannies confidence that they had the necessary skills to give children the highest standards of care. The best colleges throughout the twentieth century were thought to be the Norland Institute, started in 1892, and Princess Christian College, opened in 1901.[26] These colleges set the trend for professionalising child-care, offering a recognised and highly valued training which ensured that, by the end of the first decade of the twentieth century, children's nursing had become a respectable occupation for middle-class women.

The woman who instigated the professionalisation of nannies was Mrs Emily Ward (*née* Lord), a nursery and kindergarten teacher influenced by the theories of the German educational theorist, Friedrich Froebel. Emily set up the Norland Institute to address concerns about unedu-cated women being put in charge of upper- and middle-class children. Her motives arose partly from her doubts about the fitness of working-class girls to be nursemaids and nannies and partly from her desire to create a new career for middle-class women. How much better it would be, Emily thought, to train girls who had been brought up in conditions much closer to the habits and lifestyles of their employers but who were not clever enough to become teachers.[27]

This radical idea had major implications for both employers and employees. For employers, the indeterminate position of governesses was already a problem, as they were neither servants nor part of the family. To extend this status uncertainty to nannies would create fur-ther difficulties, and trained nannies from higher-class homes would also expect higher wages and better conditions.[28] For middle-class girls used to having servants at home, it was equally awkward. While they might try to distance themselves from the servants, they would be doing the same kind of work as young women from lower down the social scale, the class who had once been their own nursemaids.

Despite these problems, Emily Ward's vision was welcomed because it offered girls the chance to leave home and make a respectable living. Norland Institute's stated objectives were, first, 'to offer a new career to ladies' and, second, 'to supply the public with women fitted by character and training to take charge of nurseries and little children'.[29] This aim illuminates the significance of Ward's vision in a society with an empire to defend and where class divisions were so important: taking charge meant being middle class.

New entrants were generally aged between 18 and 30 and had to take an entrance exam, although evidence of good character was considered to be more important than intelligence. Because Ward's target group was women who lacked academic ability, the general knowledge test was limited, and in 1900 included a question about to make marmalade. One applicant who knew the answer, having recently made it with her mother, was stumped by another question which asked the whereabouts of particular London streets and fashionable shops she had never heard of.[30]

At both Norland and Princess Christian, nurses took practical and written exams and did not receive a qualification until they had worked for a year with a private family who was expected to write a detailed report.[31] Conditions of service, pay and conditions were made clear to employers, including rules that nurses should not have to do heavy housework such as carrying coal and cleaning grates, or eat meals with servants. These rules were often flouted by employers, a subject of frequent complaint by qualified nurses in college magazines, but one Norland nurse who read these rules on her arrival at the college in the 1930s saw them as unnecessary: 'I hardly minded if they did ask me to carry coal or eat with the servants, so pleased was I even to be here!'[32]

Princess Christian College required employers to pay nurses' salaries directly to the college for a nurse's first two years of work after gaining her probationer's certificate. After this period, if her reports were satisfactory she would be granted a nurse's certificate and could arrange her own employment.[33] At Norland, badges were awarded if students remained in the same post for a number of years, culminating in a green bar for twenty-one years' service to the same employer. This system ended in the late 1950s on the grounds that nurses who changed positions worked harder than those who stayed in one place.[34] Qualified nurses were expected to stay closely connected to the colleges, which acted as employment agencies and countersigned testimonials from employers which were sent in on an annual basis. They did not hesitate to withhold or withdraw a nurse's certificate and strike her name off their roll if she subsequently proved 'unworthy' in any way, and a forged reference resulted in instant dismissal.[35] Thus the long arm of Norland and Princess Christian remained influential throughout a nanny's working life.

A Norland long-service badge: the green bar was awarded after twenty-one years' service with the same family. *Courtesy of Norland College*

Despite its royal patronage, Princess Christian College was not as secure as Norland financially, and its records show the strain it was under to remain solvent, recruit students, and preserve its reputation. The college closed for a short period during the First World War because of a lack of funds. Another worry came in the 1920s when Princess Christian gave her name to a baby hostel for unfortunate children which also trained children's nurses. Princess Christian College was bedevilled by confusion between the two names, and anxious that nurses with an inferior training connected to children whose mothers were thought of as 'fallen women' should not be confused with its own students.[36]

These concerns can be understood in the context of the expansion of nursery nurse training colleges, which gathered momentum after the First World War. A bureau offering advice for women's work in 1912 listed seven, offering courses lasting between six and twelve months, but by 1925 there were enough to form a National Association of Nursery Nursing Colleges. By 1932 there were colleges and training centres (for which secondary-school education was advisable as an entry qualification) offering a minimum of a year's training in every part of England and Scotland.[37] No wonder Princess Christian College felt obliged to advertise for prospective students in journals such as *Nursery World* and *The Lady*. College principals also wrote promotional articles pointing out the demand for educated girls.[38]

Parents' view of nanny training depended both on the family's class position and the aspirations they had for their daughters' futures. Cathy (born in 1943) had parents who were very well off, but her stepfather had little time for children. She had always loved babysitting and, when younger, thought she would become a children's or hospital nurse. But when her ambitions changed and she wanted to go to university to read history or archaeology, her stepfather prevented her on the grounds that there would be no money in these subjects, insisting that she train at Norland instead. Amelia (born in 1955) came from a less wealthy but still privileged family. The daughter of an electrical engineer and a school librarian, she was sent to a private school in the 1960s in the hope that she would do well academically. When she failed to follow in her more successful older sisters' footsteps, she explained that:

… there was a great hole there for people like myself. There were very few options to choose. I mean, you could have gone into an airline, you know, a hostess, but I wasn't tall enough. Going into nursery nursing seemed like what I would be able to cope with and something that I knew I'd enjoyed as a babysitter.

This would certainly not have been Amelia's parents' first choice. Unhappy about the courses offered at the local technical college, they sent her to Princess Christian College.

Both Norland and Princess Christian allowed respectable women from poorer backgrounds to enrol on a reduced fees scheme, which at Norland continued on much the same terms throughout the century. To qualify, they had to agree to take on a servant role in the institution for a year before they started training. At Princess Christian these girls were called 'domestic nurses', but at Norland they were known as 'maidens'. During the early twentieth century, maidens even forfeited their own names while they were doing this work (a practice common to servants at that time) and were called Mercy, Verity, Prudence or Honour. Though it must have felt demeaning for the women concerned, the logic was that it would be easier for them to be accepted as a student nurse by the other students once they had reverted to their own names.

These servile pseudonyms might also have helped to disguise the fact that many of the maidens came from families only slightly less well off than those of the students paying full fees, yet worked in very similar conditions to servants. A missionary's daughter who had been privately educated described conditions for maidens in the early 1930s. She shared an attic dormitory with another maiden and worked from 6.30 a.m. to late at night (with two hours off in the afternoon) doing all kinds of chores, including cooking the nurses' and children's food, taking tea and hot water to the staff in the mornings, stoking the boilers, and chasing cockroaches in the kitchens late at night. While making no complaint, she was at pains to note what a good job she and the other maidens did for the college.[39] These practices continued for many years. Another student who was at the college thirty years later spoke of the trouble maidens would be in if they brought in the principal's tea one minute before or after the stroke of eight.

Cathy remembered one of the maidens who had shared her room in the 1960s: 'We asked what her father's occupation was and she said "oh, 'e was a draper" and I remember all the girls looking at each other in absolute horror – "a draper?"' Although other students interviewed stressed that there was no real social difference between nurses and maidens, their friendships told a different tale. Nurses usually stuck to the set of girls who arrived at college with them and did not socialise much with maidens.

WELLGARTH COLLEGE

Not every training college's principal aim was to assist ladies. Wellgarth Nursery Training College, set up in 1910 by the Women's Industrial Council in Hackney, sought a rather different kind of student. Its objective was to improve the prospects of working-class girls and give them the chance to have college-based training. Wellgarth was initially linked to a crèche in which working mothers could leave their babies all day, an arrangement that offered a much more concentrated training in infant care than was possible at school and allowed girls to practise on real babies. Press reports pointed out the advantages for working women in the 'notoriously poverty-stricken' neighbourhood of Lower Clapton and argued: 'The crèche will not differ largely from many others, but in the training of poor girls – the elder sisters of the babies, among others – as nursemaids the council hope to inaugurate a really valuable work'.[40] Despite its laudable aims, Wellgarth soon began to resemble the more prestigious colleges. Realising that a residential nursery was needed to give its students full training, the crèche soon closed. Places in the residential nursery went to parents who could pay 5s a week, described as 'mainly widows and widowers and married couples who belong to the stage'. This sum was far beyond the reach of mothers using the daily crèche, who had paid 4d a day. It was soon apparent that the college fees were also beyond the means of most working-class families. By 1912, students were said to be 'daughters of housekeepers in large houses, the children of shop-keepers, schoolmasters or skilled artisans' or innkeepers, small builders, bricklayers and farmers, with half already educated beyond elementary school level.[41] While girls from these backgrounds were not 'ladies', they were certainly not poor.

One reason for the fee increase was lack of state funding. The Board of Education did not recognise residential schools, which became a requirement for students and the fees (£36 per annum in 1913) placed Wellgarth out of the reach of any but secondary-school girls.[42] In 1915 the college moved from working-class Hackney to middle-class Hampstead Garden Suburb and soon had little connection with its place of origin. The Hampstead residents originally objected to the move on the grounds that the area was supposed to be residential and houses would depreciate in value – it was described by one resident as 'a tower of Babel' – but they soon came to terms with the college.[43]

A final irony can be seen in the reasons for the college's closure over sixty years later. By this time Wellgarth, like most other residential nurseries, was taking children in the care system into its nurseries,

but a shift in fostering policy led to a shortage of children. In 1978 the college had to return to running a day care centre. Shifts in women's working patterns meant that it was used not by working-class women but by the parents of the professional classes who lived in the area. It was they, not the communities for whose benefit the college had been opened, who tried unsuccessfully to mount a rescue bid when in 1979 Wellgarth College finally closed.[44]

Margaret Hutchins: a Wellgarth nurse in the 1940s. *Courtesy of Nicola Harland*

THE CURRICULUM

Some aspects of the nursery training colleges' curriculum were similar to the domestic subjects taught to girls at school and in homecraft centres, including needlework, cookery, laundry work and housewifery. During the Second World War at Wellgarth, domestic training involved the kind of service work done by reduced-fee entrants at the wealthier colleges. Students were expected to do all the housework, laundry, cooking, laying fires and cleaning at the college and were marked on their progress on a weekly basis. A former student's record of work in 1940 showed her cleaning staff bedrooms, among other tasks, and she was reprimanded if she was not sufficiently tidy in her work.[45]

Domestic subjects were taught without the benefit of modern machinery until the 1970s. In the late 1940s, Norland had no washing machines, and an antiquated milk kitchen was used for mixing formula. Not much had changed by the early 1960s. Although by this time elec-

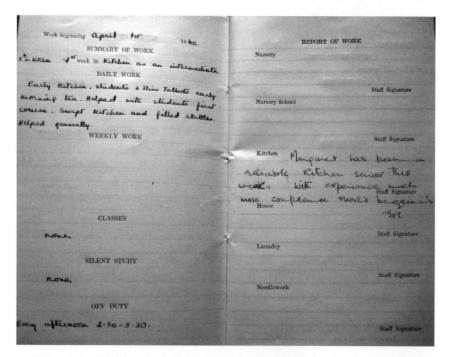

A Wellgarth student's work book. *Courtesy of Nicola Harland*

tric irons and washing machines were common in most middle-class houses, Cathy remembered doing laundry in 'horrific' conditions, in a boiling hot house with rack upon rack of drying nappies, while ironing was done with flat irons heated on braziers on pieces of material that often caught fire.

The advent of the disinfectant 'Nappy San' and washing machines in the 1970s at Princess Christian College did not make laundry much more pleasant. Amelia was terrified of going down to the roasting hot basement, where she had to scrape faeces off the nappies and put them into giant bins full of the Nappy San: 'One was already 24 hours old ready for washing and the other was the new one, and you had to make sure you got your nappies in the right one or woe betide you. You suffered for weeks after that if you got it wrong.' The big silver washing machine was even more alarming. She had to remember to close its inner lid before shutting the outer door and switching it on to fill with water. To Amelia's horror, she once forgot to close the inner door, causing the machine to break down, a sin she had to confess to the principal.

Norland student Sarah explained the logic behind domestic training:

> The point of all this was not that you were going to end up doing the cleaning and the cooking but you had to know how it was done properly so that your nursery maid or any of the cleaners under you, cleaning your nurseries, you could direct them to do it properly. You actually had to do all the domestic chores to make sure you knew the way to do it.

The possibility of going out to the colonies justified these practices:

> You had to learn how to iron with a flat iron … in case you were out in a bush somewhere and the children you were looking after still had to be turned out beautifully in ironed clothes … You had to realise that you wouldn't have electricity if you were in an embassy somewhere in a country far away.

The most important components of college training were infant care and child development. Nursery nurse manuals used for training before the

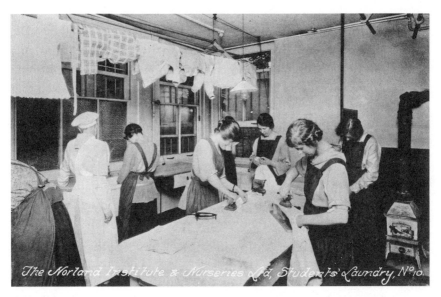

Norland nurses learning how to do laundry in the early twentieth century.
Courtesy of Nicola Harland

war, such as D.A. Kennedy's *The Care and Nursing of the Infant for Infant Welfare Workers and Nursery Nurses* (1930), were concerned chiefly with physical problems and followed the prevailing behaviourist view. Adopting strict routines and seeing nervousness in babies as the result of 'inefficient and careless handling', they advised nurses to leave them alone as much as possible and to ensure they were not the centre of attention. The courses at the leading private colleges were more child-focused, including nursery management, hygiene, practice of education, child psychology, nature study, storytelling, toys and occupations and children's games.

Much of the Norland college curriculum after the Second World War was covered in the *Handbook for Nursery Nurses* by A.B. Meering, first published in 1947. This textbook was the basis for the NNEB exam which most colleges adopted (sometimes in addition to their own qualifications); in the 1960s Cathy thought it contained everything she could possibly have needed to know. It was practical in its focus, but did not follow rigid behaviourist ideas. There were short sections on intellectual, emotional and social development, and the bibliography included works by the psychoanalyst Susan Isaacs (whose pseudonym was Ursula Wise in *Nursery World*).

Former students did not recall being impressed by the child psychology they were taught. Alison recounted:

> We did have some psychology lessons and I can remember one, she wasn't a member of staff, she was somebody who used to come in. And she said, 'When a baby wets on you, it's an honour because it's the only thing it's got that it can give you.'
>
> And you'd say, 'Yes, [but] when I've got to go and change my uniform, it's a different matter.'

Sarah commented:

> John Bowlby, that was the bible, John Bowlby's bible, *Childcare and the Growth of Love* and all this sort of thing ... Oh yes, that was a textbook, but [...] you weren't encouraged to go and get other books. I don't know where we'd have got them from either; we didn't have a library near us anywhere or no sort of library in the college to go and read other people's theories or anything like that.

Amelia, who studied at Princess Christian College in the 1970s, also had little memory of psychology being taught although, like the Norlanders, she had to do a study of one of the children in the nursery, relating theory to practice as part of her exam. In the 1970s study blocks were fitted between periods of nursery training and regarded by the girls mainly as a chance to sleep late, a break from their usual long days in the nursery.

Of equal importance to the practical training and knowledge of childcare and psychology were moral qualities. Students were marked on punctuality, neatness, personal appearance, tact, temper and general tone.[46] A nurse should not simply be competent at domestic work and baby care; she must also have the right kind of character to teach and be a good influence on children. A student edition of Froebel's *Mother's Songs, Games and Stories* (1920) used at Norland between the First and Second World Wars stressed that the teacher had the 'sacred charge of a young soul' and was supposed to teach principles such as contentment, respect for others, punctuality and to warn against greed, selfishness and cruelty.[47]

These characteristics were deemed so important that students whose conduct did not exhibit them were refused the certificate and asked to leave. Punctuality and honesty were particularly problematic after the Second World War, when some of the rules appeared old-fashioned. Norland students usually had to be in by 9.30 p.m. and remember having to miss the last acts of plays and running up the hill with nurses waiting to reprimand them if they were a minute late. By the 1960s, when social restrictions were being loosened outside Norland's walls, rules like these were secretly being flouted. In order to hear the latest bands playing at Chislehurst Caves, students used to escape through windows or sign one another in.

They were lucky not to have been caught. One student was thrown out of her college at the very end of her training because she had been caught climbing down a fire escape to go back to a dance. Her behaviour was deemed deceitful, irresponsible and untrustworthy. The fact that her probationary post employers were still willing to take her on, however, suggests that such draconian rules were no longer seen as entirely necessary in wider society. Amelia was caught by the principal at Princess Christian and grounded when she was head nurse but had refused to take responsibility for others coming in late. She was influential in changing the rules and pointed out that by the 1970s 'the world was moving forward and you couldn't place these restrictions on young women who at 18 were basically adults.'

As head girl, Amelia had campaigned successfully to relax the uniform requirements at Princess Christian, a bugbear for students throughout the century. Full uniform including starchy collars had to be worn at all times, but many students saw this as woefully out of date. Wearing the uniform correctly, including long white gloves, was a condition of the probationary year at Norland but was not always strictly enforced by employers. In the late 1960s, Flora was relieved when her employer, who had not wanted her to wear a hat, lied on the form she had to fill in for the college and said she had worn one.

BABIES IN TRAINING

Practical training in the college nurseries was regarded by students as the most important part of the training. Most colleges at one time or another had difficulty finding enough babies for them to practise on. At the beginning of the century, Princess Christian and Norland only took babies from respectable homes whose parents could afford their considerable fees. After the First World War it was harder to ensure a supply of the 'right' kind of children, and college principals would sometimes bargain with parents and reduce fees where necessary. Illegitimacy was initially an important issue. In 1926 Princess Christian College refused a baby on the grounds that his mother was not married, but by 1933 both colleges had relaxed this rule.[48] The shift in outlook reflects the gradual change in public attitudes and national policies attempting to lessen the stigma of illegitimacy. At the same time, many more colleges and residential nurseries were looking for babies. Until the 1970s, the Norland nursery children continued to be drawn mainly from embassy staff or parents who were working abroad, but Princess Christian College, like Wellgarth College, began to take children who, often through abuse or neglect, were in the care of local authorities.

From 1953 a significant number of children in the Princess Christian nursery had been placed there by Manchester City Corporation, which agreed to pay for twenty permanent places. This policy was described as 'a link between those enlightened people who worked for others at the beginning of the century and the wider conception of the welfare state which many more people are trying to work out today', but it also ensured that the college would have 'a full complement of students and children'.[49] Amelia described working with Corporation children, some of whom had been severely abused:

> Those children's clothes had to be cut off them, their bodies were
> so swollen with urine and faeces that they'd been left in … They
> were bathed and they were given beds and they were fed and
> looked after … I can't remember how long they were with us, but
> I do know that the father had found out where they were being

taken and was threatening to come and smash the place up, so we had a police guard there.

She and her fellow students had been given no warning that the work would be so challenging:

> I think parents thought it was a finishing school and I think we were too naïve to actually realise the enormity … We were given all these children who basically had a lot wrong with them, probably mentally, because of that had happened in their short lives. But it never, it didn't occur to me, I think we were naïve, we just loved them as being the children that were there.

For trainee nurses, looking after babies and young children 24 hours a day was most memorable. Two children brought up in the Norland nursery at the start of the century had generally positive memories. One boy who, unusually, stayed from the age of 15 months until he was 8 years old, looked back on his Norland childhood as extremely happy.[50] In retrospect, however, nurses were quite critical of the colleges for the way the children were treated. At Norland in the 1950s and 1960s children were kept in family groups. A nurse would be in charge of a particular baby or child, whom they slept with in the nursery and looked after for a month before moving on to a child in the next age group. While accepting of this at the time, with hindsight Alison stressed how they had practised on the children, some of whom were as young as ten days old, and suggested that the experience might have been quite traumatic for the children. She had thought about it a lot since and was critical of parents who did not see their children from one year to the next. Flora could not 'imagine how those children have grown up, how they've managed to make relationships with people.'

The nursery took no account of Bowlby's views that continuity of caregivers was essential for a child's mental health. Taught in theory, it could not be put into practice because the nurses were seen as needing experience with children of all ages. Nurses often preferred to look after young babies. The rigid, regular routines of eating, sleeping, play and exercise imposed upon them meant that few babies gave much trouble, in contrast to some older children who had too many changes of carers.

Nurses often became attached to the babies who were the subjects of their child study and recalled them in detail many years later. Amelia remembered Jimmy with great fondness, 'her baby' from 3 weeks until he was a year old. Rushing back on her day off to give him a birthday present, she was heartbroken to discover that he and his twin sister had been removed from the nursery by their mother, with no warning. She was even more distressed to hear that six months later a social worker had seen both children neglected and lying in dirty cots. Amelia could not bear to hear any further news of Jimmy. However much love nurses lavished on their special babies, they had to accept the fact that they had no control over their future.

The most vulnerable babies and children looked after by students were cared for during their period of hospital training, which usually lasted three months. In the early 1900s, Princess Christian maintained that the students should not be taught subjects such as physiology, hygiene and sick nursing in case it led them to think they were trained sick nurses. Confusion between the two categories of nurse arose because children's nurses needed a good knowledge of common ailments in order to look after delicate children, and because trained sick nurses were often recruited for children who needed extra care in their own homes. The young Ralph Bankes, heir of Kingston Lacy, who had been nearly starved to death by his nanny in the early 1900s, was coaxed back to health by 'a long train of blue-veiled hospital sisters' who, according to his sister Viola, spoiled and pampered him.[51]

Despite Princess Christian's concerns that her nurses should not be mistaken for the blue-veiled kind, most college-trained nursery nurses spent a term in a hospital. By the 1950s they were given a thorough grounding in the care of sick children as well as the delivery of babies and care of nursing mothers, taking much more responsibility for patients than they would be allowed today. Amelia, who trained at Princess Christian, had enjoyed her hospital term at Withington in Manchester in the 1970s:

I have to say it was my favourite part of the whole training ... They let me in to deliver babies and I was even there at C-sections as well, and more importantly the surgeon explained every procedure to me and explained everything as he did […] that procedure; it was just fantastic.

Cathy at Norland had also enjoyed her term at Farnborough Hospital in the early 1960s. She had sneaked into theatres disguised in a gown and mask to watch operations, including Caesarean sections. She had even managed to talk to the cricketer Colin Cowdrey (who was being treated in the men's ward) before being hustled out by the matron with the retort, 'Come along Norlanders, come out of there, you've been chatting to the men for too long.' But Cathy was also given a worrying amount of responsibility for an 18-year-old girl. On one occasion she was left in charge of a ward of twenty-two mothers: 'I was there all by myself. I remember saying to one woman in a side ward, "Would you like me to show you how to bathe your new baby?" and she said, "No, it's alright darlin', I've got twelve at 'ome. I only come in 'ere for a rest".' This story is indicative of the severe shortages in the National Health Service which Norland students were often, by default, compelled to fill.

Insensitivity and poor supervision by hospital staff seem to have characterised some nursery nurses' hospital training in the post-war years. Cathy was given a baby whose limbs had been deformed by prenatal thalidomide to take to its mother – without being told what was wrong with the baby – and had to watch the parents sobbing when they found out. Sarah's difficult experiences in a south London hospital put her off hospital nursing for life. One of the hospital nursing sisters was frequently drunk, and most were unfriendly; they looked down on the Norlanders and used them simply as spare pairs of hands. Sarah found it heartbreaking to have to take responsibility for a tiny baby in a premature unit and see it dressed up after its death in lacy clothes knitted by the ward sister, and painful to be told to give a child with hydrocephalus a bottle, only to have it die in her arms shortly afterwards.

Sarah was equally horrified when she was told to enforce the hospital practice of holding down screaming children on their beds while the parents left the ward. Not long afterwards she was shown the film 'A 2-Year-Old Goes to Hospital', made by Bowlby's colleague James Robertson,[52] which showed the harmful effects on young children of being separated from parents. These experiences can also be connected to later memories of the National Association for the Welfare of Children in Hospital started in the 1960s by academic wives in Oxford who asserted their rights to remain with their children.

Although most nannies looked back on their training as helpful to them, nursery training colleges had to work hard throughout the century to counter the perception that any woman could be a nanny, a task they still struggle to achieve today. The difficulties the more prestigious colleges faced were partly to do with class. Presenting children's nursing as an important job involved strict admission protocols but led to strange contradictions. Those who were not 'ladies' were excluded, but students were still required to learn domestic subjects without the benefit of labour-saving devices, and be waited on by poorer students who were given the work of maids. Professionalising nanny training did not remove the majority of untrained mothers' helps or au pairs who cost little to employ and were less likely to challenge a mother's authority with expert knowledge.

How far the expert knowledge nannies learned at college was focused on the child's emotional needs is questionable. While child psychology was taught after the Second World War, it seems to have had little impact on students at the time. For children in the training nurseries, the legacy was mixed. Standards of physical care were usually high, and there were many benefits for children who had been neglected in their own homes, particularly in consistent routines and the attachments they formed with particular nurses. But these could not last long, and they were moved from one carer to another or back to parents they no longer recognised. This problem became apparent when I spoke to former nursery and children's home residents who contacted me seeking their old nurses. Even when they had no memories of individual carers, they still often talked or wrote about their feelings of loss. Finally, colleges maintained that training was essential but, as we shall see in the next chapter, mothers did not always see a trained nurse from a middle-class background, however smart her uniform, as preferable to a village girl.

5

SITUATIONS VACANT, SITUATIONS WANTED
FINDING AND KEEPING A NANNY

Then I had to get a job quickly because both my parents were disapproving of me having left [a post as a hospital nurse] and I got a job. I saw an advert in the *Telegraph* for somebody to look after children … I remember going down to the interview and Betty had already interviewed one or two people. One of them smoked and of course I'd never smoked in my life and she gave me the job and I was absolutely thrilled.

Hilary (born in 1925)

I found my way to the Council for Unmarried Mothers, which was in Kentish Town, and went to see somebody who was extremely nice actually … She said would I like to become a mother's help and that, if I did, I would become a mother's help for a few months up until I was, I think until I was six weeks before the baby was due. And then I would go to a mother and baby home, and the assumption was I think that the baby would be adopted and so I felt I didn't really have any choice at all.

Hannah (born in 1947)

The almost random, largely unforeseen nature of these two women's routes into becoming a nanny was typical of the way many untrained nannies and mothers' helps first found a job. Taking a post looking after children was seldom a goal they actively and systematically pursued, but often seemed to happen by accident, out of short-term necessity, or as the line of least resistance. Although trained or experienced nannies could be more purposeful and organised in their attempts to find the right post, they too often drifted on the winds of chance.

Drawing on family and personal contacts was probably the most common way that childcare work was found. While parents often helped to get jobs for their daughters, they could also be a threat, compelling them to take any suitable job to get them out of the house and earning their keep. Fear of parental disapproval pushed Hilary into taking a job she might not otherwise have thought of doing, but her testimony also shows the importance of advertising. Using more formal recruitment methods, such as personal columns in the press, or nanny agencies, allowed employers to stipulate criteria for the job and choose from a number of applicants, rather than simply accepting personal recommendations. These were also good ways for prospective nannies to seek a wider choice of jobs, enabling them to look beyond their local area and personal contacts to find a more interesting post or better salary. Agencies that placed girls as mothers' helps and nannies were not confined to private employment bureaus; they also included nanny training colleges, domestic service training schools and centres, orphanages, children's homes and organisations aiding friendless or destitute girls and single mothers. Unlike private agencies, these institutions did not always offer girls much of a choice. As Hannah's story shows, some young women felt they had no option but to take the only post they were offered.

FAMILY AND PERSONAL CONTACTS

Family connections and personal recommendations have always been important in getting young people jobs.[1] Nannies found posts through parents, siblings, and friends in service occupations and also through informal networks of patronage among employers which meant that nurses and nannies were often passed from one family to another. This was regarded as a safer and more reliable way of finding a nanny than taking the risk of employing a complete stranger who would have intimate access to their home, possessions and children.

Some nannies stayed within their own and the employers' extended family and friendship networks for their whole working lives and helped one another find posts in the same or neighbouring households. The Selwood sisters, from a small Gloucestershire village, became an invaluable asset to the Bloomsbury circle in the early part of the twentieth century. In their teens and early twenties, several of the seven sisters became nursemaids and nannies to children of the artist Vanessa Bell and her cousins and friends. They often moved between households, with younger sisters joining older ones or replacing them after they left to get married.[2] Intergenerational family contacts were also common, with parents and grandparents passing on nannies or nannies' younger relatives to the next generation. 'Keeping it in the family' stretched as far as families employing their own nieces or cousins, a long-standing practice in servant-keeping households. In the 1960s it had become sufficiently acceptable even for upper-middle class girls to be nannies that Jane Robinson, the daughter of an army general, was willing to take a post as an under-nanny in a wealthy cousin's Kensington house. It was only a temporary job, suggested by her mother after she left boarding school, but she soon discovered that she occupied a subservient position quite at odds with her own class background. Her only knowledge of childcare came from the nanny who had brought her up. But learning to obey her nanny as a child may have made it easier for her to kowtow to the older 'grand nanny' who insisted that 'everything had to be as she wanted'. Jane was in awe of her cousin who lived a glamorous London lifestyle with little time for her children. Still, the incongruity of having a relative as their nanny, particularly one who had been brought up in the same way as them, was not lost on the children when they met Jane again in adult life. Although they said they had no memory of her looking after them, they roared with laughter to cover any feelings of embarrassment.

Ada had no network of families or wealthy cousin to employ her. Neither did she have the luxury of a boarding-school education or any choice about her future occupation when she started work as a mother's help at the age of 14. But like Jane, she did have a mother to give her a push. Mothers were often influential in finding jobs for daughters, particularly in rural areas where alternative employment was scarce. Some had high aspirations for their daughters, while others preferred them to go into service because it was a respectable job which would teach them housewifery skills they would later need as wives and mothers. Most employers in the 1920s and 1930s wanted girls aged over 16, a preference that can explained by the move from larger houses, where girls could be trained as maids or nursemaids by older servants and nannies, to smaller households where one servant did everything, including cooking and childcare.[3] By 1942, when Ada began work, women under 40 were being called up to do war service and employers were recruiting from a smaller pool of girls and young women.

Ada's first post was not a happy one. Although the job was in her home village and she cycled back home on her day off, she felt so miserable that she used to have regular crying fits. When her mother finally told her to 'do something about it', her mother's sister, a cook, found her the next job. As before, Ada had little say in where or what the job was. She was obliged to leave the village to work near her aunt in another county. There, with no previous experience of babies and 'completely innocent', she was put in charge of a 4-month-old baby, a worrying responsibility for such a young girl.

Her career initially followed a recurring pattern of taking a job found by her mother or aunt, feeling concerned that she would not be able to cope with her employers' children, and eventually tears when she left the young charges she had come to love. Even when she became more confident and applied to an agency, it was her mother who asked the questions and obtained the forms for her to fill in. Ada continued to want the security of being close to home. After she found a longer-term job with the Robinsons and became nanny to Jane and her younger brother and sister, she was at first reluctant to move when the family was stationed in Bournemouth hundreds of miles away. Her mind was changed by the faith and trust invested in her by Mrs Robinson who, Ada explained, 'was like a mother to me'.

Enid, daughter of a solicitor's clerk born in 1922, also had help from her family in finding a job but told a very kind of different tale. She too had to leave school at 14. Her parents had hoped she might go into office work like her elder sisters, but Enid declared: 'Well, Mum, I'm just not interested and I don't want to work in a stuffy old office.' As a result she was allowed to stay at home and help her mother, a common practice for girls in large families who provided much-needed domestic support and help with younger children.[4] In 1942, she was called up to do war work but was determined not to be a land girl or to go into munitions work, seeing nursing as a better option:

> My father there came up trumps. He used to work with a Mr B. Now Mr B was the secretary at a local hospital, a private small hospital, and he got an interview with the matron because they needed nurses at this hospital … But I didn't know until I got there for my interview that it wasn't an ordinary hospital, it was a mental hospital … So anyway, the matron was pretty good really, I mean she should have just washed her hands of me but she didn't. She said, 'Well, there is another job going that you might be interested in and,' she said, 'The medical superintendent and his wife have got one little boy …' [and they offered her a post as a nanny].

Enid's account of her parents' involvement in getting her a job suggests the difficulties of classifying daughters as dutiful, independent, or rebellious, as some historians have done.[5] Enid certainly portrayed herself as rebellious. Always getting her own way, she circumvented the government's attempts to sign her up for jobs in which she was not interested. She relied on her father to find her more congenial work but refused to take the job he found for her. As a result, she managed to get a post which counted as war work but also used the domestic skills she had learned from her mother. Although Enid lived independently from her parents, she looked for work where she could stay in regular contact with them. Later jobs took her away, but the pull of home remained strong and, after moving with her second employers to a lonely spot in Cornwall, she returned to her home area for her final post. 'I wanted to go home', she said; 'I was homesick … and I was, I suppose, ready to settle down. I wanted something permanent.'

Both Enid and Ada had choices in taking or leaving particular posts, but their decisions were connected with their feelings about their families. Parents exerted a pull over their daughters to stay in close touch, which was not easy to ignore. Still, family connections were only part of the story. Nannies had to go where the jobs were and accept the terms and conditions of living-in if they wanted to stay. If their employers moved to a new area they either had to go with them or give notice. Although both Enid and Ada were homesick, returning home to find new jobs could only be a temporary solution; they could not stay there for long. Wider expectations about work and marriage for women also affected the length of these women's nannying careers. They became attached to their charges, and leaving them was always painful. But, as Enid explained, she could not see her work as permanent: 'they were just jobs until the day I did meet my future husband'.

JOBS FOR 'OUR GIRLS'

Colleges and training centres were indispensable in helping their students secure their first and sometimes subsequent jobs. Indeed, in the best nursery training colleges the first post was probationary and considered part of the training, with a good reference from the employer essential for qualifying as a trained nurse. Recruiting a nurse recommended by a college was one way employers could ensure that the children would be in safe hands. Reports from the college staff could be read in the nurse's testimonial book, and all subsequent employer references were countersigned by the college to ensure that they had not been faked. If a nurse needed a job or had good reason to leave a probationary post early, as was the case for Norland nurse Alison, she could usually find a new post quite easily by contacting her college. In 1913, Wellgarth Nursery Training College had 271 vacancies for their twenty-four graduates, with nearly twelve employers competing for each nurse.[6] After the First World War, the shortage became even more acute; Norland College received requests in each morning's post 'for forty or fifty nurses, where only one, if that, can be supplied'.[7]

Domestic service training schools and centres also found jobs for their girls. Students would be recommended and employers could select the one they preferred. Sometimes employers would come to the college to make their own choice rather than having suitable girls sent to them. The initial selection process could be somewhat rough and ready. Vera, who

EIGHTH REPORT

Date of beginning duties   1 Oct. 1945

Date of Leaving   16 April 1946

Names and ages of Children in the Nursery at present time
Edward five, Humphrey 3, and Phillida
16 months.

General Remarks It was wonderful to have her back after so many war years away, and it came as a gt blow to us when she informed us she felt obliged to live at home to help her mother. If anything she has worked harder, and even more efficiently than ever. Never will the clothes be kept to such perfection again. Her darning needs to be seen to be believed, and the childrens good health is a real credit to her. The help she has given over and above the children, nurseries, etc. has been deeply appreciated. We have also been able to leave the house & children in her hand now & again, with absolute confidence.   Janet Stone.

Signature

Address   Bracken Cottage Bucklebury.

Date   15 April 1946

27

A Wellgarth College-trained nanny's testimonial book. References were given every year and countersigned by the college in red ink. *Courtesy of Nicola Harland, Phillida Gill and Janet Stone* attended the Crystal Palace Training School in the 1930s, was lined up with a group of other girls who all had to show their hands, presumably to ensure they didn't look too rough. She was very surprised when a lady employer who had a large house in Kensington with a full staff picked her, particularly as she was the smallest girl in the group. This was a good opportunity for a girl from her Welsh mining background who, without nursery training, would have probably ended up as a maid of all work.

Children's homes and orphanages routinely helped their girls find work as nursemaids, nannies or mothers' helps. So did maternal and child welfare organisations such as the National Council for the Unmarried Mother and her Child (NCUMC), which was formed in 1918. Single mothers were often rejected by their own families and needed both work and accommodation. This could usually be found in live-in service positions either during pregnancy or after the birth of the baby.[8] Pearl Bickerstaffe was helped to keep her son Rodney with her with until he was nearly 3 years old, by which time she had been accepted back home by her family. She found nursing work where Rodney could go with her, including a job as a nanny to the two children of the warden of the University Settlement at Bethnal Green. She obtained these jobs through an employment bureau run by the National Association of Maternity and Child Welfare Centres.[9]

Hannah (born in 1947), daughter of a civil servant from a small country town, was less fortunate. In 1967 she became pregnant while working in West London. Her father had warned her not to come home, and she turned to the NCUMC for help after the father of the baby abandoned her. The NCUMC annual report for 1967–68 shows only 1 in 20 unmarried women who applied for help were specifically looking for employment; the majority were either seeking accommodation or did not specify what kind of help they needed. Hannah had little idea before contacting the agency what help it might be able to offer. She was not typical of the expectant mothers seen at the office that year, who were believed to be more independent, socially confident middle-class girls.[10] Annual reports from the 1950s and 1960s made much of the training opportunities offered to such girls and claimed that unmarried mothers no longer had to earn their living in domestic work.[11] But Hannah had gone to the NCUMC out of desperation, and nothing besides a mother's help job was available to her. She disliked her new employers, but she was in a confused state and felt she had little choice but to accept the job, which involved doing housework as well as looking after two small boys.

NANNY AGENCIES

Private agencies were useful for nurses who wanted a third party to vet prospective employers. They tempted nannies, au pairs and mothers' helps with jobs offering high salaries, particularly if they were willing to work abroad. Employers found the agency useful for weeding out unsuitable applicants. Yet the supply of applicants did not always meet every mother's needs. In 1910, when Joan Kennard was trying to find a nurse for her two young boys, she consulted Mrs Boucher, owner of a popular nanny agency,[12] but felt deeply frustrated at having 'lady nurses' foisted upon her, believing they 'could give too much trouble' and was determined to 'resist to the last' if she could. It is likely that Joan worried about the limitations in the tasks a lady nurse would be willing to do, but she had to give in when no other suitable candidates were found:

> I am sorry to say that she does call herself a 'lady nurse', but we told her our objections to that and she swears that she gives no trouble in the house etc. She was very highly recommended by Mrs. Boucher and we both thoroughly liked her. She [is] a very quiet-looking, middle-aged woman, I should think sort of farmer's daughter class.[13]

Joan was reassured in part because the woman's presumed social origin was far enough away from her own to be only on the borderlines of ladyhood, and because an unsophisticated country lass was likely to cause fewer problems.

An oversupply of 'ladies' wanting to be nurses was common at this time, but parents were increasingly reluctant to employ other staff to wait on them. Wages were also a point of disagreement. Nannies willing to do housework were in short supply, but statistics from a well-known servants' registry on the eve of the First World War show 25 per cent more nurses who wanted an annual salary of £25 or more looking for jobs than there were mothers wishing to pay that amount.[14]

An article in *Nursery World* in 1926 by the Honourable Mrs de Gray highlights another problem. In the interwar years, agencies had difficulty matching employers, who increasingly wished to share childcare, with experienced nurses, who usually wanted to be in sole charge. Mrs de Gray was filled with misgivings by the 'careless, noisy, and rough specimens' of nurses in other people's houses. Her request to an agency for a nurse who 'could work under the mother's supervision and yet not be under 25' yielded nobody suitable. It produced only 'a stream of ex-typists, waitresses, prehistoric gamps and other persons who, being either weary of or unsuccessful in their jobs were deemed by the registries as suitable for nurses … but not a soul with any experience materialised'. Only by a stroke of luck did Mrs De Gray eventually find a nurse between 30 and 40 with previous experience as a 'nurse or help' willing to work under her. [15]

In a seller's market, nannies seem to have had more positive experiences with agencies. Both Enid and Ada used them to get better jobs during and just after the Second World War. Enid stayed with the London agency she had found in *The Lady* magazine because of the choices it offered her. 'I could go anywhere to work anywhere in England,' she declared. 'I had dozens and dozens and dozens of letters from them … because the world was changing … and oh there was plenty of jobs.' Ada also used an agency to move into higher-status work with a wealthier family, becoming a nanny whose main job was to care for the children and where other servants did the cooking and housework. Before being accepted at an Edinburgh agency in the late 1940s, she was interviewed and had to fill out forms with answers to questions about what she would do in particular circumstances. She thought 'they really were very, very good'. Since she'd had considerable experience in previous jobs but no formal training, being accepted on their books was particularly useful for her. It helped her get a post where she was happy to stay because she felt more at home than in the earlier jobs found by her aunt and mother.

SERVANTS OR LADIES?

Lady Nurse or Nannie under 30. Two boys 4, 2. Do own nurseries, laundress. One maid kept. State salary.

(*Nursery World*, 13 May 1936)

Agencies generally recruited nannies and employers through advertising. Although this was not the most common method of recruitment, as Lucy Delap pointed out in *Knowing Their Place: Domestic Service in Twentieth-Century Britain*, advertising columns are an especially useful source to shed light on the beliefs and assumptions of those who used them.[16] Most importantly, they demonstrate how important a nanny's social class and family background was for employers. This was particularly true before the Second World War, when class distinctions were more rigid, and it was easy for advertisers to clarify exactly what kind of nanny they required. In addition to the local press, the most common national papers and magazines that carried adverts for childcare jobs were *The Times*, *The Lady*, and *Nursery World*. Skills such as needlework, experience with children, and sometimes musical ability were considered important. However, one of the major issues employers needed to make clear in their advertisements was whether the person they wanted to look after the children should be a 'lady'.

The pros and cons of this question were not entirely straightforward. Norland College required its applicants to be ladies (also known as gentlewomen) by birth or education. They did not define exactly what being a 'lady' meant, but the common understanding of the term was that the family should not be members of the working or lower-middle classes who made their living from manual trades or clerical work or with a father in the ranks of the armed services. As Joan Kennard's recruitment problems in the early 1900s show, some propertied workers, such as farmers, straddled the borderline. Being a lady entailed subscribing to a particular code of values and, whether or not nannies were themselves ladies, they were the main channel through which these rules and values were transmitted to young children.

Expectations of a lady nurse were not supposed to be the same as those of a nurse or mother's help, and advice columnists tried to clarify the difference so that employers could recruit the right kind of person.

For example, in a household management column in *The Lady* in September 1905 a correspondent was advised that a lady nurse 'does not clean her nurseries, nor carry up coals, water or meals'.[17] Yet many advertisements for lady nurses or lady helps advised applicants that, in addition to childcare, they would be doing 'light' or 'slight' housework, or even that no other servant was kept. Some indicated that a lady was either 'preferred' or 'not objected to' or that applicants should be 'ladylike'; these were coded references to the fact that they might be expected to do some work not normally performed by ladies. The 1936 advertisement in *Nursery World* (quoted above) stated that the nanny or lady nurse had to clean the children's rooms and was expected to do laundry. The main family wash would be sent out or done by the maid, but the children's clothes had to be starched and ironed so the children could be shown off nicely. The fact that the nanny was expected to be under 30 and was asked to state her salary suggests that the employer would not have been able or willing to pay the high wages demanded by an older trained nurse.

Editors and advice columnists went to some pains to explain the consequences for the household layout and budget if a lady nurse rather than simply a nurse were employed. One important issue was where a lady nurse should eat; correspondents advised that they must have enough space in their houses for meals to be taken separately from other servants. In 1925 a lady nurse wrote to *Nursery World* to complain that when staying in a hotel with her employers she had been expected to have her meals in an upper servant's hall and associate with waiters and waitresses. She asked whether as a 'lady nurse brought up in a good family accustomed to feeding with people of my own position' she was justified in refusing to 'repeat the experiment to the extent of (probably) having to give up the post'. The editor replied:

> I take it that you were engaged as a lady nurse; that is to say that you were not engaged as a nurse, and incidentally happened to be a lady. If being a lady is part of your job, that position should certainly be upheld by your employer … This is not snobbery: it is due to yourself and others to uphold the status of the lady nurse. But I shall be very glad of other opinions.[18]

Advice was often given on the best way to manage with fewer staff, one of whom might have to double as both nurse and housemaid. While a correspondent with an experienced and reliable nurse was told to 'hang on to her at all costs', another was advised to 'get a dependable mother's help, as a lady nurse would require a certain amount of waiting upon and would not sweep or scrub the nurseries, thus making the work of the general servant more arduous'.[19] The unreasonable demands made by 'Lady Domestics' became the subject of satire, with the *Daily Mirror* in 1922 suggesting that they were of so little use that their tasks had been reduced to receiving guests and arranging flowers.[20]

NURSERY NURSES, GOVERNESSES, COMPANIONS, LADY HELPS, ETC.

Appointments Vacant
4s. for 20 words.
1s. for every additional 5 words.
Charge for Box Number 1s.

Applicants for situations are advised not to send original testimonials when replying to advertisements. Copies will answer the purpose quite as well, and in the event of being lost or mislaid no inconvenience will ensue.

A CAPABLE young Nurse-Help wanted. Doctor's house. Maid kept. Girls 2 and 3. Mrs. Gemmell, Dornhurst, Halstead, Essex. (A937)

A NURSE-HELP, middle March. Two boys day school, baby girl. All nursery duties. Good needlewoman. Well educated. Not full charge. Nursery meals. Christian family. Maid kept. Interview essential. Dolton, 5 Alexandra Crescent, Bromley, Kent. (A873)

A NURSERY GOVERNESS for only child, boy 4½. Nurseries cleaned and waited on. Country girl preferred, fond of horses and dogs. Mid-Sussex, main bus route. £40. Apply Box A952, " The Nursery World," 154 Fleet Street, E.C.4.

AN experienced Nannie. Baby 15 months. Doctor's house. 219 New King's Road, Parson's Green, S.W.6. Fulham 0395. (X576)

Advertisements for nannies, nursery governesses and nurse-helps in *Nursery World*, 1926. *Courtesy of* Nursery World

THE SHIFT TO THE MOTHER'S HELP

Nannie is unnecessary; home help doesn't sound very attractive;
mother's help doesn't convey my meaning. I need someone equivalent to the army-aide de camp who can be relied on to pull their
weight under any and every circumstance; but I feel only the celes-
tial regions will ever fulfil my requirements.
(Letter to *Nursery World*, 15 August 1946)

Lady nurses finally disappeared after the Second World War, at least in
name. By the 1950s, advertisers and agencies rarely used the word 'lady'
in relation to mothers' helps or nurses, even in *The Lady* magazine. The
column which had previously been called 'governesses, companions and
lady helps' was now titled 'Cooks, Housekeepers, Household Helps etc.',
although the issue of class was still occasionally referred to obliquely
in phrases such as 'good opportunity for the right person'.[21] The term
'nanny' (usually spelled 'nannie'), firmly rejected by Norland College
because of its working-class associations,[22] became much more wide-
spread, largely replacing 'nurse'. It was sometimes used as an alternative
to mother's help but sometimes combined with it, as nannie-help or
nannie-housekeeper, reflecting the dual roles the worker would be
expected to play.

Writing to *Nursery World* during the cold, wet summer of 1946 at the
height of post-war austerity, mothers despaired of getting any live-in
help at a price they could afford. They often had to manage with only
a daily help, which meant they could never go anywhere alone or out
in the evening with their husbands. One mother said she would gladly
have had an ex-nanny as a general help whom she could trust with the
children overnight, while a nanny insisted that although she would be
willing to lend a hand with housework on occasion, her work should
really be in the nursery. Nannies and mothers endlessly debated whether
or not housework should be included in addition to childcare, and what
the job should be called.[23] Trying to cope with 'rations, coupons, housekeeping, sickness etc.', a mother longed for a 'really jolly, understanding,
honest-to-goodness soul who is not too superior' and asked readers to
invent a title for the type of helper she required.[24] Another responded

that since nurses who 'assisted with extraneous tasks were now valued much more highly than departmental nurses' and argued that their status should be raised; 'assistant housewife would more fittingly describe the finest preparation for wife and motherhood'.[25]

Some women, who had to manage without help during the war, were critical of mothers who demanded nannies. The post-war propaganda on the undesirability of mothers leaving their children added fuel to these debates. In the mid-1950s one woman condemned a mother who wanted her child to be trained by an expert, pointing out that he was not a 'circus animal'.[26] This shift away from the employment of the 'departmental nurse' helps to explain why untrained women answering advertisements for nannies after the war were usually called by their first names rather than 'nanny' or 'nurse', which seemed too formal and old-fashioned.

As the balance between situations wanted and situations vacant shifted, employers had to look for ways to make their advertisements stand out. Incentives such as televisions, the use of a car, and sometimes even a separate flat began to be offered, and any associations with domestic service were downplayed. By the 1970s, the children's own names began to be used in their advertisements, implying it was the children who were looking for a carer rather than the mother asking for help. My employer Gill was one of the first to do this in her advert in *The Lady*, a tactic she described as 'practically revolutionary'. The success of this strategy was apparent in her recruitment of an excellent mother's help (the one who preceded me!), who had answered her advert because she particularly liked its wording.

THE RISE OF AU PAIRS

One solution for the hard-pressed mother who could not or did not wish to recruit a nanny or mother's help was to look for an au pair. Early in the twentieth century this term, which means 'equal to' or 'on a par', was often used in advertisements looking for mothers' or lady helps to indicate that the successful applicant would be treated on the same level as the family who was offering her a home. It also implied that no substantial wage would be offered, only room and board and sometimes pocket money or, where the post was for a companion to a lady with limited means, shared expenses. It was not uncommon for European girls wishing to improve their English or for French ladies offering to teach French to advertise themselves as 'au pairs'. *The Lady* had two advertisements of this kind on the same day in 1905, both stressing their qualifications as teacher and graduate, one of which was written in French and stated 'sans salaire' (without a salary).[27]

Although the term 'au pair' was still used in relation to mothers' helps after the Second World War, by the 1950s it came to be applied principally to schemes through which young women from European countries, initially mainly Germany and Scandinavia, would come to England for a year. An estimated 17,000 girls were coming to Britain each year by the mid-1950s, and the number rose thereafter. Au pairs were seen as the answer to the dilemma of the middle-class housewife who could no longer afford or was unable to recruit live-in domestic servants, and lack of space made it easier for her to house someone of similar social standing.[28] Not only were such schemes popular with girls as a way of learning English, but they also offered an easy way of travelling abroad.

Mothers looking for au pairs had to decide which nationality would suit them and their families, based on their sometimes limited knowledge of the countries with girls looking for places. Lillian (born in 1932), a Canadian academic wife and mother living in London in the late 1950s, made a conscious choice to take on Danish au pairs because she thought they would be more independent than girls from other European countries, able to speak better English and able to communicate well with the children. The fact that they would go to college each afternoon and socialise with other au pairs in the evening was important, particularly after the family moved into a small house in the provinces with very cramped conditions. Her first au pair came through an agency which gave little information, but subsequent girls (each of whom stayed for about a year) were recruited by word of mouth, a series of sisters and friends mostly coming from the same Danish village. Although she could not interview her au pairs in advance, Lillian had a list of things that they should watch out for, picked up from her mother and mother-in-law, 'for instance always testing the bath water, turn handles of pans in', and made sure that every new girl saw it.

Stella, an only child living in a London suburb whose mother was often engaged in voluntary work, saw her mother's decision to take au pairs as reflective of the 1950s' zeitgeist: many of her parents' friends had au pairs, but none of them had nannies. They came mainly through personal contacts, the first one being the niece of a Norwegian friend of her mother:

> So it suited both families. L's family knew where she was coming to and my mother didn't feel that she had a stranger coming into the house. So … I think our sort of procession of au pairs started off as … almost like a favour to a friend.

INTERVIEWING NANNIES

The suitability of au pairs usually had to be taken on trust unless the employer used an agency, but few mothers would take a nanny or mother's help without an interview. Mabel Liddiard, matron of the Mothercraft Training School, urged mothers to choose nurses carefully, taking care to find a kindred spirit who would work with her rather than against her, as well as ensuring that she was well trained in good hygiene methods.[29] But mothers needing a nanny in a hurry did not always have the time or inclination to heed such advice.

Enid's second employer, who lived on the Isle of Wight, came to London, conducted the interview at a friend's house, and engaged Enid on the spot. Within a few days Enid was on the island and realised why she had been taken on so swiftly. The mother had never had a nanny before, but with her husband returning home at the end of the war she now wanted time alone with him. Enid was thrust into a strange house with a 4-year-old child and baby who were quite unused to having a nanny. The child didn't take kindly to her new nurse and Enid's first reactions were, 'I want to go home' and that she had taken the wrong job. But she soon gained the child's confidence by talking to her and reading her stories.

Nannies more experienced in going to interviews were less likely to take the first job offered. In the late 1970s, Walter and Pamela had initially employed a part-time mother's help who was uncritical, shared their liberal views on childcare, and did not mind their untidy house. They had much more difficulty when they decided to employ a trained nanny and found that the nannies seemed to be doing the interviewing. Pamela recounted:

> I went to an agency and they sent us various people, and our problem really was that we're an academic family and we live in a slightly shambolic way. We were living in Westminster which sounds like a very posh address, it was SW1 which is a posh postcode, and when the nannies arrived for the interview, they came into this house and they thought, 'Oh God I can't cope with this'.
>
> You know, a) we didn't know what we were looking for because we'd never had the experience of a nanny before, and b) you could sort of see them, the piles of books, you know and dust and stuff like that. So we interviewed about three or four and then Susie [...] came along and she said she'd give us a try.

Mothers interviewing for the first time were sometimes at a loss to know what they were supposed to ask, particularly in cases where nannies were considered part of the family rather than an employee. Single mother Hannah noted this in her second job as a mother's help with a doctor who offered her a home in exchange for helping his wife, Jean, look after four older children. She explained:

> then I had a phone call completely out of the blue from Jean and she said, 'Would I like to come over and meet her?' and I can't remember on what premise I was meeting her at all ... So I went. I remember going to meet Jean and having a sort of strange interview where she sat on the sofa and we chatted basically and she did ask me a few questions ... and how I remember it is that she said, 'Well, would you like to come and live with us?'
>
> And I thought, 'Great, yes because I can get out of where I am, and they seem nice.'

Other mothers had clearer expectations. Beth, who worked at home in the 1970s, was initially determined to have a trained nanny, rejecting an au pair because she wanted someone whose first language was English. As a first-time mother, she also needed 'the reassurance that they had done their qualification and they knew what they were doing'. Yet she was nervous when doing the interview, feeling 'very unqualified to hire somebody' and believing that she should really still be looking after her own child. Beth's continuing discomfort with having a stranger in the house affected later interviews: she rejected one candidate, ostensibly on the grounds that she had a child but in reality because she thought the woman might be too attractive to her husband. This usually unspoken fear haunted many mothers and was sometimes a determining factor in a decision to recruit an older woman. Beth's assessment of her various nannies' likely attractions was probably accurate. When her husband later was propositioned by a nanny whom he found naked in the bathroom next to his office, she was reassured. She knew he would not be tempted (he was apparently petrified and retreated as far away as possible) because this nanny definitely wasn't his type.

Interviews in the early part of the twentieth century were usually confined to mother and nanny, but in the more child-centred post-war period children might also be present. Norland student Alison was rejected for her first probationary post because she had not interacted sufficiently with her prospective charge. Believing that she should not force herself upon the child, she had held back, and the mother saw this as a sign that she was not interested. My employer Gill was keen to find people who would be kind and loving to her children and who had the same priorities and outlook on childcare as herself. She asked me to take her 1-year-old baby for a walk before giving me the job, to ensure that the child would be happy with me.

Like Beth, Gill found the process of interviewing difficult, regarding it as a 'tedious, tedious, tedious, thing … and very fraught'. Her first mother's help had produced a list of questions at the interview relating to time off and holidays, and Gill was concerned that formalities of this kind were being given more priority than the nature of the job. Because the questions seemed out of character with the candidate, Gill decided to engage her anyway. She later discovered that the questions had come from a third party who was concerned about exploitation. Although this situation was a cause of amusement when the two women discussed it afterwards, the sensitivities it exposes are indicative of the unstable boundary between family and work. This issue is also apparent in *Nursery World*, where mothers and nannies endlessly debated whether nannies' demands for higher wages and regular time off were reasonable, given the nature of the job, or a sign that nannies were uncaring and mercenary. Mothers struggled to hold on to nannies and helps, feeling let down when they left for jobs with a better salary, with one mother longing for someone who would 'take a really human interest in her family'.[30]

CHANGING JOBS

Charges that mistresses were inhumane were common in the early part of the twentieth century and often lay at the root of nursery maids' decisions to change jobs. In a survey carried out before the First World War, some nurses declared they were fulfilled by their job, pointing out that cooks and housemaids could not 'love their saucepans and furniture as I love my babies', but others complained about mistresses treating servants as if they had no feelings.[31] Turnover was high, but employees could not force employers to give them a written character reference (or testimonial) if they left, and if they objected too strongly they might be dismissed without one, which made it difficult for them to find another job. With no unions to back them, they were in a weak position, as courts were usually unsympathetic, believing the mistresses' version of events. In 1913, when a 'saucy' maid tried to sue her mistress for unfair dismissal, she lost her case.[32]

The press often lampooned the trials of mistresses and misbehaviour of servants. In 1908, the *Daily Mirror* cartoonist W.K. Hazleden published two cartoons in this vein. 'Trials of a nurse' showed a nurse subjecting a baby to every conceivable form of neglect and abuse, smacking, shaking, swinging and tossing her into the air, while in 'Technical training in being a nursemaid' the nurse was even more incompetent. She smacked and stuck a pin into the baby, ignored her cries both as she fell into the fire and while flirting with a lover in the park, and allowed her to get soaking wet in the rain. Under the caption 'the young idea', the

'Technical training in being a nursemaid' (*Daily Mirror*, 1908), by W.K. Hazleden.
Copyright Mirrorpix

baby's elder sister imitated everything she saw the nurse doing. The final image was of a nurse throwing the baby at its mother with the retort 'mind your own baby' and an advisory caption:'give notice constantly'.[33] Here Hazleden was not simply illustrating the dangers untrained, uncaring, working-class nursemaids posed to babies. He was also criticising middle- and upper-class mothers for allowing their children to be so badly neglected, giving the message that they should really be employing a more trustworthy, trained professional nurse.

While still often critical of nannies' propensity to give notice, later in the century employers were more likely to see frequent changes of carer as advantageous. Such practices ensured that mothers would remain in charge and would always be the most important person in their children's lives. A mother writing to *Nursery World* in the 1940s believed that older, experienced nannies thought they had nothing to learn and resented her interference; she preferred younger ones, who were willing to be trained in her ways and would leave to get married.[34] My employer Gill felt similarly. Having herself been brought up by a trained nanny during the Second World War, she was determined not to relinquish her central role as mother and chose not to hire trained helps or nannies on long-term contracts because they might challenge her way of doing things. As Gill's second help I fitted her criteria and was happy to go along with her rules, although I sometimes struggled to live up to her standards, such as keeping the nursery tidy and dressing the children in the right outfits.

Mothers knew that children would often be upset when they lost a nanny and had to get used to a new one, but it was not until after the First World War that these concerns were aired publically. Children's reactions to nannies' comings and goings were discussed in some depth by psychologists in *Nursery World* who gave advice on how to help unhappy children adjust to a new nanny and explained that much depended on how the changeover was managed.

Columnist Ursula Wise had a particular interest in this issue, and stressed the importance of honesty. Writing to a woman whose daughter, after initially accepting a new nanny, began to cling to her mother, she explained that this behaviour was rooted in a lie told to the child that her old nanny was going on holiday. Wise insisted that the child must have seen through the lie and that the mother needed to acknowledge her loss. Similar problems, including tantrums, were also reported by a nurse who had recently left a post. She had been accused by her former employer of having spoiled her charge, a little girl to whom the nurse had been devoted. Wise suggested that the loss of her nurse and disturbance of her accustomed routine had aroused 'a general resentment in the child's mind' and was causing her headstrong behaviour. She advised mothers not to change nurses too often and to 'balance against the present ills, those arising from the mere facts of the change'.[35] These letters were reproduced after the author's death in a book, *Children and Parents: Their Problems and Difficulties*, which was still in print in the late 1960s.

Similar advice in an article 'Parting from Nannie', probably influenced by Anna Freud and Bowlby's work on attachment,[36] appeared in the 1946 volume of *Nursery World*. It also focused on the issue of trust, advising a mother whose new nanny was unable to manage her son's tantrums not to consider getting rid of her in favour of a more experienced nurse as this would greatly increase the boy's sense of insecurity. Parting from a nanny, if not well managed, could have an adverse effect on a child's attitude towards future relationships and his/her ability to form new attachments.[37] The importance of mothers and nannies getting on together and not becoming rivals for children's affection was also strongly emphasised.[38]

Sadly, however, it was often this kind of rivalry (though sometimes mixed with other factors) that led to a nanny's departure. Amelia, who had trained at Princess Christian College, found one situation so difficult that she decided to become a hospital nurse instead. The parents suspected that Amelia was neglecting the children, but she believed that they were unhappy about the attachment between her and her charges. The crunch came when Amelia was prevented from reading them bedtime stories: 'They took all that off me and he [the father] took charge of taking the children to bed and they used to cry, those children cried when he did that. "We want Amelia to read a bedtime story." And you start to think this is really, really horrible.'

Although such conflicts were damaging for all parties, some children were resilient enough to cope well and in retrospect saw having a number of different carers in quite a positive light. For Beth's son David, their transience was difficult – but not impossible – to deal with. His memory of his nanny Pat as 'lovely', the big hug he gave her, and his tears when she left stood out in a long line of similar partings:

> The transition period … was quite weird. You've just got used to someone and you generally got very, very attached to them if they were a nice nanny; you know, you didn't realise that they were being paid by your parents to look after you … Well, you just didn't think about it, I didn't compute that they're in a job. But to me, she was just this person that was around and if I got on really well with them, you know, it was really sad when they had to leave.

David had coped with his feelings of loss by distancing himself from his nannies and strengthening his attachment to his mother. Even if Beth wasn't always as sympathetic as nannies were when he hurt himself, he knew she would always be there for him. Nannies' comings and goings were, he thought, 'a good test perhaps of early relationship-building skills for small children because you were having to regain trust with this new person and let them into your life and hope they're nice and hope you get on well with them'. Stella's feelings of sadness when an au pair had to leave were displaced in her memory by the excitement of having someone new:

> Somebody who's going to come and be part of our family for quite a long time. What are they going to be like? … This is someone who's going to share our lives … because I quite enjoyed having them around, I never thought, 'Ugh, what are they going to be like?' I was really, really intrigued.

Never becoming too closely involved, she saw them as part of a wider group of people who were always coming and going in their very sociable household and 'just grew up with the idea that it's a nice thing to have lots of people around'.

Leaving children they loved was very hard for nannies. Whatever the reasons for their departure, partings could be traumatic. One nanny who shared her agony at leaving a much loved charge with *Nursery World* readers was amazed to receive so many letters in response expressing sympathy. Her last charge was the nearest to her heart, and although she could now think of him without the terrible heartache she used to have, the letters and gifts she sent were not acknowledged and she had heard nothing more of the child.[39]

Edith Hunt, a Suffolk nanny in the 1920s, changed jobs several times for reasons including homesickness and ill-health, and experienced two 'nervous breakdowns'. She believed that the over-ruling power that compelled her to leave her children was the will of God. Yet it was her powerful attachment to one of her charges, who would not let her out of his sight after she had been away for a short holiday, that had provoked her second collapse:

> It was and will always be the worst aspect of looking after other people's children and the wrench for both nannies and children is almost unbearable at the time. During my illness, I found it impossible to stop crying – I didn't want to eat – I didn't sleep properly … I was still under the doctor two years after.[40]

TEMPORARY WORK AND TESTIMONIALS

The disturbances and heartaches suffered by nannies and children who did become deeply attached often lay behind nannies' decisions to only take temporary positions. As Gill's mother's help I saw my job simply as a way of not being at home with my parents and earning money in the gap between school and college. For career nannies, however, temporary work was both a useful means of getting varied, interesting jobs and a way of avoiding pain. Most of the disadvantages of temporary work were not in dispute. As a Norland nurse explained in 1916, it was more tiring and sometimes also trying, the children were often difficult to manage, families were not interested in temporary nurses, and nurses had to adapt to employers' ways. Yet a more distant relationship with a family could be easier than getting too close, as a nanny writing after the Second World War discovered. Having previously had a series of temporary jobs, she was now in a permanent post with a 'sweet baby boy', but her chief worry was that if she stayed too long she would get too fond of the child.[41]

Temporary posts might involve looking after children during school holidays, covering for permanent nannies when they went on holiday, or working as a monthly nurse caring for mothers and young babies during the first four weeks of a baby's life. Testimonial books of college nurses attest to the satisfaction that could be gained from short-tem work which did not require nannies to become emotionally involved with individual children. After her probationary year, one Norland nurse worked in short-term posts from 1916 to 1940, mainly in the south of England, until she was 51 years old. She filled five volumes of the Norland Testimonial Book, either as a monthly nurse or taking charge for a few weeks in emergencies, and returning to the same employers many times over. References from employers stressed how she had helped them with feeding and dietary management and that children became much healthier and happier under her care. [42]

Trained nannies were most likely to get work as monthly nurses, but not all nurses in this kind of work had qualifications. Lillian's monthly nurse in the 1950s, who came from an Essex village, was untrained. She had previously worked as a nanny for many years and become unhappy about getting too involved with children and then being sent away. In her final long-term post, she had become very attached to a little boy, but when she left 'they gave her a coffee pot, that was that'. As a result of this experience, she began to do monthly nursing with a little caravan as her base where she planned to retire.

Most of the testimonial books which trained nannies took with them from job to job gave glowing references which should have made it easy for them to be re-employed. These letters cannot, however, be taken as an accurate reflection of how successful a nanny really was. Lillian's not very positive experience with her monthly nurse did not prevent her from re-employing her for a short period, but she regretted it afterwards as the nurse was not able to cope very well with older children. This experience seems to have been common. Many of the nannies I interviewed stressed that they much preferred working with young babies, who were less challenging and could be more easily trained, and employers often noted that nannies were most successful with babies. Some employers would write good references in order to be rid of a nanny they did not get on with. Others might have been concerned that if they wrote a bad reference the college would not keep the nanny on their books. Reading between the lines, however, it is possible to get a sense from one testimonial of why one particular nurse did not pass her probationary year.

Aileen was a Wellgarth graduate in the 1950s sent by the college into a job which involved looking after a young baby aged a month old. On the surface her report from her employer appears to have been satisfactory. She was said to have been fond of children, was recommended for a post with a young baby, and commended for her skill as a laundress, and was praised for keeping the baby clean and tidy, as well as for her ability to handle a baby with skill and confidence. Yet a note from the college principal inside the book which stated that no badge would be awarded until she completed a satisfactory year's work suggests that there had been problems. These were obliquely referred to in the testimonial's final paragraph, in which the employer stated that she was fortunate in having had an exceptionally healthy and contented baby to look after and that when she has had further experience in the nursery she would be an excellent nurse, but was best suited to the care of infants.[43] It seems likely that more information was given to the college by the employer which was not written down.

A better sense of the reasons why employers might have asked nannies to leave, why some nannies departed early, and why others stayed on can be obtained by following one nanny's life over several decades. This account is drawn from two interviews, one with the nanny and the other with the child she cared for.

JEANNIE'S STORY

Jeannie, born in 1934, had never lived with her parents, who were separated; they had business and professional backgrounds but could not give her a home. As a result, she was fostered as a young child and later brought up by grandparents who were farmers in the West Country. After her first post at the age of 15, and a six-month period of nursery training, Jeannie took a job in Kensington caring for the future actress Harriet Walter and her sister Charlotte as very young children. It was the most exciting period of Jeannie's working life, and she greatly enjoyed the social life, regularly going out with friends dancing at the Hammersmith Palais. When she came in after the 11 o'clock curfew once too often and had a stinking row with her boss, however, she was dismissed and had to look for another job, which she found in *Nursery World*.

Jeannie was not too worried by her dismissal and, given the shortage of nannies in the early 1950s, she was able to get another job without much difficulty, despite the fact that she did not have very good references. Her new employer, watching Jeannie interacting with the child Marion, took an instant liking to her and Jeannie soon became devoted to the family. They treated her very differently from her previous employers, more like a companion than a servant, and she stayed with them for ten years. Jeannie's distress at having to leave when her charge was sent to boarding school at the age of 12 must have contributed to her much more negative attitude towards her third employer, who lived in Switzerland. Here she was relegated once again to being a member of staff and was very critical of the mother, who would 'take all afternoon to have a bath' and constantly interfered with her care of the child.

By this time Jeannie was older and much more experienced, and she was able to give her notice without any worries because of the relationship she had established with her previous employer. While she was in Switzerland, Marion had written to Jeannie about how miserable she was at boarding school, and both Marion and her mother were so unhappy without Jeannie that Marion's father wrote and asked her to return to the family. Marion explained that Jeannie was able 'more or less to name her terms'. She remained with the family for the rest of her working life and Marion took responsibility for Jeannie's care in old age.

Jeannie's life history can be related to many of the concerns we have encountered in the process of the recruitment and retention of nannies. Her grandparents came from the farmer classes on the borders of gentility from which many nannies originated. She trained at a residential nursery, and although her education was limited she was probably perceived as being from the right kind of background by potential employers. She found her first job at the age of 15 through a school friend and another job through an advertisement in *Nursery World*. She gave and received notice in posts where she felt exploited by her employers and had broken their rules. As a result she did not get the perfect references that enabled some nannies to go easily from job to job. She overcame this problem by making the most of the post-war domestic labour shortage and displaying her genuine love for children at interviews. She felt able to leave babies and young children in short-term jobs where she wanted to get out without too much heartache. Yet she became so attached to one family that they became her life's work. Offering companionship as well as childcare, this family replaced her own parents, who had never welcomed her as a child.

Although in some respects Jeannie resembles the rare breed of Victorian and Edwardian nannies who stayed with families throughout their lives, she was a thoroughly twentieth-century nanny. Her history also shows the value of knowing about nannies' lives outside and beyond their jobs, their families of origin, and their continuing connections with employers in later life. We take up this important subject in the next chapter.

6

LIFE BEYOND
THE JOB

Shirley's nanny had been with her from birth, a fixed and seemingly immutable presence in her young life. But when the family lost much of their money in the stockmarket crash of the late 1920s they had to move to a much smaller house. Nanny took 5-year-old Shirley to see the new house, reassuring her she was not to worry that the house had no room for Nanny and that she would find a little corner. It was not until the day they moved that Shirley discovered the truth; returning from school to the new house, she found Nanny had disappeared without saying good-bye. It was an awful moment which she recalled vividly eighty years later, denouncing it as 'a very cruel thing to do'.

Yet this was not the last time Shirley saw her nanny, who moved on to work for friends of her parents. The child had to find a way of coping with the pain of loss, feelings that were intensified when she had to watch 'her' nanny looking after other children. Shirley pretended that it was she, not her parents, who had let her nanny go and that she was in control of the situation. She fantasised that Nanny was not these children's real nanny but, rather, she had loaned her nanny to them. This strategy made it easier for Shirley to keep in touch with her nanny, who came to her twenty-first birthday party. But the pain never entirely went away.

Shirley's story reminds us that we have to look beyond the confines of the job itself to understand what both having and being a nanny really meant. In a relationship where feelings of love and loss on parting could be so powerful that they were never forgotten, finding ways of keeping in touch could offer a life raft for both parties. For the family, knowing something about a nanny's world when she was not working for them might mean listening to stories about her childhood, meeting her relatives and other families who employed her, visiting her home, and communicating afterwards by letter or phone and in face-to-face meetings. Although having links with other families that their nanny had looked after could be difficult for a child, it was better than burying feelings about her which might take many years to recognise and never be resolved.

Sadie, one of the seven Leigh sisters, had to cope with the same kind of loss as Shirley but, unlike her, she was allowed no further contact with her former nanny. On her daily walk, she had to pass the cottage where her nanny Nellie lived, and the image of her nanny's home remained sharp in her mind into old age. But her requests to visit Nellie fell on deaf ears, and Sadie never saw her again.

For 5-year-old Hilary, who was not told that her nanny had been sent away (for fear she would infect the family with tuberculosis), feelings of sadness and loss lasted well into middle age. Her tears were initially met by empty reassurances that her nanny would come back, but after the nanny died her parents fell silent and barely admitted that she had existed. As Hilary grew up she felt she was always looking for people and could never accept their loss. But it was not until fifty years later, when she became unreasonably upset by the death of Senator Robert Kennedy, that she recognised the loss she has suffered in childhood and realised just how important her nanny had been.

These three children's experiences remind us how necessary it is to know more about nannies' lives outside the job and the connections mothers and children did – or did not – make with nannies in the longer term. This subject is significant not simply because of its importance for individuals but also as part of a wider history. Dynamics between nanny, mother and child inside households can be understood much better if we investigate the backgrounds from which nannies originated, the class and ethnic communities they inhabited, the kinds of families they came from, the ways they had themselves been mothered, and their continuing links – or lack of links – with relatives and friends.

Children visiting a nanny's family entered new territory and were introduced to different food, smells and behaviour. Yet the strangeness could be overlaid with an aura of familiarity because nannies brought something of their outside lives into every job they did. When a nanny talked about her own world, including other children she had looked after, she often made comparisons; standards were introduced to which a child and his/her mother might or might not measure up and could become sources of anxiety. But the connections that children and mothers maintained with nannies, often into old age, were helpful for all parties and kept the relationship alive even if they rarely or never met face-to-face again. And in cases where nannies and families offered one another continuing mutual support and contact throughout a nanny's life, we find deep feelings of love and reciprocity which testify movingly to the value of these relationships.

The different ways that a nanny's outside life might influence her charges' childhoods can be related in part to the extent of the social distance between them. Lucy Delap has argued that, although some nannies did feel a lasting attachment to their charges and stayed in touch with them, the love and intimacy that existed between them was inevitably 'shot through with awareness of social chasm and the ephemerality of the relationship'.[1] This situation may explain the difficulty upper-class memoirists seem to have had in finding out much about their nannies' backgrounds. Lack of any obvious sources, the short-term nature of many jobs, and the knowledge that, however much they were loved, nannies were not part of the family tends to limit accounts of nannies to brief snapshots. Few authors have tried to discover much about the early lives of their nannies, in contrast to their curiosity about their parents. Yet, however short- or long-term these relationships were, the more knowledge we have about the nanny's side of the social divide the better we will understand them. As Alison Light showed when she researched the early lives of Virginia Woolf's servants,[2] only then can we can transform the two-dimensional upstairs–downstairs mentality of some popular accounts of service relationships into something more interesting and satisfying.

NANNY TURRELL

I discovered the value of such information by investigating the early life of Annie Turrell, the first nanny to care for Viola and Ralph Bankes at Kingston Lacy in Dorset in the early 1900s. Viola had only fragmentary memories of this nanny, telling us that she had shared her baby brother Ralph's room, had been shocked that Viola and her sister had not known how to play with their little brother, and that her favourite dish was cold boiled bacon with vegetables. She had a nostalgic image of setting off for a walk 'with the Nurse and nursery maid in their grey coats, nursery maid pushing the pram, Nanny walking majestically behind'.[3] Each of these anecdotes means so much more when set in the context of Annie's past life before she came to the Bankes' household, a past which must have influenced her charges' childhoods profoundly.

Annie's upbringing was typical of that of many servants and nannies working in big country houses during this era. The census shows she was born in 1871, the seventh of eight children with four older sisters, two older brothers and one younger brother, all of whom, unusually for this period, survived infancy.[4] Her parents were agricultural labourers living in a small hamlet a few miles from the small country town of Ingatestone in Essex, an area they had lived in all their lives.[5] Annie's favourite dish, which she doubtless encouraged the cook to serve up frequently for the nursery, reflects the diet she would have known as a child: vegetables available from the cottage garden and home-cured bacon from the family pig most cottagers kept to supplement meagre wages. Bacon was a treat not often given to a youngest daughter in competition with older siblings. Its appeal would have been enhanced by the fact that the lion's share would have gone to her father and older working brothers, with meat given to younger ones only on Sundays.

Annie must have played outdoors with her siblings and children from neighbouring cottages from an early age and, despite the more protected upbringing she gave her charges, her shock at Viola not knowing how to play with her brother is understandable. Yet this memory might have been given extra salience by Viola's knowledge of a similar story which she would have read as a child or perhaps read to her own children. One of the strongest messages promoted by Frances Hodgson

The Bankes children and their nannies. Viola is on the left, next to her brother Ralph. *Courtesy of Bankes Collection, Kingston Lacy House, National Trust*

Burnett in her book *The Secret Garden* (1911) was the contrast between the unhealthy, overprotected, rich child who does not know how to play and the ruddy-cheeked nursemaid from a cottager's family who teaches her charge how to skip and play games. This romantic image of country childhood is relevant to Annie in more than one way. The

Bankes' choice of a country girl as a nanny for their children was typical of the servant-employing classes, influenced by the belief that she
would be more robust, healthy and tractable, a better influence on their
children than a city girl.[6] This sentimentalised view of rural life ignored
the harsh realities of poverty, overcrowding and agricultural depression
that in the last decades of the nineteenth century drove Annie and her
siblings away from home and into the city. Viola's description of another
nursemaid leaving 'a cosy home' to go into service shows a similarly rosy
view of a contented rural community. In fact, Dorset agricultural labourers endured some of the most squalid living conditions and embittered
class relations in England during the whole of the nineteenth century,
and arson attacks on landowners' property were still common in the
county during the 1890s.[7] Viola seemed unable to fully recognise the
envy implicit in the customary greeting given to her by the wife of one
of her father's employees: 'Nice to be you'.[8]

Annie's upbringing in a crowded cottage with seven siblings sharing
rooms and beds had another important influence on the Bankes children. As a young baby, Viola shared her nanny's bedroom and possibly
also her bed. But when her younger brother was born she was banished to her elder sister Daphne's room. The two girls were looked after
by several different nursery maids who did all the care work, including washing and dressing them. This regime in some ways repeated
Annie's own childhood experience, despite taking place in a household
that could not have been further removed in size and wealth from that
of her parents. As the youngest girl, Annie was probably removed from
her mother's bed at around the same age as Viola, replaced by a brother
who was three years younger, and cared for by her elder sisters, a very
common pattern in large families.[9]

In his autobiography *Cider with Rosie*, the writer Laurie Lee remembered a similar event just after the First World War. Lee was deeply
attached to his mother, whose bed he shared. When his younger brother
took his place, his older sisters tried to comfort him but he still thought
it 'outrageous … my first dose of ageing hardness, my first lesson in the
gentle, merciless rejection of women'.[10] Viola too became experienced
in dealing with rejection. After Annie left her post at Kingston Lacy
when Viola was 6 or 7, she was followed by a long line of nannies and

nursemaids who left or died. This series of partings from maternal figures culminated for Viola in a final and decisive break with her mother, a distant figure who disapproved of her daughter's decision to marry an Australian doctor on the grounds of his class, although the couple remained living in Britain. Viola's most intimate relationship in adult life was as far removed from her mother's world as the nursemaids and nannies who had been close to her in childhood, and she was banished forever from Kingston Lacy.

Annie's decision to move on from Kingston Lacy, which had such an important effect on Viola and her siblings, can be traced in part to the economic position of her family and the upward mobility of her generation. Unlike their parents, Annie and most of her siblings did not remain in their home village. During the last three decades of the nineteenth century, a protracted agricultural depression limited the possibilities for families to survive on the land; a quarter of full-time farm workers in England and Wales left agricultural employment between 1871 and 1911.[11] At the same time, an increasingly affluent middle and upper class required more servants, with well over a third of all working women between 1881 and 1911 employed in domestic service or other service work.[12] By the time Annie was 10, in 1881, two of her sisters were already away from home in service, one in a large establishment as a housemaid with two other maids, a cook, coachman and groom. The 1880s and 1890s saw Annie's family fragmenting further. Many of her siblings improved their prospects by joining the mass migration of the rural residents to the city and taking up in jobs in the police force and nursing. I was unable to locate Annie in the 1891 census, but she was no longer recorded at home and, by the age of 20, would have doubtless followed her sisters into service.

There was a strong incentive for children leaving poverty-stricken homes to better themselves, not simply for their own sakes but also to send money home.[12] Rather than following her two London-based sisters into hospital nursing, as girls in service often did,[13] Annie looked for ever more prestigious situations within personal service. Like her eldest sister Elizabeth, who moved from housemaid to nanny, Annie chose childcare. She probably started as a nursery maid and worked her way up to the position of head nanny. The first record of her work is in 1901, when at the age of 30 she appears in the census returns at Kingston Lacy as a 'domestic nurse'. Here she was employed by one of the principal aristocratic families in Dorset to care for baby Viola and her elder sister and had a nursery maid working under her.

Annie's pathway to becoming a nanny may explain why she stayed only a few years at Kingston Lacy. It was common for nannies to prefer new babies, and Viola makes it clear that Annie went on to look after another newborn. Having sole charge of a baby from a month old in a wealthy household, with nursemaids to assist her and not too much interference from a mother, seemed an ideal situation for most nannies. Since Viola's father died not long after her brother was born, Annie was probably looking for a new situation as her charges grew older. She left when Ralph, the youngest Bankes child, was 4 or 5. In 1911, when she was 40, we find her at Emo Court in Ireland in sole charge of the 3-year-old George Seymour Dawson, Viscount Carlow, only son of Lord Portarlington.[14] With a 17-year-old nursemaid under her, she could once again parade majestically behind a pram.

We can see in this story that although Annie had travelled a long way from her Essex rural origins, her family background remained a vital but invisible force in her career, with consequences for all the children she looked after. Her continuing importance in the lives of both sets of charges can be gauged by the bond Viola felt with Viscount Carlow when they met much later in life. The warmth they felt for one another was based on having had the same nanny, even though they had never met as children and their memories of Annie were very hazy.[15]

FRIENDS FOR LIFE: UNA SHERIFF MACGREGOR AND SYLVIA FLETCHER MOULTON

While Annie Turrell stayed with Viola only for her first six or seven years, the background of a nanny who stayed with one family for life was of even greater significance. Whether or not nannies remained with a particular family and were regarded by them as a continuing responsibility was inevitably influenced by the nanny's own home circumstances. Especially significant were the nature of her connections with her blood relatives and the family's financial position before, during, and after her working life.

In the early twentieth century, 'distressed gentlewomen' often sought work as nannies in wealthy families because they wanted or needed to earn their own living after their families had fallen on hard times. Una Sheriff Macgregor (born in 1877), who came from a genteel background, was probably in this position. One of the earliest graduates of Norland College, in 1902 she began caring for the month-old baby daughter of Sir John Fletcher Moulton, a prominent barrister and liberal MP; she stayed with her charge for more than forty years.

Una's background could not have been more different from that of Annie Turrell. Her parents were owners of the substantial Glengyle estate on the shores of Loch Katrine in the Highlands of Scotland, inherited by Una's mother Jemima Macgregor, and had family connections to Rob Roy, which may explain why her father George Sheriff had taken his wife's name.[16] The Sheriff Macgregors were able to live on private means in Kelvinside, a wealthy suburb inhabited by members of Glasgow's elite professional and manufacturing classes, in a substantial four-storey Victorian house where they kept three servants.[17] The family moved soon after George's death in 1895, however, and this change in their fortunes seems to have been a catalyst for Una to leave home and go to London to train at the newly founded Norland College. Una never returned to her birth family but in the course of her working life managed to find a situation in which she could retain aspects of the lifestyle into which she was born and develop an extraordinarily close and equal relationship with the child she looked after, one that few other nannies in her position could have known.

Like Annie, Una was good with babies, a preference noted by two previous employers, and she found her ideal situation looking after the only child of the Fletcher Moultons, who lived in a large London town house in Onslow Square. Although grander and with a bigger staff, the house was similar in style to the one in which Una had grown up in Glasgow, and she soon made herself indispensable to the family. Testimonials written by Sylvia's mother Mary show that Una was in full charge (because both parents were often absent from home) and that she had bonded closely with Sylvia from birth, putting herself 'absolutely at one with

Una Sheriff Macgregor
(1877–1943), nanny to Sylvia
Fletcher Moulton.
*Courtesy of the Mistress
and Fellows, Girton College,
Cambridge*

the child's real interests' and becoming the object of some jealousy on
the part of the child's French governesses.[18] After Mary died in 1908,
Una became even more important. Her high status is suggested by her
position on the 1911 census return, filled in by the head of household,
just below Sylvia and her father and above all other household members,
including the butler and governess.

In a testimonial in 1912, Sir John described the relationship which
Una developed with Sylvia as having 'almost completely ceased to be
the original one of being a nurse to a child. The thoughtful and intel-
ligent child of 10 years old makes demands on her which are as exacting
as those of years ago but they have completely changed in character.'
It is tempting to wonder how far the character of Sir John's own relationship with Una had changed after his wife's death, but Sylvia and
Una certainly seem to have been developing a more equal relationship,
facilitated by their similar class backgrounds. The bond between them

had important consequences for both women later in life. It is not clear
how far Una kept in touch with her mother and sisters in Scotland, but
her brother's demise in the Boer War not long after her father's death
and her mother's sale of Glengyle in 1918 to the Glasgow Corporation
Water Board for less than half its original purchase value suggests that
the family estate, which would have been depleted of much of its labour
force during the war, was no longer giving the Sheriff Macgregors a
viable income.[19] Una could probably not have relied on her family for
support. The friendship that developed between Sylvia and Una, helped
by their similar family backgrounds, became much more important for
both women than relationships they had with their own relatives.

Sylvia had no siblings and little or no contact with her father during
the war. Put in charge of the production of explosives and poison gas,
Sir John, now Lord Moulton, shipped Sylvia and Una off to New York[20]
and supposedly had to be reminded that he had a daughter when the
war ended. He died in 1921, not long after Sylvia and Una's return from
the United States, and the two women remained living together. In 1933,
Norland awarded Una a green bar for more than twenty-one years' service in the same family.[21] Sylvia never married, and Una's continuing
love and support must have been hugely important, enabling her in 1929
to become one of the first woman barristers called to the Bar. Una died
in 1943 but remained a significant presence in Sylvia's life. So strong were
her feelings for her beloved Da (as she called Una) that when Sylvia died
in 1989 she gave explicit instructions that her ashes were to be buried
not with her family but at the foot of her nanny's grave in Barcombe
Churchyard, Sussex.[22]

SHARING A NANNY

Such a powerful and lasting bond between nanny and child which
lasted was probably a rarity. But feelings of love, gratitude and sometimes also guilt that a child had not done enough for his or her nanny
in old age were common. These emotions were often complicated by
the gulf between the child's and the nanny's backgrounds and by the
nanny's divided loyalties between her own family and those of different

employers. Loving and losing the same nanny might create a bond for some children, but for others, having to share her with her own relatives or with children she had looked after in earlier jobs (even if the families never met), could provoke jealousies or at least feelings of unease.

The children looked after by Agnes Gregory (born in 1871), nanny to the middle-brow novelist Pamela Frankau, her sister Ursula, and her nephew Tim, were in this position. Agnes's background was much more similar to Annie Turrell's than it was to Una Sherriff Macgregor's but, like Una, she formed a strong attachment to a particular family which lasted from 1906 until her death in 1965. Agnes did not continue working for and living with one family until she died. Only the wealthiest families could afford this commitment. Although Mr Frankau was the son of a wealthy cigar merchant, he was unreliable, spent little time with his family, and divorced his wife after the First World War, leaving the family struggling financially. Agnes stayed with the Frankaus until after Pamela and Ursula were grown up, and during the 1920s lodged in Battersea on call to the family whenever she was needed.[23] Yet her devotion to them was not exclusive. Rather, it ran in tandem with her loyalty to her blood relatives and to other families for whom she worked before and between her jobs with the Frankaus.

Agnes was born in Southampton, the daughter of a sailor who died when she was 4 years old. She grew up with her mother and younger sister in the household of her widowed grandfather, a coachman. Her mother had also been in service, and Agnes trod a pathway familiar to many other girls from her background. She was employed as nurse-maid or nanny for two or more families before she started work for the Frankaus at the age of 35; she moved on to work for at least one other family after Pamela and Ursula had grown up; and she came back to look after Ursula's young son Tim from his birth in 1936 until the early 1950s, when she finally retired.

For Tim, knowledge of his nanny's other families was something he accepted but kept at a distance. Agnes had talked about them and some-times visited them, but Tim never felt comfortable enough to discuss the visits with her: 'They weren't secret but we just didn't ask. Well, my mother must have known, but I didn't ask who these people were.' Like his mother and aunt, these shadowy figures had been cared for by the

A child in a tin bath, 1940s. Tin baths which had to be filled by hand were still common in older working-class houses. *Copyright Everett Collection, Shutterstock*

nanny he adored. Yet they were not part of Tim's family, or even distant relatives, and their relationship to him was never discussed.

Children who shared a nanny sometimes encountered one another for the first time at her funeral. Gillian was in a similar position to Tim. Her nanny had been with Gillian from her birth in 1940 and stayed with her parents into old age, but had also kept in touch with other families from an earlier period of her working life. At the funeral Gillian dealt with this slightly awkward situation by avoiding talking to her nanny's 'other children'. She thought that the realisation of their secondary position in their nanny's life prompted them to leave right after the funeral service without making contact either with Gillian's family or with the nanny's relations. Gillian thought this situation was normal because she believed that she and her siblings were Nanny's 'real children', although what the feelings of the 'other children' were we shall never know.

Both Gillian and Tim remembered spending time with their nannies' relatives. Gillian was excited by the differences between the hotel run by her parents and her nanny's sister's house. Gillian's memory of watching the tin bath being brought in and filled with hot water in front of the fire reminds us how common it was not to have access to piped hot water or bathrooms in the 1940s and '50s.[24] For a child used to modern conveniences, it was a thrilling experience. Tim also enjoyed staying at the home of his nanny's sister, whose husband had been a bricklayer, but was more conscious of the class tensions these encounters could engender. As a child, he welcomed visits from his nanny's niece and her family, who came up to London to go to C&A Modes, a chain clothing store. But Tim was also aware that these occasions were 'rather a nightmare' for his mother, who tried to make sure she was out at work when they visited.

Negotiating class differences could be confusing for children, particularly when a nanny's family went out of their way to provide luxuries for their guests that the children were not allowed at home. Sadie Leigh, who lived in a substantial country house in the interwar years, was faced with this dilemma when she accompanied her second nanny Norma on a visit to her mother:

Joan [Sadie's sister] and I were going to go and have tea with Mrs East in her little cottage and previously we used to ask Norma if we could have fish paste for our tea and Norma used to say, 'Good heavens, your father can't afford these luxuries, you shouldn't ask for them, eat the jam that's on the table.' Well, when we went to tea with Mrs East my mother had said, 'She's very, very poor so don't ask for anything, you may only get water to drink' ... And she had fish paste sandwiches, but of course we couldn't eat them because we'd been told she was so poor we mustn't have anything ... And on the way back Norma kept telling us off ... for not eating them. She said, 'Now, you've always asked for them and now you say you don't like them.'

Sadie, too, regarded this situation as normal:

Well, those are the sort of things that occur all the time if you're brought up by staff because you don't want to hurt anybody or upset anybody and you're treading on eggshells a lot of the time but you don't realise that you are.

FAMILY CONNECTIONS AND LIFELONG LABOUR

Social distinctions were felt particularly acutely in the highly stratified upper-middle-class Leigh household, where the children were taught how to recognise the difference between ladies and women by their governess. For families that were downwardly mobile and had to learn to live with fewer servants, distinctions between a nanny's family and their own became more blurred. When the Plant family was in financial straits, their nanny (who, like the Frankau nanny, was also named Agnes) doubled as a parlour maid. Only Nanny could be trusted to produce the salver ready for visiting cards if the mother was out or to show visitors into the sitting room in the correct way. The Reverend Plant's salary was only a modest £300 per annum, and soon after the advent of war in 1914 spiralling prices obliged the family to give up Agnes, along with their other staff.[25]

The Plants were fortunate, however, that, rather than going on to another job, Agnes, who was still a young woman, went home to look after her widowed mother, a grandmother figure known by the

Plant children as 'Nanniemigger'. The family continued to make use of Agnes's labour without having to pay her a salary, a situation some might consider exploitative. In her memoir *Nanny and I*, Ruth Plant (born in 1909) explained that she did not miss her nanny because she was regularly sent to stay with her for long holidays or when she was in quarantine to avoid infection. Indeed, the whole Plant family stayed at their nanny's house for one summer, perhaps because it was the only holiday they could afford. Agnes continued to live in her home village after her mother died, supporting her sister Edie and helping with her nephews. Yet Agnes did not give up her involvement with the Plants, who continued to see her as part of their family. Ruth's aunt Aggie lived as a lodger with Edie in her rambling farmhouse, which Ruth described as 'an ideal retreat for spinster ladies of moderate means with "treasures" like Edie and Nanny to look after them'.[26]

The love between the Plant family and their nanny was deeply felt on both sides, particularly by the children. Ruth's older brother offered Agnes a home after her mother died. Yet it was by no means an equal relationship. A 'treasure' is a valuable object, but what was most treasured by the Plants was their nanny's capacity to look after them. Agnes related her lifelong reluctance to wear coloured clothes and her preference for the grey and black colours of her former uniform to the time when Ruth's mother stopped her from wearing a favourite blue pinafore to answer the door to callers. She never forgot this legacy of service.

For the family who benefited from a nanny's lifelong devotion, her death was hard to bear. The Plants comforted themselves by imagining Agnes as keeping an eye on her charges from her heavenly home. Ruth visited a medium after she died and was rewarded with a vision of 'a little white-haired lady who comes to you with affection and thanks' who laid on Ruth's knee balls of wool in the bright colours her nanny had never felt able to wear in life.[27]

Nannies could also serve the next generation of a family in an unpaid capacity long after their original employment was a distant memory. Where a nanny and child were not too far apart in age and formed a close bond, they became almost like sisters, with the nanny assuming the role of aunt to her former charges' children. Sarah and her charge Bessie had this kind of relationship, yet it too was not without complications. Sarah had been taken on by Bessie's mother to look after a much younger sister. Although Bessie had not got on well with her earlier nannies, Sarah was different. Only eight years her senior, Sarah acted like a warm and loving older sister towards her, providing emotional security that the child had not received from her rather stern mother. As an adult Bessie rejected her background and joined the Communist party. While Sarah had no interest in politics and remained in a subservient position within Bessie's mother's family, the two young women became lifelong confidantes. Bessie's daughter Sandra explained the dynamic between them:

> On principle her [Bessie's] politics made her want to have an equal relationship with Sarah but my mum didn't have many close friends really … She never really allowed herself any kind of emotional life … So I think Sarah was kind of an anomaly really and a hugely important one. All through her life she would go and stay with Sarah down in the country and they would sit and talk and share their lives. I think Sarah was probably about the only person in her life that she really shared her thoughts and feelings with.

Sarah was equally important to Bessie's children, who called her Aunty Sarah, became deeply attached to her, and spent long holidays with her in Wales. Like Bessie, Sandra found physical warmth and security in her relationship with Sarah:

> There was just a general sense of being accepted for yourself and just being loved for yourself and you didn't have to try terribly hard and if I got … I always got rather anxious about things and Sarah would just come and make it alright, you know, it doesn't matter, you don't have to be anxious like this. So yes, hugely important, this big bosom that you could just lean against and yes, being in bed with her and just mooching around with her, you know, and being accepted and she was very good with children.

Eventually Sandra came to realise that, though deeply buried, inequalities between Sarah and Bessie persisted and true reciprocity had never existed. Bessie looked down on Sarah's husband and had no interest in her children, who were never invited to stay with Bessie's family although, as Sandra pointed out, it would have been nice for them to have a base in London. Sarah's son must have been aware of the social distance between the families and felt some resentment towards Sandra and her sisters. Tellingly, he described the dessert the girls were allowed to choose on the last day of their holidays as 'good riddance pudding'. As an adult Sandra came to recognise with some degree of pain that the love Sarah gave her was not really for her but an aspect of her devotion to her mother Bessie: 'We saw her almost as surrogate mum but we weren't her surrogate children, not really, she didn't. Her eggs were not in our basket.'

It is difficult to assess how far the lifelong labour nannies devoted to the families that had employed them constituted exploitation. The continuing mutual love between a nanny and child created conditions in which a nanny might be treated in later life much like a grandmother or aunt. Yet shadows of the past hung over these relationships. Agnes's retention of her black and white uniform is an obvious clue. But so also is Sarah's equivocal status as 'aunt' to Sandra, based primarily on the love and loyalty she felt for Sandra's mother Bessie and clouded by the legacy of service.

OBLIGATIONS IN OLD AGE AND DEATH

This lack of clarity about the nanny's status as family member or friend affected the extent to which families assumed obligations to her in old age. Children who felt closer to their nannies than their mothers were most likely to pay the debts they felt were owed. The most famous case is Winston Churchill. At the age of 18, Churchill wrote to his mother protesting the family's ingratitude towards his beloved Nanny Everest. She was an elderly woman whom they were 'cutting adrift' because they had 'no further use for her', expecting her to find a new place and begin all over again, and the young Churchill denounced such proceedings as 'cruel and rather mean'. Unable to prevent his nanny from moving back to an old employer, and determined to help her, he sent payments for her support for the next two years until her death, and he and his younger brother paid a local florist for many years to put flowers on her grave.[28]

These attempts to care for nannies in old age show them to be almost – but not quite – family members. The Desboroughs' nanny Harriet Plummer stayed with them until after the youngest daughter had grown up, and was thought of as a family friend. Ettie Desborough's biographer Richard Davenport-Hines describes the deep and authentic love between Harriet and her charges and their mother's doubts after Harriet's death that 'the children would ever have such love given to them again'.[29] The youngest boy Ivo's letters to Harriet from boarding school show just how close she was to them; he confided in her miserable feelings he could not bear to tell his mother, longing for his nanny to come and visit him and begging her to take him home.[30]

Davenport-Hines notes that when Harriet had a stroke and became distressed and confused, Lady Desborough and her daughter were 'as attentive to her as sisters' and points to letters signed by Ettie as 'your affectionate friend'.[31] Yet, where servants were concerned, friendship is always a relative term. The census shows that Harriet's father died before she was 8 years old, leaving a widowed mother who had worked as a charwoman to support her family and had later taken in boarders to survive. Despite the affection Ettie felt for Harriet, she did not treat her as a social equal and reacted to her illness by sending her to an institution rather than having her looked after in Taplow Court. The family could easily have afforded to provide this care but, in the interwar years, when mental incapacity was regarded as incurable,[32] they may have seen institutionalising her as inevitable. Yet arguably they owed it to their nanny in return for so many years of devoted service. Harriet's letters to Ettie from the institution may be confused and rambling, but also show her desperate wish to go home to Taplow Court. Complaints about the matron and nurses suggest Harriet was subject to harsh regimes that were all too typical of institutional life for the mentally ill in this period, including being held down, force-fed food she disliked, and separated from other residents. The deferential tone of her letters and the gratitude Harriet expressed to Ettie even when she was desperately unhappy show the distance between them.[33]

We must be careful not to romanticise relationships between nannies and families, however strongly they expressed their mutual attachment. In the end Ettie's treatment of Harriet was not really so different from the Churchill family's ungrateful attitude to Nanny Everest. Harriet was their employee, and the devotion she felt for the Desboroughs and for Taplow Court, where she had lived since her teens, did not qualify her to be considered 'one of the family' when she became a burden to them rather than a support.

The deep feelings that adult children had for their nannies were often expressed in moving tributes after the nanny's death. In an obituary in *The Times* for Una, Sylvia described her as a 'lifelong friend', and in his autobiography Winston claimed Nanny Everest as his dearest and most intimate friend for the first twenty years of his life. Yet neither Sylvia nor Winston explained their relationship in the inscriptions they put on their nannies' graves. Sylvia and Una's gravestone in a Sussex churchyard simply shows their names, while the inscription on Nanny Everest's grave reads 'Erected in Memory of Elizabeth Anne Everest who died 3rd July 1895 by Winston Spencer Churchill and Jack Spencer Churchill'. In neither case is there any mention of the relationship between them.[34]

A nanny's gravestone (1909), on right. Note that the inscription is set apart from those of her employers on the family monument. *Courtesy of Desmond Ryan*

The Frankau family's relationship to their nanny Agnes was also ambiguous. Tim was very upset when she died at the age of 93 in 1965 and felt he should have done more for her. Her will showed she had left her Post Office savings and most of her possessions to him, his mother, and his aunt. The Frankau family arranged the funeral and put up a gravestone. But on failing to get a response from Agnes's nephews about the wording of the inscription, her former charges Ursula and Pamela were perplexed about what they should write. In the end nothing was said about Agnes's relationship either to the Frankaus or to her own family. Most gravestones memorialise a dearly loved wife, mother, daughter or sister, but the inscription on Agnes's grave simply reads 'dearly loved', giving no indication of who was doing the loving.

A NANNY'S LOVE HAS FAR TO GO

Nannies' feelings about families they had worked for are equally powerful and complicated. Those who did not go on to have children of their own felt an especially strong need to continue to love and be loved by their charges. Emily (born in 1903) centred her life on the children she cared for. At the age of 90, she still looked after children in the village where she lived and kept in touch with many of her former charges. Although she firmly rejected the idea that she was a substitute mother, Emily was anxious to make it clear that a nanny was more important than a mother and that, while she accepted that the children belonged to their parents, she was sure they had loved her best. She explained: 'They saw this beautiful lady coming in, and they loved her coming in, but there was no rushing up mummy, mummy and tears and arms round their necks, not like, not like nanny.'

Emily's determination to raise the status of nannies above mothers and her unconscious though obvious hostility to her employers can be traced partly to her own family background. Her mother was incarcerated in a mental institution when Emily was 14, a terrible stigma in the early twentieth century, which she hid from her early employers. Her dread of her mother's illness, which was commonly believed to be hereditary, and fear of bringing up a child who 'wasn't right' explain why she had no children of her own. But she had been compensated through her work. For Emily, the name 'nanny' embodied all the love and care that was lacking in a mother. The hardships she had experienced in childhood enabled her to help the families for whom she worked later in life. She had shared their tragedies and was now 'able to share the grandchildren coming along'.

In an attempt to make her many children into one family, Emily had placed their photos together in one frame, creating a strange group distinguished by the changing fashions of her working life which stretched from the 1920s to the 1960s. Although leaving each of the children had been heartbreaking, from the perspective of old age Emily saw her relationship with them as a blessing. Most importantly, being a nanny had enabled her to have the family she had always wanted without the necessity of marrying: 'I always had in mind having my own home,' she said, 'and having all the children you see, getting things for the children, and now you see it's come true, the children do come and they do come and they do bring their children.'

Having a place in the lives of their charges was particularly important when it was not simply for the nanny's own benefit but also helpful for the children. Doreen (born in 1936), who worked as a nanny during the 1960s, felt that continuing contact was necessary for a boy and two younger girls in one family who experienced major disruptions and trauma during their childhood. The children's parents separated and divorced while Doreen was living with them and, a year after she left, the mother committed suicide. Doreen explained that these children's lack of 'a family unit' meant they needed extra support. She stayed in touch because she had once been part of that unit and was still needed.

Nannies gave children a sense of security and continuity in case of parental divorce, which became increasingly common after the Second World War. The Leigh sisters and both generations of the Frankau family (Pamela, Ursula and Tim) had parents who divorced during their childhood, and the children were grateful to their nannies for helping them weather the storm. However, staying in contact with her former charges was not easy for Doreen when they went to live with their father and his new wife and family. Their father was Jewish and did not approve of Doreen because she was not. The children had to be careful not to let him know they were in touch with her, cutting phone calls short and sending cards in secret. To lose a nanny and then a mother in tragic circumstances must have been extremely traumatic for the children. But because Doreen was an outsider in the family unit, had been rejected by their father, and could not give them the long-term security they needed at a distance, they struggled to stay in touch with her. Doreen wondered why the boy had stopped sending her cards; but for two years the girls did not feel able to tell her that in his late teens their brother, who had been the one to find his mother's body, had also committed suicide. While both girls invited Doreen to their weddings, only the youngest, who had moved to Australia, continued to communicate with her, responding to the long letters Doreen sent her with a round-robin letter every Christmas.

Former nannies who went on to have children of their own often did not stay in touch with the families they had worked for. Yet they still found the skills they learned on the job useful later in life. It was common for nannies to go on to take other jobs involving childcare, such as childminder or playgroup worker, when they were married and nursery nurse, school matron or foster mother when they were single. For Margaret, a Wellgarth nanny from a middle-class background who disliked 'being treated like a maid', fostering was preferable to nannying because there was no mother to spoil the children and she could train them in her own way. From the 1950s to the 1970s she fostered more than fifty children alongside her own child, taking every child she was offered by the Social Services department and receiving letters of gratitude from some of the parents. Yet she also kept in touch with an employer from the 1940s and in the 1970s returned briefly to help her former charge during her first few weeks after childbirth. The family regarded her help as invaluable, for she was 'the only person who could have fitted in so well'.[35]

Marriage and the birth of a nanny's own children could often separate nannies from former charges, though not always permanently. In the 1950s, the Robinson daughters Matilda and Jane had been bridesmaids for their nanny Ada. Although Ada still thought of them as 'her' children and returned to see them as often as she could, it was harder to stay in touch after she had a daughter of her own. Later she refused to comply with Mrs Robinson's request that she might like to go back for a week and tidy the house for them, and she did not see any of the Robinsons again for many years.

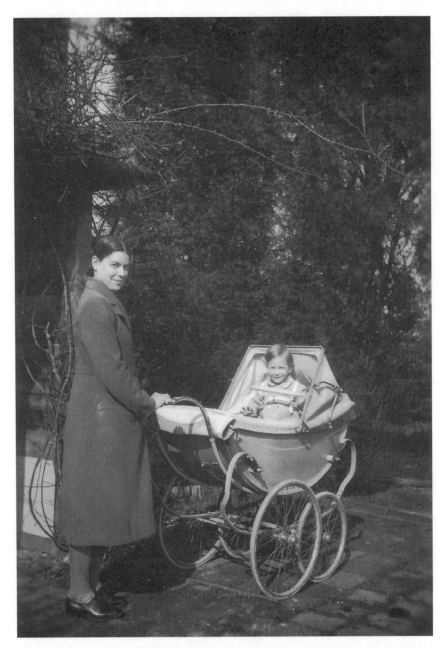

A 1940s nanny and child. This nanny kept in touch with her former charges and offered her help and expertise when the boy's younger sister became a first-time mother. *Courtesy of Nicola Harland, Phillida Gill and Edward Stone*

A nanny 'grandmother' looking after her former charges' children, *c.* 1985. *Courtesy of Joy Lori*

NANNIES ABROAD

Class and religious differences were factors in separating Ada and Doreen from the children they had cared for, but at least they lived in the same country. British nannies who worked abroad and foreign au pairs who worked for British families were much less likely to maintain any long-term contact. Au pairs and host families often failed to understand one another's manners and behaviour, and although most au pairs eventually adapted to the host family's ways of doing things, investment in the relationship was limited on both sides as the job was not expected to last more than a year or two. When more serious difficulties arose, an article in *The Times* in 1960 suggested, they were usually in equal measure between girl and householder and were often based on a lack of understanding of the degree of change young girls experienced in an alien country, cut off for the first time at the age of 16 or 17 from contact with their immediate families.[36]

How far nannies and au pairs felt at home in their host family and country depended both on their employment conditions and on their own attitudes. There was no language barrier for British nannies employed in the United States, but they still commented on the foreignness of American society, airing their grievances in the correspondence column of *Nursery World* and training college magazines. Though some felt the wages and living conditions were too good to miss, others were less sure. For example, in 1926 one nanny mentioned overheated rooms and her thwarted attempts to open windows, strange names for familiar products which made it difficult to explain what she wanted in shops, and her surprise at American people's horror when she tried to walk with her charges through city streets to get to a park. In such circumstances London was preferable to New York, and she was reluctant to return to the United States, in the short term at least, warning other nurses not 'to expect Eldorado'.[37]

Most young nannies and au pairs working for foreign families went abroad because they wanted to travel, have new experiences in an unfamiliar country, and perhaps learn another language. Although they may have liked children, childcare was not usually their main motivation in taking the job. Some were vulnerable and homesick and (in the case of au pairs) became objects of concern to those who aimed to ensure they were not exploited as cheap labour.[38] Others enjoyed a vibrant social life outside the job and, if the family allowed it, might also entertain friends at home. But neither party usually felt the need to stay in touch in the longer term.

As an inexperienced 19-year-old, Fiona was 'desperate to leave home and have adventures', so she travelled to Israel to join a kibbutz, with no intention of becoming a nanny. Three months of picking up dead turkey chicks soon changed her mind and she went in search of new entertainments:

I went down from Northern Israel to Southern Israel, a place called Eilat near the Sinai. It was just after the '67 war and Israel occupied Sinai and I went down there to look about because it was a groovy place to be, through the Negev desert, hitchhiking there, and I stayed in someone's flat. Everybody knew somebody who knew somebody who knew somebody and people were hanging out on the beach and there was sort of an international youth culture. Then somebody said, 'Do you want to stay here? I know a family who have been looking for a nanny.' And I didn't particularly want to go back to the kibbutz so I went and met the family and lived with them for three months.

While her job as a nanny could hardly be described as 'groovy', learning about Jewish culture, coupled with opportunities to go out in the evenings and meet men, made it worthwhile. The family were Zionists, and Fiona found out a lot about Israeli politics and the Jewish religion and customs, including Shabbat songs. She had a lot of fun with the children, sleeping outside with them and camping in the Sinai Desert.

While the job offered Fiona new experiences, the household was not a happy one. She was one in a long line of nannies in a family that had lost a daughter and then adopted a replacement for her. Fiona thought the parents were remote as a result of repressing their grief. She did not bond strongly with the children, who were unsettled by bereavement and frequent changes of carer. So she turned down the family's request for her to stay with them when they went on holiday, preferring to work her passage back to Italy on a yacht, and although Fiona sent presents to the children after she left, they soon faded in her memory.

Fiona took a second job as a nanny in an equally random way in her mid-twenties at a ski resort in France where she was 'trying to become French'. By then a trained teacher, she was much more aware of the needs of her charges. The two grandchildren of a French-born English duchess had been looked after by a series of nannies (four in one season) who were unable to cope with them. Fiona coped much better than her predecessors, but this was a short-term job. She became aware that the 4-year-old had become very attached to her when he raced down the hall and jumped into her arms when she returned a few weeks later to be paid for her month-long employment. She also realised the cost to children of emotional neglect and overindulgence, and the experience affected her own feelings about having children. 'I remember clearly thinking, "well I've done little children, that's done, tick." It didn't make me want to have children at all.'

British children looked after by a series of foreign au pairs also had to learn not to get too attached to them. Stella knew that au pairs should be treated as 'family' but also that they were not the same as her relations and she had to be a little bit more on her best behaviour. Au pairs' 'social life was completely separate'; she was not allowed in their bedrooms, and they usually went to a club with other au pairs on their days off. Although au pairs brought a little of their culture into the family, making the occasional foreign dish, plaiting her hair in the Scandinavian style, and teaching her a few words of Swedish, very little remained after they left. None stayed in touch beyond sending an occasional Christmas card or returned to visit again: 'It wasn't that sort of relationship. It wasn't ever "you must come and see us".'

Yet for some mothers, the outside lives of au pairs were part of their attraction. Lillian, the Canadian academic, was used to having help in the house as her own parents, who were from 'modest backgrounds', had moved into the middle classes and employed maids and household helps when she was a child. Historian Ross McKibbin argued that middle-class families like Lillian's in small houses with maids living on top of them felt some relief after the collapse of domestic service after 1940 because 'it re-established the privacy of middle-class life'.[39] The enforced intimacy of sharing a house with a servant might have been difficult at times,[40] but, for Lillian, sharing her home with au pairs from rural farming communities in Denmark offered considerable benefits.

Having an au pair was not simply a cheap way of getting the housework done, but was also a chance to learn about Danish life and customs. Lillian liked to listen to their stories, and their company offered her relief from loneliness. She was also repeating a pattern in her own family history. As a housewife in the 1940s, Lillian's mother had been lonely and become attached to Anna-Maria, a working-class Italian university student who had helped in their house in the country. As a young girl Lillian had also been fond of Anna-Maria and was much closer to her than she could have been to any of the maids.

The outside lives of foreign nannies and au pairs in short-term jobs were not easily shared with employing families, and chances to learn more about an au pair's country of origin and culture could easily be missed. While Lillian enjoyed the company of young women from a different culture, Stella's story shows a more limited social and emotional investment in their au pairs, which did not include intimacy or long-term involvement. While Fiona learned a lot about Jewish culture and Israeli politics from her host family, the attractions of working abroad had much less to do with time spent with the children than with her social life and friends she made away from her job.

NANNIES' FRIENDSHIPS

Nannies were in particular need of friends because the job could be very lonely. Most nannies who I interviewed made this point, and it was also a frequent complaint in letters to magazines. Loneliness was often a catalyst for nannies to move to another job, bringing them nearer to family and friends or offering them better opportunities for a social life. The editor of *Nursery World* saw the magazine as having a role to play in helping nannies make friends, not only through the correspondence column 'Over the teacups' but also through the '*Nursery World* Friendship League' set up in 1926. Its aim was to put nannies and mothers (with or without nannies) living in the same neighbourhood in touch with one another 'so that they might go ·for walks together and find companionship for themselves and possibly also for their children'.[41] Nannies regularly wrote to this column from all over Britain, a service which continued until after the Second World War. They were most commonly looking for someone to share off-duty time and/or afternoon walks with the children but, as with any lonely hearts column, it is not possible to tell how successful they were in finding friends in this way. Nannies who trained together found another way of combating loneliness. They maintained friendships by chain letters which were sent round the group and added to by each member, with some groups also having annual get-togethers, a practice that often lasted into old age.

Au pairs often had more structured opportunities than nannies to socialise with others in their off-duty hours, particularly if they lived in London or a sizable town. Not only might they meet other au pairs in the English language classes they attended, but organisations set up to provide friendship and leisure activities encouraged them to join

THE NURSERY WORLD

"The Nursery World" Friendship League

Enquiries from nurses wishing to be put in touch with others living in the same neighbourhood or to correspond with nurses living abroad will be published in this column FREE OF CHARGE.

When replying, will you please enclose your letter in a stamped unaddressed envelope with N.W.F.L. No.— (whatever number you are answering) in the top left-hand corner, and forward it in another envelope to the Editor, " The Nursery World " Friendship League, Bouverie House, Fleet Street, E.C.4.

N.W.F.L. No. 1733 (Dorking or Guildford).—Nannie, aged 20, would very much like to meet another nannie of the same age for half-days. Very fond of all amusements.

N.W.F.L. No. 1736 (Willesden Green).—Nurse (22) would like to meet another for daily walks. Charges aged 3 and 6 years.

N.W.F.L. No. 1737 (Broughton Park, Manchester).— Hospital-trained nurse (22), with sole charge of baby, aged 7 months, would like to meet another for walks and off-duty. Fond of all amusements.

N.W.F.L. No. 1740 (Esher).—College-trained nurse would like to meet another college nurse for occasional afternoon walks. Charge aged 13 months.

N.W.F.L. No. 1741 (Sheffield).—Nursery governess (21) would like to meet another governess or lady nurse for half-days. Fond of all amusements and sport and would like to join a club or dramatic society.

N.W.F.L. No. 1744 (Blackdown).—Nannie (15½) would like to meet another nannie for off-duty in or near Aldershot.

N.W.F.L. No. 1745 (Farnham or Winchester).—Nurse (24) would like to meet another for off-duty. Keen on all forms of amusement.

Nursery World Friendship League. *Courtesy of* Nursery World churches and youth clubs. In some London boroughs, activities were targeted specifically at au pairs. For example, in 1962 Hendon Borough Council gave an annual grant of £25 to support clubs for foreign girls which met during the afternoons from 4 p.m. to 6 p.m. in church halls throughout the borough and included programmes of talks, film shows and quizzes.[42]

Nannies in towns might readily find others to go out with in the evenings. But for those who were given little time off or found it difficult to synchronise off-duty hours, socialising with other nannies in parks such as Kensington Gardens was the simplest way to find friends. This habit was often formed in childhood when they had taken the babies they minded out in prams in a gang with other girls. They continued this practice later in life, gaining companionship and sociability in what was often quite a lonely job. For some it could be a lifeline; they greatly enjoyed gossiping and comparing their jobs with others in similar positions. But nanny networks were often hierarchical, confined to nannies of similar ages and backgrounds and excluding nursemaids, who were expected to mix socially with servants. When he lived with his grandparents in Windsor during the Second World War, Tim remembered his nanny, Agnes, getting together with a whole crowd of other nannies, 'Nanny Lothian, Nanny Dickson, Nanny this, that and the other', while he danced and sang 'strange songs' with the other children. But if she met children on a walk with a nursemaid rather than a nanny, she refused to speak to them. Such snobbery may explain why Vera, daughter of a Welsh miner who became a Kensington nanny in the 1930s and had enjoyed being part of the pram parade, chose to spend her days off alone rather than making arrangements to meet other nannies in the park.

Nannies living in the country had fewer choices of friends and were often lonelier, particularly if they considered themselves a cut above the servant classes. Their employers' attempts to find friends for them did not always work well. Alison described an outing between mismatched nannies when she was working on the Isle of Wight that ended when she suggested having tea at home and her companion was determined to go to a pub where she could 'meet fellas'. When Alison explained that she could not understand why anyone would want to buy tea out when she could have it at home, her companion responded, 'You'll never meet a fella if you don't go into a pub'. Alison did not wish to meet the sort of men who frequented pubs.

Nannies working for British families in non-European countries, where racial sensitivities were more salient than class barriers, seem to have had the best social life. Nannies employed by officers in the armed services had the chance to go out with British military men as well as other officers' nannies. After a relatively quiet life in Britain, Ada had twenty-six other nannies to socialise with when the family was posted abroad to North Africa; she found a boyfriend for the first time and eventually became engaged. With little time apart from the children and so much responsibility, Ada valued her private life and outings with friends. But Matilda, the younger Robinson daughter, was less willing to allow her nanny a life apart from the family. Looking down from an upstairs balcony, she poured water over Ada and her boyfriend, who were sitting underneath, and was punished with a few sharp slaps.

Emily had a similar experience to Ada in Egypt, where she had a marvellous time going to dances and having lots of partners. But she had a much lonelier time in South America, where she was stuck looking after one very difficult child. For many nannies, friends and fun outside the job – or the lack of them – were as likely to make them want to stay in or leave a post as the relationships they made within it.

Nannies' family backgrounds, social connections and friendships away from the job shaped their lives and relationships with their charges as much as did conditions on the job. The links forged between nannies and their charges were often strong and could last a lifetime. But, however close they became, nannies' different social origins cast long shadows over these relationships, affecting the ways in which obligations were discharged or ignored. Nannies who remained in or closely connected to a household may have been much loved and thought of as 'family', but the rules governing the relationship were never quite the same as those among kin.

Some children and nannies failed or struggled to stay in touch with one another, meeting an array of barriers. These included the social prejudices of the children's parents, the claims of a nanny's relatives (including her husband and children of her own), and the needs of another employer's family which had taken precedence. Some nannies saw the job as temporary, wanting to move on to get a better job or to travel and make new friends. But aspects of themselves and their outside lives remained with the family. Children were not supposed to become overly attached, but a nanny's presence in the household often had long-lasting influences on those they left behind.

In Chapter 7 we look at a different kind of nanny influence which affected many more of the British population: the appeal of the fantasy nanny in fiction and film.

7

IMAGINARY NANNIES IN FICTION AND FILM

I very much liked the idea of having the sort of colourful nanny I'd read about in books … There was Eloise's 'Nanny' – an unflappable, loving stout British woman in bustled skirt with whalebone pins in her hair … Or the much skinnier and brightly attired Julie Andrews as both wunder-nanny Mary Poppins, or Maria the ex-ex-original guitar-playing nun turned nursemaid in *The Sound of Music*.[1]

The majority of the British population never employed or were cared for by a nanny and never worked as a paid carer. They based their conceptions of the tasks nannies did and the relationships they had with their charges and employers on fiction, particularly novels and films. Even families who had nannies compared their actual nanny with imagined nannies; this exercise was always interesting, could be instructive and even reassuring. I look at these fictional versions separately because they had a disproportionate influence on popular thinking. Small in number but great in weight, they deserve a chapter to themselves.

Only a few well-known novels and films feature nannies as central characters. We could almost count the really well-known ones in Britain (those whose reputation outlived their first appearance) on the fingers of one hand. But they figure in the background of many tales. Often known simply as Nanny, Nana or Nurse, they serve important purposes. Some were loving, comforting figures, representing a place of safety to which children could return. But they could also be restrictive. Trying, usually unsuccessfully, to prevent children growing up and achieving independence, nannies often replaced parents in stories as objects upon which to project feelings of frustration and rage. We rarely get much insight into the feelings of fictional nannies, but in adult fiction and films they occasionally emerged as characters in their own right. These sources offer views of nannies' motivations and engage with children's feelings of powerlessness in the face of uncomprehending adults, and they also speak to parents' concerns about giving up control of their children.

What makes all these stories interesting, whether famous or not, is the way in which they have helped to define our ideas about nannies more generally. Books were mainly consumed by middle-class audiences, with nannies in children's stories often loved as much by the adults who bought them as by the children who heard or read them. Films and TV programmes had a much wider reach. Whether nannies were angelic beings who loved children more than their parents and offered comfort and safety or annoying, even devilish, creatures who imposed senseless restrictions and at worst were harmfully neglectful, they seemed to rule the world. Yet the ways in which fictional nannies and their employers behaved changed in some important ways over the twentieth century, and we need to set each story in a wider context to understand why this was so.

THE NOT-SO-GOLDEN EDWARDIAN AGE

I begin with the anonymous nurse in Hillaire Belloc's satirical cautionary tale, 'Jim', which first appeared in 1907.[2] This rhyme tells the story of a boy who was eaten by a lion because he ran away from his nanny and is remembered fondly by many older people today who learned to recite it as children.[3] Its ironic ending, 'Always keep a hold of Nurse for fear of finding something worse', suggests that having a nanny was only marginally better than being devoured by a wild beast, and the nurse's smile in the original illustration to the poem, which shows her informing the parents of their child's fate, suggests she was not sorry he was gone.

The self-satisfied smirk on the face of Jim's nurse contradicts the picture of a selfless angel so common in childhood memoirs, a particularly

Jim's nurse informing his parents he had been eaten by a lion. Illustration to the poem 'Jim' by Basil T. Blackwood, *c.* 1907.

pervasive image in the mid-twentieth century. But this hostile portrayal of a nanny in a children's poem at the start of the century is not really so surprising. Upper- and middle-class children often had mixed feelings about being cared for by nannies from a lower social class than their own and resented being restricted to the nursery and having only occasional access to their parents. The fact that Jim was spoiled by his friends, given 'Chocolate with pink inside and little Tricycles to ride' and taken to the zoo for a treat only increased his frustration with being forced to stay with his nurse. While his dreadful fate was supposed to be a warning to children who misbehaved, it would certainly not have endeared nannies to its readers. It was the graphic description of a child being eaten by a lion that made the verse so popular, a gruesome demise that has appealed to children across the decades. The spoiled child, doting parent and hated nurse also appear in an anonymous rhyme published around the same time: 'Willie with a fearful curse threw the coffee pot at Nurse. As it struck her on the nose, Father said: "How straight he throws!"'[4]

The idea of a nanny as a place of safety, however disagreeable, was common in children's stories dating from this period. As restraining characters, nannies were the targets of children's abuse and bad behaviour much more frequently than mothers. Indian nurses got particularly poor treatment, reflecting racist and imperialist stereotypes that presented British culture as superior in every way to that of colonial subjects.[5] In Frances Hodgson Burnett's *The Secret Garden* (1911) the subservient ayah waited hand and foot on her charge. Fearful that Mary's crying would disturb her mother, she allowed Mary to get her own way too often and as a result shouldered the blame for defects in her character. So harmful was Mary's upbringing shown to be that the child was pictured raining abuse on her absent nurse who had the misfortune to be taken seriously ill:

> [Mary] pretended that she was making a flower-bed, and she stuck big scarlet hibiscus blossoms into little heaps of earth, all the time growing more and more angry and muttering to herself the things she would say and the names she would call Saidie when she returned. 'Pig! Pig! Daughter of Pigs!' she said, because to call a native a pig is the worst insult of all.[6]

Mary could only be cured of the faults caused by her Indian upbringing by being transported to England. Yet, rather than contrasting Indian ayahs with traditional English nannies, Burnett rejected the entire idea of a nursery regime. Instead, Mary was placed in the care of Martha, a hearty young servant girl from the Yorkshire moors, an area of England commonly believed to foster sturdy independence. Neither selfless nor subservient, Martha expected Mary to look after herself. As Mary became more self-reliant, she improved in health and temper, turning into a much nicer child than she could ever have been with her ayah in India.

Children's nurses were insulted by being called pigs in India, but in England even a dog could be a nanny. In the hugely popular play *Peter Pan* (1904), by James Barrie,[7] Nana the Newfoundland dog was the ultimate protector nanny who tried desperately to prevent the Darling children from being lured away to Neverland. Nana was trained by Mrs Darling to look after the children because her husband could not afford to pay a nurse, and the dog became a symbol of safety and reliability.[8]

She was the figure whom the children longed for when they found Neverland frightening. She stayed with the family long after they had grown up; by this time she had become the classic old retainer, coddled by her former charge, Wendy, who kept a bed for her in the nursery.[9] We can also see the advantages of Nana being a dog rather than human, as dogs tend to do as they are told, particularly when they grow old. If we consider Nana's human as well as her dog-like qualities, however, it becomes clear that Barrie's opinion of nannies was not much higher than Hodgson Burnett's. Nana was both a victim and the butt of jokes. Because Mr Darling thought she was getting above her station, lording it in the nursery and showing up his failings as a father, he fed Nana his son's nasty medicine and banished her to the kennel.

Barrie had a difficult relationship with his own mother[10] and idealised both Wendy and her mother as maternal substitutes for the boys who had lost their mothers. But Nana was depicted as a stereotypical childless spinster and as such an object of ridicule. She was taken in by the Darlings because she belonged to 'no one in particular'. Prim and interfering, she would peep into prams to make sure that careless nursemaids were looking after their babies properly and follow them to their

This early twentieth-century photo of a dog dressed as a nursemaid was probably inspired by a production of Peter Pan. *Copyright Chippix / Shutterstock*

homes to complain to their mistresses. She was also 'a lesson in propriety' and believed in old-fashioned remedies, contemptuous of 'all this new-fangled talk about germs'.[11] Like a Victorian old maid, she was redundant for most of the story, as all the exciting parts happened in Neverland where the children had to be resourceful and look after themselves.[12]

The marginalisation of nannies in *Peter Pan* and *The Secret Garden* must have struck a chord with many upper- and middle-class children who longed for holidays where they could escape from day-to-day nursery routines. It is little wonder that the most appealing stories show children getting away from nannies. Edith Nesbit's series of children's books, which have remained in print ever since they were written in the early 1900s, were part of this trend. These books also give insights into the social dynamics of Edwardian middle-class families, which to contemporary eyes do not reflect well on the children in the tales.

In Nesbit's books, the adults who counted were not nannies or nurse-maids but other characters, usually from the children's own background, who engaged with and learned from them, did not try to confine them, and played with them at their own level.[13] Nesbit's second marriage in 1917 was to a working-class sailor[14] but her stories depict a yawning social divide between the classes with children kicking against servants' authority and looking for ways to escape them. In *The Story of Amulet* (1906) the four older children are left in temporary care of their 'old Nurse' who fussed over her former charges. Although she spoiled them, they were miserable at the thought of staying with her and worried that she might prevent them from having any fun. As the youngest child Jane pointed out, 'We must get Nurse to see how old we are now or we'll never have any time at all.'[15]

In *Five Children and It* (1902), the same children were equally dismissive of their nursemaid Martha. Jane mocked her and her fellow servants' pretensions when she took their baby brother on an outing to visit a cousin: 'I expect they pretend they're their own babies, and that they're not servants at all but married to noble dukes of high degree, and they say the babies are the little duke and duchesses'.[16] Mocking nursemaids who aped their betters is a low point in the portrayal of nannies in children's stories.

The expanding number of children's books published in the Edwardian period marks the beginning of Britain's love affair with childhood. As families became smaller after the First World War and children's value to the nation rose, so also did the status of their caretakers.

NANNY KNOWS BETTER: CHRISTOPHER ROBIN AND *BALLET SHOES*

It took the war to make the British really appreciate the importance of infant life. The demise of so many young men and publicity about the high infant death rate woke the nation's conscience, and 'the contented child' soon came to be seen as 'the pillar of the State'.[17] Nannies' work was part of this wider mission, and they tended to be portrayed more positively in books published after the war. As trained children's nurses became sought after for their professional and personal skills, so too did nannies in fiction begin to engage more directly with children's feelings and desires.

A.A. Milne's collections of verses *When We Were Very Young* (1924) and *Now We Are Six* (1927) shows this new approach. Nannies in his poems were not repressive but sympathetic characters in tune with children's needs. Christopher Robin is an only child, more typical in this period than the five or more children in most of Nesbit's Edwardian tales.[18] His nanny is pictured in various poems taking him for walks, playing with him, and helping him find a beetle she had accidentally let out of a matchbox.[19]

In his memoir *The Enchanted Places* (1974), Milne's son Christopher, who was the model for Christopher Robin, endorsed his father's interpretation of his relationship with his nanny. Christopher remembered her as hugely important in the first nine years of his life, 'almost a part of me', and connected her with his teddy bear, immortalised in *Winnie the Pooh* (1926). We can see the influence of psychoanalytic thinking on Christopher's memories of his nanny, as he explained: 'When a child plays with his bear the bear becomes alive and there is at once a child–bear relationship which tries to copy the Nanny–child relationship'.[20] His father made similar connections in the poem 'Us Two'. As they stuck together holding hands and looking for dragons, Pooh was a comforting nanny for Christopher Robin, while the boy felt more courageous and grown-up by becoming a nanny for Pooh.[21]

Christopher did take issue with his father over the portrayal of his nanny in other parts of the book. In the poem 'Brownie', he was particularly critical of the lines, 'I think it is a Brownie but I'm not quite certain (Nannie isn't certain too)' and 'They wriggle off once because they're all so tickly (Nanny says they're tickly too)'. Far from seeing the nanny in the poem as reassuring and in tune with the child's fantasies, Christopher thought she was not really listening. He was determined that this image should not be associated with his own dear nanny:

What Nanny actually says on both occasions – and you can hear her saying it, not even pausing in her sewing, not even bothering to look up – is, 'That's right, dear.' Undoubtedly this is the truth about some Nannies. But as I hope I've now made quite clear, NOT MINE.[22]

So important was Christopher's nanny that her departure was traumatic.[23] In the poem 'Buckingham Palace', Christopher Robin's nurse Alice was 'marrying one of the guards', but nothing is said about what this event would mean for the child. An Oedipal fantasy, usually associated with a boy's rivalry with his father and emerging sexual desire for his mother, led the real Christopher to see the man who waited for many years to marry his nanny as a rival. Christopher begged her not to go and to marry him instead to no avail, and in the end she went.

During the interwar years, nannies might delay marriage for a few years, particularly if they had ageing parents to support. The shortage of men in relation to women after the First World War meant that a significant proportion of nannies would remain single and, in the 1930s, as times got harder and families were smaller, changes of job were common. The frequent comings and goings of nannies, as well as of parents in families who lived or worked abroad, intensified children's need for stories in which a nanny would always be there. This fantasy was realised most powerfully in one of the earliest girls' career novels, Noel Streatfeild's *Ballet Shoes*, published in 1937. This story appealed as much to lower-middle-class children, who would have never known nannies first-hand but still loved the idea of a warm motherly person who would never leave them, as it did to upper-middle-class children. The book was an enduring favourite, with the author still receiving fan mail nearly fifty years later, by which time it had sold over ten million copies.[24]

One of its central characters was Nana, a stout, comfortable, old-fashioned nanny who continued to look after her first charge Sylvia into adulthood and then took care of Sylvia's three adopted children, known as the 'Fossils', becoming the equivalent of a grandmother. On one level Nana was much like the classic Edwardian nanny. Sylvia remained 'in awe of Nana', who ruled the roost, insisting that the children be given nice sensible names, believing in having 'my nurseries to myself', and brooking no interference. She stuck to rigid routines, such as the conviction that 'nicely brought up children should be out of the house between 12 and 1 even on a wet day'.[25]

'An old-fashioned nanny', *Harmsworth* magazine, 1900.

At the same time, Nana was the driver of a new regime which eventually led the Fossil children out of the nursery into the world of work. When Sylvia ran out of money and could no longer afford to keep the children at school, Nana refused to be paid and suggested taking in boarders who helped to educate the children. She encouraged Sylvia to send them to a stage school so that they could earn their own living and help support the household.

Despite the reduced circumstances of many middle-class families, preparing their children for careers as performers was quite radical. Acting was now considered a respectable career, and stars of the ballet, theatre and screen attracted big audiences, but Sylvia had to be persuaded that her children should have stage careers and was convinced that Nana would disapprove. Nana, however, saw it as a way of solving their financial problems and allayed Sylvia's worry that the children were too young. She pointed out that 'little children grow up' and that she supposed that 'Anna Pavlova [a famous ballerina] was a little child once'.[26] When the youngest girl Posy was determined to go to Czechoslovakia to train at a famous ballet school, Nana agreed to go with her, enabling the child to realise her dreams.

What makes Nana such an appealing character is that she represents safety, order and love without too much restriction or control.[27] Nana's Edwardian origins did not make her any less popular with a late twentieth-century audience than she was in the 1930s. What could be better than an old-fashioned nanny who gave all her time to children without the distraction of a husband, encouraged their ambitions, and continued to be there to love and support them when they succeeded?

MARY POPPINS AND 'OTHER PEOPLE'S BABIES'

Another fantasy which attracted children in the 1930s was the idea that a nanny who had left would return. Mary Poppins, heroine of a series of children's books created by the Australian-born children's writer P.L. Travers, fitted this bill. So well-known has Mary Poppins become that her name is now shorthand for the perfect nanny. Yet the Mary Poppins in Travers's books was a much more contradictory and sometimes frightening figure than the popular image derived from the 1964 Walt Disney film. Like Nana in *Ballet Shoes*, the original character was a product of the Depression. The family, who lived in 'the smallest house in the lane', was plagued by financial anxieties.[28] After the Banks family's old nanny left without giving notice and the mother was helpless, Mary Poppins restored order. Yet she still left them at the end of every book, obliging them to cope alone until she came back, which she always did in the next book.

One reason for the books' popularity is that they gave expression to children's deepest fears, which explains the frequency of stories portraying children who have lost parents or other significant figures in their lives.[29] As journalist Caitlin Flanagan points out, these books all hinge on something fundamental: 'Is the person on whom a child relies for the foundation of his existence – food and warmth and love at its most elemental – about to disappear?'[30] The nanny who answered this question was a very different character from the reliable Nana in *Ballet Shoes* who never left. A much more complex and enigmatic figure, the original Mary Poppins represented the contradictions many children experienced in their relationships with nannies: not simply order and security, but also magic and adventure, as well as fear, sadness and grief.[31]

One of Mary Poppins' most striking characteristics was that nobody ever knew what she felt because she 'never told anybody anything'.[32] The children could never tell who she was, what she might do next, and what new and magical world she might take them to. Although she was often sharp and impatient and could be scary, she gave the children respect as individuals in ways their parents did not. They felt safe with her in the nursery as she tucked them into bed smelling of warm milk and toast. Mary Poppins created order and routine and gave children boundaries, always doing what she said she would do. She always knew best, representing the new order of nannies who would not defer to a mother's authority. She stood in clear contrast to Mrs Banks, who was an ineffectual, absentminded mother and something of a snob.

In the first book, Michael was worried about Mary Poppins' possible departure from the day she arrived, repeatedly calling out anxiously, 'You'll never leave us, will you?' One of the early signs that Mary Poppins would be a 'good enough'[33] mother figure to the children is that she knew he needed an answer and finally responded, 'I'll stay till the wind changes'.[34] When the wind finally did change, Mary Poppins kept her word. She departed without notice after giving Michael one of her treasured possessions. The effect of this on the Banks children was cataclysmic. Michael suddenly burst into tears: "'She gave it to me," he wept. "She said I could have it all to myself now. Oh, oh, there must be something wrong! What is going to happen? She has never given me anything before."'[35] Travers sensitively described the physical effects of the children's anxiety and their vain attempts to reassure one another. When Michael called his mother a 'cruel woman' because she had denounced Mary Poppins' sudden departure as 'outrageous', 'preposterous' and 'discourteous', the child shook his fist at her and wailed: "'Mary Poppins is the only person I want in the world"'.[36]

We might assume that this outburst would have stuck cruelly at his mother's heart, but Mrs Banks was merely baffled. Concerned only about finding a replacement, she showed no empathy or understanding of the child's distress. Travers was portraying a very different conception of the mother–child relationship than the one we hold today. Yet it would have been familiar to many mid-twentieth-century readers whose mothers were not their main carers. When Michael began to cry again it was not his mother who comforted him but his elder sister Jane. Denying her own sense of loss, Jane gave Michael the portrait of Mary Poppins which had been left under her pillow, whispering, "'You have it for to-night darling"', and she 'tucked him in just as Mary Poppins used to do.'[37] The real gift Mary Poppins gave Jane was a capacity to care. This legacy was reinforced at the end of the second book. As Mary Poppins prepared to leave the family again, she told Jane to look after her younger siblings and placed her hand on the pram, passing on to her young charge the skills of a loving nanny rather than an absent mother.[38]

Mary Poppins was popular with readers whose nannies had left because it offered them a fantasy that they would return. But the books' appeal stretched much further, including children who had never had nannies and those with nannies who did not leave. One young reader with a nanny she disliked but who stayed with her family for nearly fifty years explained why she found the series so compelling. She discovered Mary Poppins at the age of about 10 and wrote to Travers asking for more. To this unhappy child, the Bankses seemed like a shinier and cosier version of her own family and whatever was wrong with Mary Poppins seemed minor compared to all that was wrong, or merely missing, in her own nanny.[39]

A sadder image of a perfect nanny emerged during the 1930s in the poem 'Other People's Babies' by the playwright, humorist and social-reforming MP A.P. Herbert, which was published in *Punch* magazine and his collection *Ballads for Broadbrows* (1930). Herbert's own devoted nanny had stayed with the family after his mother died when he was only seven, and went on to look after some of his own children.[40] But Herbert was aware that this was not always the case. His wistful, humorous verse (which he later turned into a song) revealed the feelings of an elderly nanny who could not return to or stay with one family and tells more of the hardships of her life than the pleasures.

The 61-year-old nanny reflected mournfully that she had been mother to dozens of babies but none of them were hers and she was nobody's wife. Although she could boast that she had bathed 'the Honourable Hay', he did not remember her, and her hard work and long hours went unrewarded. She was given notice as soon as the babies could crawl and, unlike widows, had no pension.[41] The song was performed and recorded by the British actress Norah Howard in a revue staged by Herbert at the Palace Theatre in London in 1934.[42] It was a big hit, catching the public imagination around the time when the plight of elderly women deprived of the chance of marrying by the First World War was being brought to the nation's attention in a campaign to give spinsters pensions at the age of 55.[43] According to the author, it was still occasionally sung nearly forty years later.

NANNIES IN THE POST-WAR YEARS: FROM *BRIDESHEAD REVISITED* TO *NURSE MATILDA*

Nannies were in short supply during the Second World War, and the post-war advent of the welfare state did little to remedy the situation. Nostalgia for a lost golden age of nannies and concern about the new household order can be found in a number of adult novels. Perhaps the most famous of these is Evelyn Waugh's *Brideshead Revisited* (1945) whose account of the destruction of a pre-war English upper-class family and their stately home included descriptions of the family's faithful Nanny Hawkins. The youngest child, Sebastian, estranged from his blood relatives and carrying a teddy bear that represented his inability to grow up, remained deeply attached to his nanny into adulthood. She stayed in the house after the family had fled, her physical disintegration symbolising the demise of a whole way of life. When the hero Charles Ryder revisited the house during the war after it had been requisitioned by the army and found Nanny Hawkins still there, he reflected: 'She who had changed so little in all the years I knew her, had lately become greatly aged. The changes of the last few years had come too late to be understood [by the nanny]'.[44]

Nancy Mitford covered similar territory. In her partially autobiographical novel *The Pursuit of Love* (1945), an upper-class family who managed to avoid being evicted from their stately home were thankful to hang on to their nanny for a new generation of babies. The reverence with which the young mothers treated their shared nanny is shown by their willingness to wait on her in the absence of other servants, mending and washing and doing any necessary chores rather than looking after the children themselves. The narrator, wife of an Oxford don, made it clear just how unsatisfactory she thought the new nannyless households were:

> I have seen too many children brought up without nannies to think this is at all desirable. In Oxford the wives of progressive dons did it often as a matter of principle; they would gradually become morons themselves, while the children looked like slum children and behaved like barbarians.[45]

The welfare state had much more profound effects on British social and economic relationships than simply removing nannies and servants from middle- and upper-class households. It was at this point that nannies began to be associated with the state, the implication being that that too much protection was being given to its citizens. The social anthropologist Geoffrey Gorer made this connection in 1951 as he reflected on the significance of Mary Poppins. He pointed out how different Mary Poppins' charges were from the active children in Nesbit's Edwardian stories and regarded this shift as a reflection of changes in the English character. Passive children like Jane and Michael Banks, who had expected to be looked after and entertained by their nannies, were now expecting to be looked after by the government. Gorer suggested the welfare state was much like a nanny, keeping its citizens in order, arranging their lives, and giving them treats if they were good and obedient and did not try to take any initiative.[46]

In fact, the generation of children brought up without nannies but with free education, healthcare and orange juice were not quite as passive as Gorer believed. By the 1960s the idea of having someone to keep children in order seemed increasingly appealing, and fictional nannies had a higher profile than ever before. At the nadir in nanny employment rates, nostalgia for nannies peaked and the Hollywood star Julie Andrews made nannies famous in two hugely popular Academy Award-winning films, first *Mary Poppins* in 1964, quickly followed in 1965 by *The Sound of Music*. They were accompanied by a new series of children's books, *Nurse Matilda* (1964) and its sequels (reincarnated in the recent *Nanny McPhee* film series) which featured another nanny with a cure for children who misbehaved.

Nanny nostalgia was at its height when many middle-class mothers managed on their own or without full-time help. The welfare state did not extend to providing childcare; rather, mothers were urged to stay at home and look after their own children. Liberal parenting styles were common, as many mothers followed the new childcare expert Dr Spock's advice to be flexible and responsive to the child. But some found it hard both to treat children as individuals and to keep discipline and saw Spock's regimes as turning children into 'absolute horrors'.[47]

Christianna Brand, author of the *Nurse Matilda* stories, offered a solution for children who needed to have firm limits set on their behaviour. Daughter of a colonial family, Christianna spent many of her childhood holidays with her cousin Edward Ardizzone, who became one of the best-loved illustrators of children's books. They first heard the *Nurse Matilda* stories from their grandmother as cautionary Victorian tales told as a warning to naughty children. Many years later they retold and illustrated the stories for publication.[48] The books found an audience

in the 'naughty' 1960s generation by showing children with lax parental boundaries the value of 'tough love'. Spock himself embraced this
approach in the late 1960s, as he 'retreated from his early permissiveness
and advocated much stricter disciplining'.[49]

Nurse Matilda owed a debt to Mary Poppins, particularly in her habit
of disappearing at the end of each book. But the children she was sent
to tame were much naughtier than the Bankses, and their mother was
both ineffective and unwilling to believe her children could possibly
behave badly. Speaking to parents' fears that they might be overwhelmed
by their unruly offspring, Brand made the Brown family have so many
children that new ones were constantly appearing, interchangeable in
their naughtiness. Nor could the nannies hired by their parents keep
them under control. 'Not a week passed by but the fat nanny or one or
two of the starchy nurses or the French governess or the skinny little
nursery maid gave notice and had to be replaced by a new fat nanny or
starchy nurse or foreign governess or skinny little nursery maid.'[50] Nurse
Matilda proved to be the answer, teaching the children lessons by giving
them doses of their own medicine such as forcing them to carry on
eating when they gobbled their food until they were so full they cried
for mercy.

Nurse Matilda was much uglier than Mary Poppins, with rusty black
clothes, a bun, a potato nose, and a huge tombstone tooth. Yet, like many
monsters and witches in fairy tales, her ugliness was a cloak under which
she hid her true nature. And, just as Christopher Robin's nanny and
Pooh Bear were part of him, containers for the child's anxious feelings,
so Nurse Matilda carried the bad parts of the Brown children. They had
made her ugly, but she made them good. As they learned her lessons,
her ugliness gradually diminished and she was revealed as the beautiful, loving, but still firm nanny they all needed. Running exhausted up
a dark road, they finally called for her, 'and in that one moment – how
could it have happened that to each child it seemed as if those loving
arms came around him and he was lifted up gently and his weary head
cradled against a kind shoulder'.[51]

NANNIES MAKE THEMSELVES REDUNDANT

Hollywood exploited nostalgia for kind, loving nannies to the full in *Mary Poppins* and *The Sound of Music*. In the film, Mary Poppins is radically different from Travers's original character. Disney's young daughter first brought the stories to Walt's attention in the early 1940s. He had to fight long and hard to get the author to sign over the film rights, and although she finally approved the script she was far from happy with the final product. As Disney was aware, much of his American audience would have found the idea of a nanny bringing up children without any input from their parents unpalatable, so he changed the story in important ways, setting it in the Edwardian period but making it in tune with 1960s values.[52]

Not only was Mary young and pretty, but her job was to ensure that the family would never need a nanny again. Mrs Banks was distracted from her maternal responsibilities by her political activism in the campaign for women's suffrage. Mr Banks was a cold, authoritarian father who refused to heed the message that his children were running away because they needed parents to love them, rather than a strict nanny. The film was not simply nostalgic but critical of Edwardian upper-class values. It strongly backed the post-war ideal of a breadwinning father and a mother who stayed at home and did not need servants.[53]

The film can also be linked to the social upheavals of the 1960s, particularly middle-class women's discontent with being confined to the home. Feminist writer Betty Friedan described their predicament as 'a problem with no name' and gave them a public voice in her best-selling book *The Feminine Mystique* (1962). But *Mary Poppins* the movie rejected this view, showing the dangers of women's activity outside the home. Mary's job was done when she had reformed both parents and helped them take responsibility for their own children. At that point she left the family alone under the authority of a kinder, more compassionate Mr Banks, happily flying kites together in the park, a scene which reinforced the message about the importance of child-friendly fathers.[54]

The Sound of Music had a similar theme. Its heroine Maria was a former nun who found work as a nursery governess. Her self-imposed task was not to discipline naughty children but to help the Austrian von

Trapps recover from the disciplinarian regime imposed on them by a father who treated them like a military squad. Maria adopted the relaxed approach that was characteristic of the decade. She taught the children to act more like normal children, insisting that they wear play clothes rather than uniforms. Constitutionally unable to follow the rules of the convent, she was lively and spontaneous. Ultimately, she liberated the children and their father from the tyranny of Nazi rule. The final scenes which show the family escaping to freedom over the mountains would have been particularly appreciated by British and American audiences inculcated in Cold War ideology, who were terrified of being taken over by totalitarian regimes.[55]

Maria conveniently fell in love with Baron von Trapp, and the nanny was transformed into a wife and mother. Maria was of peasant origin, but her marriage into the aristocracy did not disturb relations between the classes any more than did Mary Poppins introducing the Banks children to chimney sweeps and bird-food sellers. Neither film was revolutionary, but their focus on nannies did not suggest a return to old-fashioned pre-war values. Some social levelling would have been seen as natural in the 1960s when the dominance of white, heterosexual, middle-class men was being challenged by social protest movements on all fronts. Rather than disrupting traditional hierarchies, both films used nannies as the key to bringing men back to the home. As heads of nuclear families, fathers (together with their wives and children) were shown to be the bedrock of post-war society, while nannies were ultimately redundant.[56]

NANNY AS THREAT: THE OLD MAID

At the same time that Julie Andrews was making young nannies famous, another equally well-known Hollywood star, Bette Davis, turned an older nanny into an object of fear. The Hammer horror film *The Nanny* (1965), based on an American novel by Evelyn Piper, was transposed into a British setting and related to British social issues. The plot centred around an elderly spinster nanny who allowed a child to die in the bath (a boy in the book, a girl in the film) and attempted to kill the child's older brother Joey. Both the book and the film subverted the romantic view of nannies serving several generations of the same family. This transgenerational nanny was very different from the comforting Nana in *Ballet Shoes*. Nanny (as she was known) had become too dependent on the Fane family and would not let go of Mrs Fane, Joey's mother, who had been her last child, infantilising her and making her weak and dependent, unfit to be a mother herself.

More sinister still was Nanny's relationship with Joey. The boy feared and hated her and knew she was trying to kill him. Nanny's psychological state is eventually explained in the book, and her motivations for wanting to murder Joey become clear:

> Mrs Fane is the perfect child because she would never not need Nanny. Or, she corrected herself, would be perfect except for the boy Joey. Because Joey would lose Nanny her last child. His presence would *banish* Nanny. He would force his mother to leave Nanny. How perfect otherwise … since Nanny wasn't up to the care of an authentic child – all that running after – all those modern ways which Nanny was too old a dog to learn. Yes, if there were no Joey, Nanny would have the perfect job which would last until she died.[57]

Yet this chilling scenario still does not tell the whole tale. Another explanation given in the film for why the nanny was so unbalanced can be linked to the social concerns of 1960s Britain. In a decade with rising numbers of single mothers, many of whom gave up their babies for adoption, the film showed the possible emotional consequences of having a baby outside marriage. For it turned out that Nanny was not simply a spinster with frustrated maternal instincts; she was an unmarried mother whose neurosis was caused partly by her abandonment of her own child.

Another important aspect of the film can be connected to post-war interest in children's mental as well as physical health. Joey was sent to a residential school for emotionally disturbed children, but the psychiatrist failed to diagnose his problems or make sense of his hatred of middle-aged women. Joey's parents were also out of touch with him. His stern authoritarian father and emotionally fragile mother, who was dominated by her nanny, were powerless to protect their son because they could not understand his behaviour or feelings.

As was the case with the other two 1960s films, the nanny's eventual departure (in this case to a mental institution) reunited a troubled family.[58] On the surface, *The Nanny* ended happily. But Joey's desperation to make his mother strong and well in the final scene is telling. Just as the 'nanny state' was alleged to be disempowering British citizens, so too Nanny's domination left Joey's mother disabled. As Joey told his mother he would look after her just as Nanny used to do, Mrs Fane's mournful face suggests that she would never fully recover and become a proper mother to her son again.

ABSENT MOTHERS

All the nanny films of the mid-1960s were in line with contemporary thinking about the importance of mothers' close relationships with their children. But broken or dysfunctional families could not always be mended by the return of a mother. In a decade with rising rates of family breakdown and divorce, fictional nannies, like some of their real-life counterparts, could become the only emotional refuge for children in the face of loss.

A trilogy of adult middle-brow novels, *Clothes of a King's Son* by Pamela Frankau, showed just how important a nanny could be, not as a replacement wife and mother, but as a permanent support for a family fragmented by death and divorce. In these books, Blanche Brigstock looked after the Adair children, whose mother had died and whose itinerant showman father was unreliable and often insolvent (much like Frankau's own). Brigstock, as she was called by the children, was the only secure mother figure in their lives. Like Nana in *Ballet Shoes*, she remained their anchor and moral guardian as the children grew into young adulthood.

Brigstock was in fact the alter ego of Frankau's much loved nanny Agnes, whose story of intergenerational care we encountered in Chapter 6, and to whom the author dedicated the first volume, *Sing for your Supper*. Always on call, with the children firmly at the centre of her life, Brigstock was unconditionally loyal to the Adairs. Like Agnes, she was waiting in the wings with no life of her own, ready to step in whenever

The author Pamela Frankau with her nephew Tim. *Courtesy of Tim D'Arch Smith*

she was needed. For example, during the children's holidays from boarding school, she came back to look after them. Unlike Edwardian children, who struggled to get away from their nurses, the Adairs could hardly wait to see Brigstock again. So important was she to them that after their father remarried, the youngest child ran away to live with his nanny and let the rest of the family go to the United States without him. [59]

H.E. Bates explored the feelings of a child who lost both his mother and his nanny in *The Distant Horns of Summer* (1967). This novel reflects the influence of Bowlby's and Winnicott's ideas on attachment: the child must have a 'good enough' mother, and discontinuity of care generates emotional difficulties. The story centres on James, a 6-year-old boy whose mother had left and whose father had gone abroad with a lover. It depicted the sad consequences when James was placed in the care of Gilly, an unhappy, inexperienced 17-year-old girl. While she was supposed to be looking after James, Gilly was seduced and abandoned by an older man and eventually disappeared (her suicide is hinted at but left to the reader's imagination). The consequences for James were traumatic. He had become attached to Gilly, who had accepted the child's need to talk to imaginary friends (who were more reliable and comforting than any of the adults in his life). Gilly's disappearance led to the return of his former nanny Miss Garfield, an unsympathetic older spinster who showed no understanding of James's feelings.

The most heartbreaking episode comes near the end of the book when James realises he has been abandoned by Gilly. Miss Garfield had refused to answer his questions, 'Where has Gilly gone?' and 'Why don't I have Gilly now?', and James was determined not to hold her bony, dry hand. Betrayed and with his trust in adults broken, when his father arrived home with his lover, waving with excitement as they got out of the car, James would not respond or even recognise them. [60]

NANNY STILL KNOWS BEST

The desire for a firm but loving nanny who would neither abandon nor betray children remained alive in the public imagination throughout the post-war period, and by the early 1980s nannies were being portrayed on television. The 1970s ITV soap opera about domestic service, *Upstairs, Downstairs*, did not include a nanny but another BBC historical drama set in the same period did. *Nanny*, starring Wendy Craig (who played Joey's mother in the 1965 film *The Nanny* and had the initial idea for the programme) was broadcast on Saturday nights. It ran for three seasons from 1981–83, attracted a very large audience and good reviews, and coincided with the beginning of a new wave of nanny employment.

The heroine, Barbara Grey, was one of the new breed of professional nannies who challenged both the traditional nanny and old-fashioned parents with progressive ideas and theories about children. Trained at a fictitious college (which the programme made clear was more advanced in its thinking than either the Norland or Princess Christian colleges), the child-centred nature of the training is obvious in the principal's advice to new graduates starting out on their first post. 'Children need to be wanted,' she proclaimed, and nannies must always remember that they are not there to replace the mother but to be her understudy.

Nanny Grey took this advice to heart as she progressed through several different jobs. She took both upper-class parents and older nannies to task for their lack of consideration for children's needs. Her liberal views on punishment, coupled with her willingness to reject rigid routines, play rowdy games, listen to the child's point of view, and allow children to reject unpalatable nursery food in favour of cake, all suggest the influence of post-war childcare theories. Most importantly, her attempts to get parents to pay more attention to their children can be linked to debates about distant fathers and working mothers which dominated the feminist and anti-feminist agenda in the 1970s and early 1980s.

So concerned was Nanny Grey about the quality of children's relationships with their parents and continuity in their care that she gave her opinion in no uncertain terms and, as a result, was either asked or chose to leave several employers. Her determination to be on the children's side even led her to threaten a mother who was having an affair. Nanny made it clear that she would tell her employer's husband unless she promised to give up some of her work as a design consultant and promote the long-serving nursery maid to become nanny in her place. In a different family, Nanny Grey facilitated the return of an older nanny to an unhappy little boy whose parents had told him she was dead, and took the father to task for ignoring and even hitting his son when he craved attention. In a third situation she expressed concerns about the adverse effects of a mentally ill mother beating and then kissing her son, which led the child to have masochistic desires rooted in a fantasy that his mother was a cruel nanny. [61]

This episode reveals the influence of Freudian psychology which often shaped interpretations of the nanny–child relationship in the 1970s and 1980s. In *The Rise and Fall of the British Nanny*, Gathorne Hardy (who later became consultant to *The Nanny* TV series) also drew attention to the erotic associations aroused by nannies. The supposed sexual availability of young nannies, as with other servants, has often been the subject of comic stereotyping. [62] For example, in the men's leisure magazine *London Opinion* a cartoon published on the eve of the Second World War showed two children in prams commenting on a nanny who was chatting up a soldier, with the caption, 'Does she know many soldiers?' 'Why, she could call the roll of the Brigade of Guards if they lost it any morning'. [63] By the 1960s, humour of this kind had coalesced in the figure of oversexed (usually Swedish) au pairs. Although in 1961 *Stranger on the Shore*, a BBC TV series featuring a French au pair girl, was family viewing, [64] by the early 1970s the figure of the au pair had become increasingly sexualised, verging on soft porn (as shown in the 1972 film, *Au Pair Girls*). [65]

Nanny Grey was young and attractive, but her love affairs were more prosaic and her sex appeal muted, never a threat to her employer's families or involving removing her clothes. In some ways she was the forerunner of today's Supernanny, who changes jobs frequently in order to keep the audience's interest and to educate new sets of parents. Grey often told parents how much she loved their children, and the children expressed love for her. Yet because her own feelings had to take second place and she was determined not to replace the mother, we never witness the kind of distress that so many nannies and children felt when they parted. Subordinating her own needs like a good angel, Nanny Grey moved on to reform another family.

Despite her disapproval of mothers spending too long in the workplace, Nanny Grey offered a new model for nannies and working mothers of the Thatcher era, and the series boosted the number of applicants at Princess Christian College.[66] Inspired by Wendy Craig's programme, the BBC news programme *Nationwide* ran a feature on nannies in February 1981, an era of high unemployment. It pointed out how desperate parents were to find nannies, with five times as many jobs on offer as applicants. But there was also some ambiguity in the programme's message, shown through an interview with a newly qualified Norland nanny in sole charge of a 5-month-old baby whose mother was a high-powered executive. The young girl was talked into admitting, that despite her need for a job, she didn't approve of mothers leaving their babies with nannies. Like Nanny Grey, she found it hard to hide her feelings from the parents.[67]

The doubts raised by the media towards the end of the twentieth century about the desirability of mothers leaving their children's care to others are voiced by a very different kind of nanny from the caricatures of old spinster nurses we saw at its start. Over the course of the twentieth century, as perceptions of children's needs changed, images of nannies in fiction followed suit. As old-fashioned nannies became rarer, and upper- and middle-class parents became more involved in their children's upbringing, so did fictional nannies become more understanding and less restrictive. When the mother–child relationship took centre stage after the Second World War and child psychology found a wider audience, nannies were shown both as useful deputies for mothers and their good angels.

Nannies loved and were loved by children and showed parents how to give their children a better standard of care. They also took children into imaginary, sometimes scary, worlds from which parents were excluded. At the same time, bad or inadequate nannies stood as stark warnings to parents that they should be paying more attention to their children. The love and care Nanny Grey gave to children, her understanding of their feelings, and her determination not to replace their mothers was powerful medicine. Above all it offered parents the reassurance that they could now leave their child in safe hands, because Nanny really did know best.

8

Epilogue
NANNIES TODAY

You've been very, very naughty.

(Jo Frost, Supernanny)

A bespectacled, black–uniformed nanny around 40 with her hair in a bun wagging her finger at a disobedient child, Jo Frost bears more than a passing resemblance to Mary Poppins. As Supernanny in the hugely popular Channel Four television series, she has tamed our children for the past ten years and keeps the idea that 'nannies know best' alive in Britain today. Yet the popularity of this programme, now exported all over the world, rests as much on ideas about nannies in the past as it does on our need for help in bringing up children today.[1] On one hand, Jo is a dominatrix (an image carefully engineered by the production company in the United States), the stern nanny who puts children on the infamous 'naughty step' (some parents went so far as to send in photos of their children looking miserable there).[2] On the other, she is the nice nanny who cuddles and is loved by children and whose sound advice on childcare makes parents feel safe.

As with many twentieth-century nannies, Jo learned on the job and has made a career out of looking after other people's children. She has inspired 'a mixture of devotion and derision': love for her 'warm manner and ability to transform families', ridicule for her combination of 'guile, babble and boundless enthusiasm', and criticism for her lack of a man

'You've been very, very naughty'. *Copyright Shutterstock*

or children of her own.[3] A softer, maternal side has been revealed in more recent photos, which show her with her hair down, and wearing sleeveless summer frocks, and in press reports in which she states that she still wants to get married and either have or adopt children of her own.[4] Perhaps her image contains these contradictions because we feel ambivalent about her: she doesn't simply offer parents lessons in childcare but represents their guilty wishes to get rid of their children, at least temporarily. Decca Aitkenhead pointed out in an article in the *Guardian* newspaper that what Supernanny ultimately offers, and what people evidently want, is a regime for making children less inconvenient:

'As the blurb on Frost's latest book puts it so succinctly, "Want your life back? You need Supernanny!"'[5]

The advice given by Jo Frost and another popular childcare guru, Gina Ford (an ex-midwife who is also criticised in the press for being childless), harks back to Truby King half a century earlier, stressing the importance of firm boundaries and regular routines and not allowing the child to get the upper hand. It is in striking contrast to the more permissive parenting styles promoted during the era of 'stay at home' mothers.[6] Frost and Ford have found a ready audience in a decade when nannies have been needed once again. In 2010, nearly two-thirds of mothers with partners and children under 4 were employed.[7] Although only the rich can afford full-time nannies, the employment of childminders rose steadily during the 1980s[8] and is common among working mothers of the professional and upper classes today.

These mothers are under new pressures. More likely to be mature women than younger mothers, they have high aspirations for their children but hold demanding jobs and work very long hours. In a competitive environment where women are supposed to be able to 'to do it all' and 'have it all', mothers often take out their frustrations on their nannies. The owner of White House Nannies, an agency in Washington, most of whose clients are in very high-powered positions, describes mothers expressing criticisms of their nannies much as British upper- and middle-class mothers did half a century ago. The fantasy these American mothers have of an English Mary Poppins-type trained nanny palls as they discover, 'the fancier your baby nurse, the harder it is to remember that you're the baby's mother.' They become desperate to get rid of 'the pedigreed Knightsbridge drill sergeant her clients had thought they hired to help them bond with their babies – instead of ordering them around in their own homes and nurseries'.[9] Personal stories of jealousy and rivalry between working mothers and nannies are also sometimes in the news in Britain, most often from the mother's point of view but sometimes from the nanny's.

Tensions of this kind have produced far more books about nannies in the last two decades than ever before. Rather than the nostalgic glimpses of a golden age in books like *The Years of the Nannies*[10] and the 'good' and 'bad' nanny films and novels of the 1960s, the media today presents a much wider range of images. Advice books such as *The Perfect Nanny* tell parents how to manage their nannies, while novels focus on strains and friction between nannies and employers or on romantic and sexual relationships with nannies (lesbian as well as heterosexual).[11] Many of these books are American in origin, but some have high sales in the UK. *The Nanny Diaries* (2002), in which a nanny vilified wealthy New York families who both spoiled and neglected their children,[12] was made into a TV series. It touched 'a hot cultural nerve' and launched an avalanche of other books which the *New York Times* described as 'showcasing complex and imperfect nannies whose personal problems intersect with thorny larger questions about race, class, immigration and parenthood'.[13]

One of the most popular recent books on both sides of the Atlantic is *The Help*, a partially autobiographical novel (also made into a film) which displaces current concerns about race, class and parenthood onto the past. Its heroines are black household helps in the American South during the early 1960s who, like nannies and ayahs in the British colonies, offered love and care to white children who often grew up to despise them. Helps were women like Aibleen who brought up seventeen kids and 'knew how to get them babies to sleep, stop crying, and go in the toilet bowl before they mamas even get out of bed in the morning'.[14] *The Help* was written by Kathryn Stockett, who had herself experienced this upbringing and who makes the character most like her the key to its plot, in which the helps are given the chance to publish their own stories. Stockett depicts the pride these women took in their domestic skills and their love for their charges, as well as their feelings of anger and powerlessness in the face of racism and exploitation. She exposes the dependence of mistresses on their maids and white mothers' neglect of their own children. Whatever the historical realities of these relationships, the story is powerful. Yet it is also lopsided; the mother's side of the story is never told.

A number of non-fiction books seek to give a realistic picture of nanny employment today by interviewing both mothers and nannies. *Perfect Stranger: The Truth about Mothers and Nannies* (2007) and *and nanny makes three: Mothers and Nannies tell the truth about work, love, money and each other* (2007) expose all-too-familiar conflicts.[15] Academic studies of nannies in the United States have offered explanations for these tensions. They show how motherhood and care have become commodified and highlight the unequal relationships between mothers and caregivers. Not all of these writers see nannies simply as victims of this system. Tamara Rose Brown's *Raising Brooklyn* (2008) argues that New York nannies today are creating strong links and support networks with others of their kind.[16]

While research on nannies in Britain is more limited than in the United States, investigations in both countries show many similarities but also some significant differences between nanny relationships and employment in the early and mid-twentieth century. Nannies are now more likely to come from another country and to be mothers themselves, often leaving their own children behind to be cared for by female relatives or neighbours. This pattern has created what sociologist Arlie Hochschild has described as a 'global care chain' in which nannies' love, time and energy are diverted from their own offspring (who are its rightful recipients but do not get the same level of care or attention) onto the children of their employers.[17] In the previous century, as was sometimes the case for ayahs who took British children home by ship, a nanny's children might lose touch with their mother for many years. Today, however, nannies can now keep in daily touch by Skype and email on a computer or smartphone,[18] giving them an illusion that they are still caring for their own children.

Another change is in the way in which children's relationships with mothers and nannies are valued. Recent research on attachment supports Bowlby's views that a child needs a warm, close relationship with a maternal figure and continuity of care in the early years.[19] Some mothers see nannies as giving their children that continuity and security more effectively than day nurseries and communal childcare, which are often believed to be second-rate in Britain. Yet there are also conflicts. Women's anxiety that if they leave their children they are not proper mothers can clash with their desire to achieve success in the workplace. Wealthy employed mothers have become more competitive and have high expectations of their nannies.[20]

As Rosie Cox explains, mothers now want nannies who 'speak multiple languages and who are able to play a range of musical instruments'. They have to 'supervise homework, take charges to myriad after-school activities and help them to feel at home with high culture in museums and galleries'. These activities are seen as necessary for children to achieve a competitive edge over their friends and classmates. As in the past, parents often consider the background of the nanny to be as significant as her qualifications. Nannies are often micro-managed, expected to record all their activities and sometimes watched very closely.[21] The advent of webcams makes surveillance by mothers easier than in the past. The supposed need for surveillance has been highlighted by cases of abuse, most notoriously the controversial case of 19-year-old British nanny Louise Woodward who in the United States in the 1990s was convicted of shaking to death a child in her care.

Despite the higher salaries and improved conditions that the 'best' nannies can command, a nanny's earnings must be less than the mother's in order for the mother to feel she isn't 'working for nothing'. A nanny's work will always have a lower value than a mother's. We can find many similarities with past practices in low rates of pay, long hours and demands for flexibility, with nannies being required to fit in with employers' hours and childcare needs. But because British nannies are now often mothers themselves, it is not just the nanny but also her own children who lose out. The fact that a father's salary is rarely taken into account in deciding if a nanny is affordable[22] also points to a perspective that is missing in this book and reinforces the widely held assumption that it is women, not men, who are responsible for the care of their children. The recent arrival of a male student at Norland College, dubbed a 'manny', and increasing numbers of male au pairs, coupled with statistics showing that one in seven families today have 'stay at home' dads, are signs that gender expectations are beginning to change.[23]

Interviews I did with a mother, Valerie, two nannies, Amanda and Sylvia, and Anna, a young woman cared for by nannies, reveal personal dynamics in the nanny–mother–child triangle that are remarkably similar to those fifty or a hundred years earlier. Nannies are still both insiders and outsiders in the family and split into 'good' and 'bad'. The impact of losing a loved nanny is still strong, and good transitions between nannies are as important as ever for children.

The polarisation of nannies into all-good and all-bad figures is particularly striking in the story told by Valerie. The first nanny, June, whom she employed in the late 1990s, was like an extension of herself, complementing her role as a mother and never feeling like a rival. She blended well into family life and fitted into all of Valerie's routines. June's departure was 'awful'. Valerie and the children labelled the nanny who succeeded her 'evil', which must have intensified their attachment to the lost nanny. This new nanny crossed boundaries in the family that June had never come near. Valerie felt threatened by her dishonesty (toys and jewellery went missing) and attempts to get too close to the family. Behaviour such as giving a child a cuddle, which was seen as 'natural' in June, was regarded with great suspicion as an inappropriate demand for love. Valerie compared her experience with this nanny to the film *The Hand that Rocks the Cradle*, in which a jealous nanny attempts to kill a mother and abduct her children. When she discovered that a previous employer had similar problems, Valerie not only sacked her 'evil' nanny but tried to ensure she would never work for any family again.

Nannies still struggle when they part from children they love and have conflicted feelings about leaving their jobs. Amanda had been particularly upset about leaving a child whose behaviour was so difficult he had 'a nanny a week'. This boy had been badly neglected by his mother and, while Amanda stayed considerably longer than the other nannies, she could not bear to stay in the job. Transitions between jobs were generally easier for Sylvia, who still works as a nanny. She was older than Amanda, had been trained, and had children of her own. She had good relationships with the families she worked for and knew how important continuity was for her charges. She usually stayed with children until they went to school and kept in touch with the families afterwards.

The account given by Anna suggests how easy it still is to ignore children's voices. The long line of live-in nannies who looked after Anna and her sister until the age of 12, many coming from abroad, prompted her to write a dissertation on the subject on the grounds that no one had written about nannies from a child's perspective before. Aware of the career opportunities it gave her mother (compared with those of mothers who stayed at home), Anna maintains that employing nannies is a good idea. Yet her reflections reveal the long-term costs to children of having so many nannies:

I knew them really well then, and now I just don't know them, and they'd kind of look at me and … Maybe they'd remember things that I don't remember. But then … I'd like to … talk to them about things that I don't remember, but I don't know how significant I am to them.

Anna's intimate knowledge of her nannies when she was a young child is very different from the limited contact she has today (some nannies found her on Facebook and still send her messages). Yet the value she places on their memories of her as a young child and her concern about just how important she was for them are messages we should not ignore.

Finally, we return to Ada and the Robinson family, whose relationships span a period of more than sixty years. The sporadic contact Ada had with the Robinsons after she married has changed in recent years. Meeting her youngest charge Nigel after he had become ill was bittersweet. Her joy was mixed with sadness that she had not been in touch with him before, and she was heartbroken to hear of his death not long afterwards. However, reconnecting with Matilda and Jane has been a happy and healing experience for all parties. Matilda remembered Ada as a ghostly presence, 'just a being who was around us, who was just there for us all the time'. Her older sister Jane recalled her nanny as 'somebody to cushion, somebody to relate to; you were never alone'. Jane kept in contact with her nanny by letter and phone, but Matilda had not. She was unsure how much Ada had loved her compared to her baby brother, and was dogged throughout her life by a deep sadness and disappointment that her mother had not looked after her in the way that she believed a mother should.

Visiting Ada again after the interview Matilda did with me and realising how much she had been, and still was, loved by her nanny, has helped Matilda understand and resolve those feelings. Their story – and those of the many other voices we have heard in this book – testify to the importance of nannies, not just for these individuals but for families throughout Britain, both in the past and today.

ARCHIVES

Bankes Papers, Dorset History Centre.
Baron Chelwood Papers, East Sussex Record Office.
Bowlby Papers, Wellcome Library, London.
British Cartoon Archive, University of Kent.
British Newspaper Library, Colindale
Census England, Wales and Scotland 1841–1911
Chamberlain Papers, Special Collections, University of Birmingham.
Desborough Papers, Hertfordshire Record Office.
Edwardians, UK Data Archive, Colchester, Essex.
Geoffrey Gorer Papers, Sussex University Special Collections.
National Institute of Housecraft Collection, West Glamorgan Archive Service,
    Civic Centre, Swansea.
Norland College Archive, Bath.
Nursery World, Hammersmith
Oglander Papers, Isle of Wight Record Office.
Oral evidence on the Suffragette and Suffragist Movements: The Brian Harrison
    Interviews, Women's Library, London.
Oral history interviews with parents, nannies and children, held by the author.
Overseas Au Pair Girls 1961–1965, London Metropolitan Archive.
Princess Christian College Archive, Greater Manchester Record Office.
Wellgarth Training School Records, London Metropolitan Archive.

BIBLIOGRAPHY

Anon, *Little Willies* (Boston, MA: Carol Press, 1911).

Ashford, B., *A Spoonful of Sugar, A True Story of Life as a Norland Nanny* (London: Hodder & Stoughton, 2012).

Attar, D., *Wasting Girls' Time: The History and Politics of Home Economics* (London: Virago, 1990).

Avebury, Lady D. (ed.), *Nanny Says (as recalled by Sir Hugh Casson and Joyce Grenfell)* (London: Souvenir Press, 1987).

Bailey, J., *Parenting in England 1760–1830* (Oxford: Oxford University Press, 2012).

Banerjee, S., 'Blurring boundaries, distant companions: non-kin female caregivers for children in colonial India (nineteenth and twentieth centuries)', *Paedagogica Historica*, 46:6, December 2010.

Bankes, V., *A Kingston Lacy Childhood: Reminiscences of Viola Bankes* (Stanbridge, Dorset: The Dovecote Press, 1986).

Barrie, J.M., *Peter Pan or the Boy Who Would Not Grow Up* (first published 1904).

Barrie, J.M., *Peter Pan: Peter and Wendy* (first published 1911).

Bates, H.E., *The Distant Horns of Summer* (Harmondsworth: Penguin, 1969).

Beddoe, D., *Discovering Women's History: A Practical Guide to Researching the Lives of Women Since 1800*, 3rd edn (London and New York: Longman, 1998).

Belloc, H., *Cautionary Tales for Children: Designed for the Admonition of Children Between the Ages of Eight and Fourteen Years* (London: Duckworth, n.d. (1920s?)).

Blaffer Hrdy, S., *Mothers and Others: The Evolutionary Origins of Mutual Understanding* (Cambridge, MA: Harvard University Press, 2009).

Bowlby, J., *Can I Leave my Baby?* (London: The National Association for Mental Health, 1958).

Bowlby, J., *Childcare and the Growth of Love* (Harmondsworth: Penguin, 1953).

Brand, C., 'Nurse Matilda' (1964), in *The Collected Tales of Nurse Matilda* (London: Bloomsbury, 2007).

Brendon, V., *Children of the Raj* (London: Weidenfeld & Nicolson, 2005).

Brown, T.M., *Raising Brooklyn: Nannies, Childcare, and Caribbeans Creating Community* (New York: New York University Press, 2008).

Buettner, E., *Empire Families: Britons and Late Imperial India* (Oxford: Oxford University Press, 2004).

Bull, A., *Noel Streatfeild* (London: William Collins, 1984).

Búrliková, Z. and Miller, D., *Au Pair* (London: Polity Press, 2010).

Burnett, F.H., *The Secret Garden* (London: William Heinemann, 1911).

Burton, E., *Domestic Work: Britain's Largest Industry* (London: Frederick Muller Ltd, 1944).

Butler, C.V., *Domestic Service* (London: Bell and Sons Ltd, 1916).

Cannon, C. (ed.), *Our Grandmothers, Our Mothers, Ourselves: A Century of Women's Lives* (London: Ogomaos, 2000).

Carey, T., *Never Kiss a Man in a Canoe: Words of Wisdom from the Golden Age of Agony Aunts* (London: Boxtree, 2009).

Chaney, L., *Hide and Seek with the Angels: A Life of J.M. Barrie* (London: Hutchinson, 2005).

Cohen, D., *Family Secrets: Living with Shame from the Victorians to the Present Day* (London: Penguin Viking, 2013).

Cox, R., 'The au pair body: sex object, sister or student?', *European Journal of Women's Studies*, 14:3, August 2007, pp.281–96.

Cox, R., 'Competitive mothering and delegated care: class relationships in nanny and au pair employment', *Studies in the Maternal*, 3:2, 2011.

Crawford, P., '"The sucking child": Adult attitudes to child care in the first year of life in seventeenth-century England', *Continuity and Change*, 1:1, May 1986, p.34.

Crosse, K., *Find, Hire and Keep The Perfect Nanny: A Parent's Guide* (London: New Holland Publishers, 2009).

Davenport-Hines, R., *Ettie* (London: Wiedenfeld & Nicolson, 2008).

Davidoff, L., *Worlds Between: Historical Perspectives on Gender and Class* (London: Polity Press, 1995).

Davidoff, L., *Thicker than Water: Siblings and their Relations 1780–1920* (Oxford: Oxford University Press, 2012).

Davidoff, L., Doolittle, M., Fink, J. and Holden, K., *The Family Story: Blood, Contract and Intimacy, 1830–1960* (London: Longman, 1999).

Davin, A., *Growing Up Poor: Home, School and Street in London 1870–1914* (London: Rivers Oram Press, 1996).

Davis, A., *Modern Motherhood: Women and Family in England c. 1945–2000* (Manchester: Manchester University Press, 2012).

Davis, S. and Hyams, G. (eds), *Searching for Mary Poppins: Women Write About the Intense Relationships Between Mothers and Nannies* (New York: Hudson Street Press, 2006).

De Courcy, A., *Debs at War: 1939–1945: How Wartime Changed their Lives* (London: Phoenix, 2005).

Delap, L., '"For ever and ever": Child-raising, domestic workers and emotional labour in twentieth-century Britain', *Studies in the Maternal*, 3:2, 2011.

Delap, L., *Knowing Their Place: Domestic Service in Twentieth-Century Britain* (Oxford: Oxford University Press, 2012).

Di Ciacco, J.A., *Colours of Grief: Understanding a Child's Journey through Loss from Birth to Adulthood* (London: Jessica Kingdom Publishers, 2008).

Dick, D., *Yesterday's Babies: A History of Babycare* (London: The Bodley Head, 1987).

Fildes, V., *Breasts, Bottles and Babies: A History of Infant Feeding* (Edinburgh: Edinburgh University Press, 1986).

Fildes, V., *Wet Nursing: A History from Antiquity to the Present* (London: Basil Blackwell, 1988).

Fildes, V., 'The English wet nurse and her role in infant care 1538–1800,' *Medical History*, 32, 1988, pp.142–73.

Flanagan, C., 'Becoming Mary Poppins: P.L. Travers, Walt Disney, and the making of a myth', *The New Yorker*, 19 December 2005.

Frankau, P., *Sing For Your Supper* (London: William Heinemann Ltd, 1963).

Frankau, P., *Slaves of the Lamp* (London: William Heinemann Ltd, 1965).

Frankau, P., *Over The Moutains* (London: William Heinemann Ltd, 1967).

Fraser, R., *In Search of a Past: The Manor House, Amnersfield 1933–1945* (London: Verso, 1984).

Freud, A., 'A two-year-old goes to hospital: scientific film by James Robertson', *International Journal of Psycho-Analysis*, 34, 1953, pp.284–7.

Freud, A., and Burlingham, D., *Infants Without Families: The Case For and Against Residential Nurseries* (New York: International Press, 1944).

Froebel, F., *Mothers' Songs, Games and Stories*, trans. Frances and Emily Lord (students' edition) (London: Mr William Rice, 1920).

Gardam, J., *Old Filth* (London: Abacus, 2004).

Garrett, E., Reid, A., Schürer, K. and Szreter, S., *Changing Family Size in England and Wales: Place, Class and Demography, 1891–1911* (Cambridge: Cambridge University Press, 2006).

Gibbs, M.A., *The Years of the Nannies* (London: Hutchinson and Co., 1960).

Giles, J., *The Parlour and the Suburb: Domestic Identities, Class, Femininity and Modernity* (Oxford: Berg, 2004).

Graham, P., *Susan Isaacs: A Life Freeing the Minds of Children* (London: Karnac Books, 2009).

Gregson, N. and Lowe, M., *Servicing the Middle Classes: Class, Gender and Waged Domestic Labour in Contemporary Britain* (London: Routledge, 1994).

Grenby, M.O., *Children's Literature* (Edinburgh: Edinburgh University Press, 2008).

Gunn, S. and Blee, R., *The Middle Classes: Their Rise and Sprawl* (London: Phoenix, 2002).

Hamlett, J., *Material Relations: Domestic Interiors and Middle-Class Families 1850–1910* (Manchester: Manchester University Press, 2010).

Hardyment, C., *Dream Babies: Childcare from John Locke to Gina Ford* (London: Francis Lincoln Ltd, 2007).

Herbert, A.P., *Ballads for Broadbrows* (London: Ernest Benn Ltd, 1930).

Herbert, Sir A., *APH: His Life and Times* (London: William Heinemann Ltd, 1970).

Herman, N., *My Kleinian Home: A Journey Through Four Psychotherapies* (London: Free Association Books, 1988).

Highsmith, P., *Eleven* (Harmondsworth: Penguin, 1970).

HMSO, Report on Post-War Organisation of Private Domestic Employment, Cmd. 6650 (London: HMSO, 1945).

Hochschild, A., 'The nanny chain', *American Prospect*, 19 December 2001.

Holden, H.M., 'The War Time Residential Nurseries at Dyrham Park', Final Report to the National Trust, January 2009.

Holden, K., *The Shadow of Marriage: Singleness in England, 1914–1960* (Manchester: Manchester University Press, 2007).

Holden, U., *Tin Toys* (London: Virago, 1986; 2013).

House of Commons Debates, vol. 239, 1930.

Howie, D., *Attachment Across the Life Course* (London: Palgrave, 2011).

Hufton, O., *The Prospect Before Her: A History of Women in Western Europe, vol. 1, 1500–1800* (London: HarperCollins 1995).

Hughes, K., *The Victorian Governess* (London: Hambledon Press, 1993).

Hunt, E., *Diary of a Suffolk Nurse* (Suffolk, England: Mrs Lainsin, Horringer (undated, *c.* 1968).

Hunt, F. (ed.), *Lessons for Life: The Schooling of Girls and Women, 1850–1950* (Oxford: Basil Blackwell, 1987).

Isaacs, S., *The Troubles of Children and Parents* (London: Methuen & Co., 1948).

Isaacs, S., *Children and Parents: Their Problems and Difficulties* (London: Routledge and Kegan Paul, 1968).

James, H., *The Turn of the Screw*)(1898), Project Gutenberg E-book No. 209 http://www.gutenberg.org/files/209/209-h/209-h.htm.

Kaplinsky, C., 'Shifting shadows: shaping dynamics in the cultural unconscious', *Journal of Analytical Psychology*, 53:2 April 2008. pp.189–207.

Kennedy, D.A., *The Care and Nursing of the Infant for Infant Welfare Workers and Nursery Nurses* (London: William Heinemann, 1930).

Kline, B., *White House Nannies: True Tales from the Other Department of Homeland Security* (New York: Tarcher/Penguin Group, 2006).

Lee, L., *Cider with Rosie* (Harmondsworth: Penguin, 1959; 1967).

Lewis, L., *The Private Life of a Country House* (Stroud: Sutton Publishing, in association with The National Trust, 1992).

Light, A., *Mrs Woolf and the Servants* (London: Penguin, 2007).

Longford, E., *All in the Family: Parenting the 1950s Way* (Stroud: The History Press, 2008).

Macdonald, C.L., *Shadow Mothers, Nannies, Au Pairs, and the Micropolitics of Mothering* (Berkeley, CA: University of California Press, 1954; 2011).

Maggs, C., *The Origins of General Nursing* (London: Croom Helm, 1983).

Mayer, M., *The Nannies* (New York: Dellacoret, 2005).

McBride, T., 'As twig is bent': the Victorian nanny', in A. Wohl (ed.), *The Victorian Family: Structures and Stresses* (London: Croom Helm, 1978).

McKibbin, R., *Classes and Cultures in England 1918–1951* (Oxford: Oxford University Press, 1998).

Mclaughlin, E. and Kraus, N., *The Nanny Diaries* (New York: St Martin's Press, 2002).

McLeer, A., 'Practical perfection? The nanny negotiates gender, class, and family contradictions in 1960s popular culture', *National Women's Studies Association Journal*, 14:2, summer 2002, pp.80–101.

Meering, A.B., *A Handbook for Nursery Nurses* 4th Edition (London: Bailiere, Tindall and Cox, 1964).

Meldrum, T., *Domestic Service and Gender, 1660–1750: Life and Work in the London Household* (Harlow, England: Pearson Education, 2000).

Merkin, D., 'Nannie dearest', in S. Davis and G. Hyams (eds), *Searching for Mary Poppins: Women Write About the Intense Relationships Between Mothers and Nannies* (New York: Hudson Street Press, 2006).

Miller D., 'Getting THINGS right: motherhood and material culture', *Studies in the Maternal*, 3:2, 2011.

Milne. A.A., *When We Were Very Young* (London: Methuen, 1924).

Milne, C., *The Enchanted Places* (Harmondsworth: Penguin, 1976).

Musson, J., *Up and Down the Stairs: The History of the Country House Servant* (London: John Murray, 2009).

Myrdal, A. and Klein, V., *Women's Two Roles: Home and Work* (London: Routledge and Kegan Paul, 1956; 1968).

National Council for the Unmarried Mother and her Child (NCUCM), Annual Report, April 1967–March 1968.

Nesbit, E., *The Story of the Treasure Seekers* (London: T Fisher Unwin, 1899).

Nesbit, E. *Five Children and It* (Harmondsworth: Puffin Books, 1902; 1959).

Nesbit, E., *The Story of the Amulet* (Harmondsworth: Puffin Books, 1906; 1959).

O'Keefe, D., *Good Girl Messages: How Young Women were Misled by their Favourite Books* (London: Continuuum, 2000).

Patterson, D., *The Family Woman and the Feminist: A Challenge* (London: William Heinemann, Medical Books Ltd, 1945).

Pear, T.H., *English Social Differences* (London: George Allen and Unwin, 1955).

Pearson, L., *A Nice Clean Plate: Recollections 1919–1931* (Norwich, England: Michael Russell Publishing Ltd, 1981).

Perrin, R., *Agriculture in Depression* (Cambridge: Cambridge University Press, 1995).

Piper, E., *The Nanny* (London: Secker and Warburg, 1964).

Plant, R., *Nanny and I* (London: William Kimber, 1978).

Pooley, S., 'Domestic servants and their urban employers: a case study of Lancaster, 1880–1914', *Economic History Review*, 62:2, 2009.

Plummer, R., *The Maid's Tale* (London: Coronet/Hodder & Stoughton, 2011).

Quennell, P. (ed), *Mayhew's Characters* (London: Hamlyn, 1951).

Raymond, D., 'A biography of Pamela Frankau', vol. 1. (unpublished autobiography).

Renarde, G., *Nanny State, Lesbian Kink* (New York: eXcessica Publishing, 2012).

Renton, A., *Tyrant or Victim; A History of the British Governess* (London: Weidenfeld & Nicolson, 1991).

Rutter, M., 'Maternal deprivation, 1972–1978: new findings, new concepts, new approaches', *Child Development*, 50:2, June 1979, pp.283–305.

Sayers, J., *Mothering Psychoanalysis: Helene Deutsch, Karen Horney, Anna Freud and Melanie Klein* (London: Hamish Hamilton, 1991).

Sayers, J., *Boy Crazy: Remembering Adolescence, Therapies and Dreams* (London: Routledge, 1998).

Schappell, E., 'The best laid plans', in S. Davis and G. Hyams (eds), *Searching for Mary Poppins: Women Write About the Intense Relationships Between Mothers and Nannies* (New York: Hudson Street Press, 2006).

Smart, C., 'Good wives and moral lives: marriage and divorce 1937–1951', in C. Gledhill and G. Swanson (eds), *Nationalising Femininity: Culture, Sexuality and the Second World War* (Manchester: Manchester University Press, 1996).

Snell, K.D.M., *Annals of the Labouring Poor* (Cambridge: Cambridge University Press, 1985).

Steedman, C., *Labours Lost: Domestic Service and the Making of Modern England* (Cambridge: Cambridge University Press, 2009).

Stockett, K., *The Help* (London: Penguin, 2010).

Streatfeild, N., *Ballet Shoes* (Harmondsworth: Penguin, 1936; 1975).

Streatfeild, N., *Gran-Nannie* (London: Michael Joseph, 1976).

Stretton, H., *Little Meg's Children* (London: Religious Tract Society, 1868).

Summerfield, P., *Reconstructing Women's Wartime Lives: Discourse and Subjectivity in Oral Histories of the Second World War* (Manchester: Manchester University Press, 1998).

Swan, J., '*Mater* and Nannie: Freud's two mothers and the discovery of the Oedipus complex', *American Imago*, 31:1, 1974, pp.1–64.

Szumsky, B.E., '"All that is solid melts into the air": the winds of change and other analogues of colonialism in Disney's *Mary Poppins*, *The Lion and the Unicorn*', 24:1, January 2000.

Thane P. and Evans, T., *Sinners? Scroungers? Saints? Unmarried Motherhood in Twentieth-Century England* (Oxford: Oxford University Press, 2012).

Thompson, T., *Edwardian Childhoods* (London: Routledge and Kegan Paul, 1981).

Todd, S., 'Young women, work and family in inter-war rural England', *The Agricultural History Review*, 52:1, 2004.

Todd, S., *Young Women, Work, and Family in England, 1918–1950* (Oxford: Oxford University Press, 2005).

Tomalin, C., *Jane Austen: A Life* (Harmondsworth: Penguin, 2012).

Truby King, M., *Mothercraft* (London: Simkin, Marshall Ltd, 1934).

Van Dijken, S., *John Bowlby, His Early Life* (London: Free Association Books, 1998).

Waugh, E., *Brideshead Revisited*, 4th edn (London: Chapman & Hall, 1945).

Wright, B., *A History of the National Nursery Examination Board* (London: Council for Awards in Children's Care and Education, 1999).

Young-Breuel, E., *Anna Freud: A Biography* (London: Summit Books, 1988).

Zeepvat, C., *From Cradle to Crown: British Nannies and Governesses at the World's Royal Court* (Stroud, England: Sutton Publishing, 2006).

Zweiniger-Bargielowska, I., 'Housewifery', in I. Zweiniger-Bargielowska (ed.), *Women in Twentieth-Century Britain* (London: Pearson Education, 2001).

NOTES

Author's Note

1 Blaffer Hrdy, S., *Mothers and Others: The Evolutionary Origins of Mutual Understanding* (Cambridge, MA: Harvard University Press, 2009).

2 Holden, U., *Tin Toys* (1986) (London: Virago, 2nd edn 2013, p.18).

3 Macdonald, C.L., *Shadow Mothers, Nannies, Au Pairs, and the Micropolitics of Mothering* (Berkeley, CA: University of California Press, 2011).

1 Introduction: Hidden Lives

1 Nannies were routinely called by diminutive forms either of their surnames or first names.

2 See, for example, Rose Plummer's personal testimony in *The Maid's Tale* (London: Coronet/Hodder & Stoughton, 2011).

3 Most of the participants' birth dates and nanny experiences fall between the 1920s and 1970s.

4 *Nursery World*, 21 April 1926. See also 'That old-fashioned nannie', *Nursery World*, 9 December 1925.

5 Holden, U., 'Miss Caryer and long ago days' (unpublished manuscript, 2009).

6 Bowlby, J., *Can I Leave My Baby?* (London: National Association for Mental Health, 1958).

7 Macdonald, *Shadow Mothers*, p.xi.

8 Hostler, P., *Nursery World*, 20 December 1956. *The Child's World* (1953; 2nd edn 1965) is a collection of Hostler's articles.

9 Interview with Amelia by author (1994).

10 Delap, L., 'For ever and ever: Child-raising, domestic workers and emotional labour in twentieth-century Britain', *Studies in the Maternal*, 3:2, 2011. See www.mamsie. bbk.ac.uk; accessed 1 May 2013.

11 Gorer, G., 'Nanny transformed' (1952), Sussex University Special Collections (thereafter SUSS) Manuscript Collections, Gorer papers. Box 70.

2 Living Inside the Mother–Nanny–Child Triangle

1   Interview with Beth by author (2011).
2   Davis, S. and Hyams, G. (eds), *Searching for Mary Poppins: Women Write About the Intense Relationships Between Mothers and Nannies* (New York: Hudson Street Press, 2006, p.xxi).
3   Email from Pat to author (2011).
4   Lewis, L., *The Private Life of a Country House* (Stroud, England: Sutton Publishing, in association with The National Trust, 1992, pp.12, 93). Lavinia Pearson, *A Nice Clean Plate: Recollections 1919–1931* (Salisbury, England: Michael Russell Publishing Ltd, 1981, pp.5, 31).
5   Pearson, *A Nice Clean Plate*, pp.5, 8.
6   Bankes, V., *A Kingston Lacy Childhood: Reminiscences of Viola Bankes* (Stanbridge, Dorset: Dovecote Press, 1986, p.22).
7   Wood, G. and Thompson, P. (eds), *The Nineties: Personal Recollections of the Twentieth Century* (London: BBC Books, 1993, p.128).
8   Ibid.
9   Bankes, *A Kingston Lacy Childhood*, p.20.
10 Ibid., pp.10–11. Alice died in 1907.
11 A former servant, Margaret Powell, had become famous touring the country reading from her autobiography. BBC TV series *Servants: The True Story Of Life Below Stairs*, episode 3, 'No Going Back', 10 December 2012.
12 Thompson, P. and Lummis, T., *Family Life and Work Experience Before 1918, 1870–1973*. See http://www.esds.ac.uk/qualidata/online/data/edwardians/introduction.asp; accessed 1 May 2013.
13 Ibid.
14 Lewis, *Private Life of a Country House*, p.93.
15 Colls, C., 'The ups and downs of a nurse's life', *Norland Quarterly*, December 1909.
16 Letter from Ivy Chamberlain to Austen Chamberlain, 8 December 1907, Cadbury Research Library: Special Collections, University of Birmingham, AC/2/26.
17 Herman, N., *My Kleinian Home: A Journey through Four Psychotherapies* (London: Free Association Books, 1965, p.19).
18 Avery, Lady D., (ed.), *'Nanny Says' (as recalled by Sir Hugh Casson and Joyce Grenfell)* (London: Souvenir Press, 1987, pp.13–18).
19 Pearson, *A Nice Clean Plate*, p.9.
20 'Tony Bowlby talking to Juliet Hopkins and Sadie Bowlby at the Old Rectory, Ozlworth', Wellcome Library, Archives and Manuscripts (thereafter WLAM), PP/BOW/N, 1–2 May 1991. Bankes, *A Kingston Lacy Childhood*, p.22.
21 Letter from Joan Kennard, 1 West Eaton Place, London, to her mother, Florence Oglander, Nunwell, Brading, 15 April 1909, Isle of Wight Record Office (thereafter IOWRO), Oglander Correspondence, OG/CC/2277E.
22 Lewis, *Private Life of a Country House*, pp.46–7, 94.
23 Pearson, *A Nice Clean Plate*, p.12.
24 Email from Noreen Torrey to author (2011).
25 Dick, D., *Yesterday's Babies: A History of Babycare* (London: Bodley Head, 1987, p.91).
26 1950s Silver Cross baby coach advert, 'Land of Lost Content' Museum. See http://www.edu.lolc.co.uk/wiki/index.php/Pram#Definition; accessed 1 May 2013.
27 Letter from Joan Kennard (c/o Miss Woodward), Villa d'Albret (St Malo), to her father, John H. Oglander, 27 September 1910, IOWRO, OG/CC/2318.

28 V&A Collections. See http://collections.vam.ac.uk/item/O571341/phedre-fashion-design-madame-elizabeth-handley/; accessed 1 May 2013.

29 Harriet Plummer to Lady Desborough, 26 May 1916, Hertfordshire Record Office (hereafter HRO). Papers of Lord and Lady Desborough, of Hon. Lady Salmond and of other members of the Grenfell family, including Julian Grenfell, with a large quantity of correspondence, 1802–1971, D/ERvC2086/52.

30 Lewis, *Private Life of a Country* House, p.13. Pearson, *A Nice Clean Plate*, pp.26–7. 'Combinations' were combined vest and pants with buttons at the seat, wool in the winter and cotton in the summer.

31 *Norland Quarterly*, Christmas 1926, No. 84.

32 *Nursery World*, 12 February 1936.

33 Pearson, *A Nice Clean Plate*, pp.26–7.

34 Lewis, *Private Life of a Country Houseouse*, p.13.

35 Interview with Tony Bowlby.

36 Herman, *My Kleinian Home*, p.19.

37 Pearson, *A Nice Clean Plate*, p.11.

38 Davidoff, L., *Worlds Between: Historical Perspectives on Gender and Class* (London: Polity Press, 1995, p.109); Swan, J., '*Mater* and Nannie: Freud's two mothers and the discovery of the Oedipus complex', *American Imago*, 31:1, 1974, pp.1–64.

39 Gathorne Hardy, J., *The Rise and Fall of the British Nanny* (London: Wiedenfeld & Nicolson, 1993, p.98).

40 Sayers, J., *Boy Crazy: Remembering Adolescence: Therapies and Dreams* (London: Routledge, 1998, pp.18–20).

41 Wolfe, F., 'Room for a child', *The Lady*, 30 August 1945.

42 Interview with Evelyn Phelps Brown by Sophie Bowlby (her niece), WLAM, PP/BOW/N.2.

43 Pear, T.H., *English Social Differences* (London: George Allen & Unwin, 1955, pp.199–200).

44 Pearson, *A Nice Clean Plate*, p.9.

45 De Courcy, A., *Debs at War: 1939–1945: How Wartime Changed Their Lives* (London: Phoenix, p.6).

46 See Van Dijken, S., *John Bowlby, His Early Life* (London: Free Association Books, 1998, Chapter 1). Bowlby developed these ideas further in his trilogy, *Attachment and Loss*.

47 Bowlby, U., 'Ursula's world', vol. 1, pp.51–2, WLAM, PP/Bow/p.4/3/2.

48 Light, A., *Mrs Woolf and the Servants* (London: Penguin, 2007, p.126).

49 Fraser, R., *In Search of a Past* (London: Verso, 1984, pp.4–5, 97).

50 Ibid., p.101.

51 Kaplinsky, C., 'Shifting shadows: shaping dynamics in the cultural unconscious', *Journal of Analytical Psychology*, 53, 2008, pp.189–207.

52 St Aubyn, The Hon. Mrs, 'About the modern nurse', *Nursery World*, 25 December 1925.

53 Dawber, J., 'Employers and Nurses', *Nursery World*, 30 December 1925.

54 Colls, C., *Norland Quarterly*, December 1909.

55 'Over the teacups', Miss Ritchie, *Nursery World*, 23 December 1925, p.112.

56 Bateson, J., 'A mother's advice to nurses: an answer in effect to "those interfering mothers"', *Nursery World*, 10 February 1926.

57 Interview with Pamela by author (2010).

58 'Over the teacups', *Nursery World*, 20 January 1926, p.208.

59 This information came from Sophia's sister, Betty.

60 Norma rejected a gardener's offer of marriage in the grounds that 'he was not good enough for her family'.

61 'Correspondence from employers', *Norland Quarterly*, December 1909.

62 Macdonald, *Shadow Mothers*.

63 'Letters from nannies to Mrs Beamish with news of Tufton and John CLW/1/6/2, n.d.', Baron Chelwood Papers, East Sussex Record Office.

3 Continuity and Change over Time

1   Fildes, V., *Wet Nursing: A History from Antiquity to the Present* (London: Basil Blackwell, 1988, p.2).

2   Ibid., pp.1–5.

3   The terms 'nurse' and 'wet nurse' were sometime used synonymously. See Bailey, J., *Parenting in England 1760–1830* (Oxford: Oxford University Press, p.214).

4   Fildes, *Wet Nursing*, p.10. Meldrum, T., *Domestic Service and Gender, 1660–1750: Life and Work in the London Household* (Harlow: Pearson Education, 2000, p.152).

5   Fildes, *Wet Nursing*, pp.10–11.

6   Bailey, *Parenting in England*, p.216.

7   Crawford, P. '"The sucking child": Adult attitudes to childcare in the first year of life in seventeenth-century England', *Continuity and Change*, 1:1, May 1986, p.34.

8   *The Complete Serving Maid* (1729) cited in Meldrum, *Domestic Service*, p.152.

9   Notebook/diary by Mrs Henry II, p.9, February 1787. Bankes Papers, Box 8C/76, Dorset History Centre. Porter was beer, generally considered safer to drink in this period than water.

10 Hufton, O., *The Prospect Before Her: A History of Women in Western Europe, vol. 1, 1500–1800* (London: HarperCollins, 1995, p.196); Crawford, 'The sucking child'.

11 Meldrum, *Domestic Service*, p.152.

12 Bailey, *Parenting in England*, pp.36, 216; Tomalin, C., *Jane Austen; A Life* (Harmondsworth: Penguin, 2012, p.6). See also Fildes, V., *Breasts, Bottles and Babies* (Edinburgh: Edinburgh University Press, 1986, p.202).

13 Fildes, *Wet Nursing*; Fildes, V., 'The English wet nurse and her role in infant care 1538–1800', *Medical History*, 32, 1988, pp.142–73; Hufton, *The Prospect Before Her*, p.197.

14 Davidoff, *Worlds Between*, p.109.

15 Nesbit, E., *The Story of the Treasure Seekers* (London: T Fisher Unwin, 1899, Chapter 1).

16 Lancaster had a large number of shopkeepers, artisans and white-collar workers but relatively few wealthy or professional families. Pooley, S., 'Domestic servants and their urban employers: a case study of Lancaster, 1880–1914', *Economic History Review*, 62:2, 2009, p.408.

17 Single (not currently married) men with children were three times as likely to employ servants in Lancaster as married men; Ibid., p.417.

18 Steedman, C., *Labours Lost: Domestic Service and the Making of Modern England* (Cambridge: Cambridge University Press, 2009, Chapter 8); HMSO, *Report on the Post-War Organisation of Private Domestic Employment*, Cmd. 6650, June 1945; Patterson, D., *The Family Woman and the Feminist: A Challenge* (London: William Heinemann, Medical Books Ltd, 1945, p.36).

19 McBride, T., '"As twig is bent": the Victorian nanny', in Wohl, A. (ed.), *The Victorian Family: Structures and Stresses* (London: Croom Helm, 1978, p.50); Davidoff, L., *Thicker than Water: Siblings and their Relations* (Oxford: Oxford University Press, 2012, pp.70, 376, n. 86); Davin, A., *Growing up Poor: Home, School and Street in London 1870–1914* (London: Rivers Oram Press, 1996, pp.4–5).

20 McBride, 'As twig is bent', p.50. 1899 [C.9346] Wages of domestic servants. Board of Trade (Labour Department). Report by Miss Collet on the money wages of indoor domestic servants, House of Commons Parliamentary Papers Online.

21 Pooley, 'Domestic servants and their urban employers', p.420.

22 Steedman, *Labours Lost,* Chapter 8.

23 *Wages of domestic servants* (1899).

24 Ibid., excluding nurse housemaids.

25 Wages in the rest of England and Wales and in Scotland were about £5 less on average.

26 Musson, J., *Up and Down the Stairs: The History of the Country House Servant* (London: John Murray, 2009, p.225).

27 Hamlett, J., *Material Relations: Domestic Interiors and Middle-Class Families 1850–1910* (Manchester: Manchester University Press, 2010, Chapter 3).

28 Davidoff, *Worlds Between*, p.112.

29 Hamlett, *Material Relations*, p.119.

30 On governesses, see Hughes, K., *The Victorian Governess* (London: Hambledon Press, 1993), and Renton, A., *Tyrant or Victim; A History of the British Governess* (London: Weidenfeld & Nicolson, 1991).

31 Hamlett, *Material Relations*, p.118; Delap, *Knowing Their Place*, p.93.

32 Women's Library 8/SUf/B/168a, Mrs Dorothy Adams interviewed on 4 August 1977 by Brian Harrison; 8SUF/B/166 Margaret Ridgeway interviewed on 16 July 1977 by Brian Harrison.

33 In the 1980s a set of bells was still working in a two-storey late Victorian house in Bristol with only three bedrooms, two reception rooms, and a modest sized kitchen and scullery.

34 Gunn, S. and Blee, R., *The Middle Classes: Their Rise and Sprawl* (London: Phoenix, 2002, Chapter 2).

35 James, H., *The Turn of the Screw*)(1898), Project Gutenberg E-book No. 209 http://www.gutenberg.org/files/209/209-h/209-h.htm.

36 Buettner, E., *Empire Families: Britons and Late Imperial India* (Oxford: Oxford University Press, 2004, p.43).

37 Banerjee, S.M., 'Blurring boundaries, distant companions: non-kin female caregivers for children in colonial India (nineteenth and twentieth centuries)', *Paedagogica Historica*, 46:6, December 2010, p.780.

38 Platt, K., *Home and Health in India and the Tropical Colonies* (1923), cited in in Buettner, *Empire Families*, pp.38–42.

39 Ibid., pp.53–5, 88. 'Mem-sahip in Bombay', *Nursery World*, 4 February 1943.

40 Brendon, V., *Children of the Raj* (London: Weidenfeld & Nicolson, 2005, p.163).

41 Fielding, A.M., 'The monkey', *Illustrated London News*, 15 November 1951, p.21, Issue 5873A.

42 Buettner, *Empire Families*, pp.55, 58.

43 Gardam, J., *Old Filth* (London: Abacus, 2004).

44 Duffell, N., *The Making of Them: The British Attitude to Children and the Boarding School System* (London: Lone Arrow Press, 2000).

45 This information was obtained by email from Amy's son (2010).

46 See Cannon, C. (ed.), *Our Grandmothers, Our Mothers, Ourselves* (London: Ogomaos, 2000, pp.49–51) for an intergenerational story reflecting these changes.

47 Plant, R., *Nanny and I* (London: William Kimber, 1978, pp.37, 66–7).

48 Garrett, E., Reid, A., Schurer, K. and Szreter, S., *Changing Family Size in England and Wales: Place, Class and Demography, 1891–1911* (Cambridge: Cambridge University Press, 2002, p. 1).

49 Holden, K., *The Shadow of Marriage: Singleness in England, 1914–1960* (Manchester: Manchester University Press, 2007, Chapter 2). In the 24–35 age group the 1921 census showed 11 marriageable men to every 9 marriageable women.

50 Ashford, B., *A Spoonful of Sugar: A True Story of Life as a Norland Nanny* (London: Hodder & Stoughton, 2012, p.181).

51 HMSO, Report on Post-War Organisation of Private Domestic Employment, Cmd. 6650, 1945, Table 1, p.25. Of the trained nurses and nursery governesses, 1 in 7 was over 55.

52 Gathorne Hardy, *Rise and Fall of the British Nanny*, p.182.

53 Rea, L., 'Four in the family', *Good Housekeeping*, June 1933.

54 See, for example, Truby King, M., *Mothercraft* (London: Simkin, Marshall Ltd, 1934, pp.4–5, 67).

55 Kennedy, D.A., *The Care and Nursing of the Infant for Infant Welfare Workers and Nursery Nurses* (London: William Heinemann, 1930, p.49).

56 Brendon, *Children of the Raj*, p.187.

57 Carey, T., *Never Kiss a Man in a Canoe* (London: Boxtree, 2009, p.103).

58 Graham, P., *Susan Isaacs: A Life Freeing the Minds of Children* (London: Karnac Books, 2009, pp.208–15).

59 Isaacs, S., *The Troubles of Children and Parents* (London: Methuen & Co., 1948).

60 This book was never published.

61 Bowlby, U., 'Happy Infancy', c. 1948, p.16. WLAM, PP/BOW/M.8.

62 Swan, '*Mater* and Nannie'.

63 Young-Breuel, E., *Anna Freud, A Biography* (London: Summit Books, 1988, p.35).

64 Freud A. and Burlingham, D., *Infants Without families: The Case For and Against Residential Nurseries* (New York: International Press, 1944); Sayers, J., *Mothering Psychoanalysis: Helene Deutsch, Karen Horney, Anna Freud and Melanie Klein* (London: Hamish Hamilton, 1991).

65 *Norland Quarterly*, 126, Summer 1941, p.2; *Nursery World*, 23 September 1943.

66 Hardyment, C., *Dream Babies: Childcare from John Locke to Gina Ford* (London: Francis Lincoln Ltd, 2007, Chapter 5).

67 *Nursery World*, 1 April 1943.

68 Judith Lewis found this to be the case in her research on the requisitioning of country houses during the Second World War (personal communication).

69 Burton, E., *Domestic Work: Britain's Largest Industry* (London: Frederick Muller Ltd, 1944, p.16).

70 *Report on the Post-War Organisation of Private Domestic Employment*, pp.6, 18–19.

71 Patterson, *The Family and the Feminist*, pp.36–7.

72 'Au pair', Home Office leaflet from Ministry of Information (undated, c. 1960s). Information for the Foreign Visitor and Worker issued by the Friends of The Island and the British Vigilance Association, April 1956, in 'Overseas au pair girls 1961–1965', London Metropolitan Archive (thereafter LMA), ACC/1888/026.

73 'Information for the Foreign Visitor and Worker'.

74 Delap, *Knowing Their Place*, pp.127–34.

75 See Búrliková, Z. and Miller, D., *Au Pair* (London: Polity Press, 2010).

76 Delap, *Knowing Their Place*, p.134.

77 Rachel Billington, foreword to Longford, E., *All in the Family: Parenting the 1950s Way* (Stroud: The History Press, 1954; 2008).

78 Myrdal, A. and Klein, V., *Women's Two Roles: Home and Work* (London: Routledge and Kegan Paul 1956; 1968, p.127).

79 This was also the case for widowers and some divorced men.

80 Smart, C., 'Good wives and moral lives: marriage and divorce 1937–1951', in C. Gledhill and G. Swanson (eds), *Nationalising Femininity: Culture, Sexuality and the Second World War* (Manchester: Manchester University Press, 1996, p.93). There was less than one divorce per thousand of the population in 1963; Myrdal and Klein, *Women's Two Roles*, p.24.

81 Davis, A., *Modern Motherhood: Women and Family in England c. 1945–2000* (Manchester: Manchester University Press, 2012, pp.39–40).

82 Although au pairs were not supposed to be left in charge of children, this rule was frequently flouted.

83 Gregson, N. and Lowe, M., *Servicing the Middle Classes: Class, Gender and Waged Domestic Labour in Contemporary Britain* (London: Routledge, 1994).

84 Rutter, M., 'Maternal deprivation, 1972–1978: new findings, new concepts, new approaches', *Child Development*, 50:2, June 1979, pp.283–305.

4 Nannies in Training

1 Interview with Sarah by author.

2 Hunt, F. (ed.), *Lessons for Life: The Schooling of Girls and Women 1850–1950* (Oxford: Basil Blackwell, 1987); Attar, D., *Wasting Girls' Time: The History and Politics of Home Economics* (London: Virago, 1990).

3 *Queen*, 5 July 1913; *Girls' Club Journal* (undated). Wellgarth Training School (Herafter WTS) Cuttings, LMA Acc/3816/07/07/001.

4 WTS Cuttings, *New Health*, April 1927.

5 *Norland Quarterly*, 1970, p.7.

6 Davidoff, L., Doolittle, M., Fink, J. and Holden, K., *The Family Story: Blood, Contract and Intimacy, 1830–1960* (London: Longman, 1999, pp.162–3).

7 For example, Stretton, S., *Little Meg's Children* (London: Religious Tract Society, 1868). An illustrated version was republished in 1905. See http://www3.shropshire-cc.gov.uk/etexts/E000109.htm#X01; accessed 1 May 2013.

8 Davin, A., *Growing Up Poor: Home, School and Street in London 1870–1914* (London: Rivers Oram Press, 1996, p.88).

9 Quennell, P. (ed.), *Mayhew's Characters* (London: Hamlyn, 1951).

10 Attar, *Wasting Girls' Time*.

11 *Report on Elementary Education*, PP 1899, LXXV, pp.451–3, 'Occasional work for wages by girls', cited in Beddoe, D., *Discovering Women's History: A Practical Guide to Researching the Lives of Women since 1800*, 3rd edn, Table 3.1, pp.68–9; Davin, *Growing Up Poor*, pp.166–9.

12 Ibid., p.153.

13 Storey, J., *Our Joyce* (1987), quoted in Davidoff et al., *Family Story*, p.208.

14 Attar, *Wasting Girls' Time*.

15 Butler, C.V., *Domestic Service* (London: Bell and Sons Ltd, 1916, pp.114–15).

16 *House of Commons Debates*, 21 May 1930, vol. 239, cc 414–5W.

17 Bi-Monthly Reports for Wales, includes Salford and Lincolnshire, 1967–1968, D/D NIH 4/3; Student record cards for Dan-y-Coed, Swansea, 1972–1978, D/D NIH 4/4; National Institute of Housecraft Collection, West Glamorgan Archive Service, Civic Centre, Swansea.

18 Unpublished memoir by Jenny Sabine.

19 *Nursery World*, 28 January 1943.

20 'A real war job', *Nursery World*, 28 February 1943.

21 Ashford, B., *A Spoonful of Sugar: A True Story of Life as a Norland Nanny* (London: Hodder & Stoughton, 2012).

22 Imperial War Museum Film and Video Archive, *Heirs of Tomorrow* (1945) UKY 540.

23 Holden, H.M., 'The War Time Residential Nurseries at Dyrham Park', Final Report to the National Trust, January 2009.

24 Wright, B., *A History of the National Nursery Examination Board* (Council for Awards in Children's Care and Education, 1999, pp.43–9).

25 *Nursery World*, 18 October 1956.

26 Lists of nurses in college newsletters show that by 1956 Princess Christian College had trained more than 1,200 children's nurses.

27 Stokes, *Norland 1892–1992* (Hungerford: The Norland College, 1991 pp.1–5)

28 Ibid., p.6.

29 Norland Testimonial Book (1893), NCA.

30 Stokes, *Norland 1892–1992*, pp.17–18.

31 Ibid., pp.18–19.

32 Ashford, *A Spoonful of Sugar*, p.67.

33 Princess Christian (hereafter PC) College Annual Report 1907, Greater Manchester Record Office (hereafter GMRO), M753, 2006/33 Box 1.

34 Stokes, *Norland 1892–1992*, p.109.

35 PC Annual Report 1907, p.6; Ashford, *A Spoonful of Sugar*, p.68.

36 *The Creche News*, February 1924; History of the Princess Christian College, p.5, GMRO, GB127, M753 2006/33 Box 1.

37 'The Women's Work Bureau', *Quiver*, August 1912, WTS cuttings Acc/3816/07/07/001; Biscoe, V., *300 Careers for Women* (London: Lovat Dickson, 1932, pp.162–3).

38 *Women's Employment*, 15 April 1927 and 1/30 August, GMRO, GB127, M753, Box 6.

39 'I remember', unpublished memoir by Dorothy Ada Borough, 9/9/2003, NCA.

40 WTS cuttings, *Birmingham Daily Mail*, 7 January 1910, and *Manchester Despatch*, 8 January 1910, LMA. Acc/3816/07/07/001.

41 Ibid., *Irish Catholic*, 31 December 1910; *Morning Leader*, 10 August 1911; *Manchester Guardian*, 22 November 1911; *Newcastle Evening Mail*, 8 December 1911; *Evening Standard* and *St James Gazette*, 25 June 1914.

42 Ibid., *London Teacher*, 4 July 1913.

43 Ibid., *Hampstead and Highgate Express* (undated), *c.* March 1915.

44 Ibid., *Hampstead and Highgate Express and Golders Green News*, 15 December 1978.

45 WTS, Work Record Book 1940 (courtesy of Nicola Harland).

46 Norland Testimonial Book, 1932.

47 Froebel, F,. *Mothers' Songs, Games and Stories*, tran. F. and E. Lord (students' edition) (London: Mr William Rice, 1920, pp.xxxv and xxxiii).

48 Sub-Committee minutes, 30 March 1926, 21 February 1933, GMRO, GB127, M753 Box 4.

49 The Princess Christian College: A History, 1910–1957, pp.6–7, GMRO, GB127, M753 Box 1.

50 Stokes, *Norland 1892–1992*, p.41.

51 Bankes, *A Kingston Lacy Childhood*, pp.22–3.

52 Freud, A. (1953), 'A 2-year-old goes to hospital': a scientific film by James Robertson.

5 Situations Vacant, Situations Wanted: Finding and Keeping a Nanny

1 National juvenile labour market statistics showed over a quarter of young women in 1925 and 1950 used family connections to find work. Todd, S., *Young Women, Work, and Family in England, 1918–1950* (Oxford: Oxford University Press, 2005, p.9).

2 Light, *Mrs Woolf and the Servants*, pp.124–6.

3 Todd, S., 'Young women, work and family in inter-war rural England', *Agricultural History Review* 52:1, 2004, pp.89–90.

4 Ibid., p.86.

5 See Summerfield, P., *Reconstructing Women's Wartime Lives: Discourse and Subjectivity in Oral Histories of the Second World War* (Manchester: Manchester University Press, 1998, Chapter 2).

6 *Queen*, 31 October 1914.

7 *Norland Quarterly*, March 1919, p.12.

8 Thane, P. and Evans, T., *Sinners? Scroungers? Saints? Unmarried Motherhood in Twentieth-Century England* (Oxford: Oxford University Press, 2012, pp.69, 118).

9 Interview with Rodney Bickerstaffe for *Sinners? Scroungers? Saints?* Rodney later became general secretary to the trade union Unison.

10 The National Council for the Unmarried Mother and her Child (hereafter NCUMC) Annual Report, April 1967–March 1968, p.14.

11 NCUMC, Annual Report 1959–60, quoted in Thane and Evans, *Sinners? Scroungers? Saints?* p.118.

12 Mrs Boucher continued to advertise in *The Times* and other magazines until the early 1960s.

13 Letter from Joan Kennard, Grosvenor Hotel, London, to her mother, Florence Oglander, Nunwell, Brading, I.W., 19 June 1910. IOWRO OG/CC/2309A.

14 Butler, *Domestic Service*, p.63.

15 de Gray, the Hon. Mrs, 'Finding a Nurse', *Nursery World*, 26 May 1926.

16 Delap, *Knowing Their Place*, p.33.

17 *The Lady*, 14 September 1905.

18 *Nursery World*, 30 December 1925.

19 *The Lady*, 1/15 April 1915.

20 Delap, *Knowing Their Place*, pp.106–17.

21 See, for example, *The Lady*, 27 January 1955, p.118.

22 Ashford, *A Spoonful of Sugar*, p.67.

23 *Nursery World*, 18 April, 27 June, 11 July, 19 September, 10 October 1946.

24 Ibid., 15 August 1946.

25 Ibid., 5 September 1946.

26 Ibid., 25 October 1956.

27 *The Lady*, 12 January 1905.

28 Delap, L., *Knowing Their Place: Domestic Service in Twentieth-Century Britain* (Oxford: Oxford University Press, 2012, p.133).

29 *Nursery World*, 27 June 1946.

30 Butler, *Domestic Service*, pp.33, 35–6, 50–1.

31 Delap, *Knowing Their Place*, p.86.

32 British Cartoon Archive, University of Kent, 'The trials of a nurse to the well-to-do' WH2251. 'Technical training in being a nursemaid', WH4742. See http://www.cartoons.ac.uk/; accessed 27 February 2013.

33 *Nursery World*, 15 August 1946.

34 Isaacs, S., *Children and Parents: Their Problems and Difficulties* (London: Routledge and Kegan Paul, 1948; 1968, pp.3–4, 48–50).

35 Although Bowlby's work on maternal deprivation was not widely circulated until the 1950s, Anna Freud's report on evacuation and wartime nurseries had been publicised in *Nursery World* in 1943.

36 'Childhood problems: parting from Nannie', *Nursery World*, 7 March and 21 November 1946.

37 Ibid., 21 November 1946, and 20 December 1956.

38 Ibid., 22 August 1946.

39 Hunt, E., *Diary of a Suffolk Nurse* (Suffolk: Mrs Lainsin, Horringer House (undated, *c.* 1986), p.43).

40 *Norland Quarterly*, March 1916, p.9; *Nursery World*, 15 August 1956.

41 NCA, *Norland Testimonial Book 1916–1940*.

42 WTS Records, Student testimonial book and correspondence. Acc/3186/07/03/001.

6 Life Beyond the Job

1   Delap, *Knowing Their Place*, p.94.

2   Light, *Mrs Woolf & the Servants*.

3   Bankes, *A Kingston Lacy Childhood*, pp.10, 15–16.

4   Children living in the country were usually healthier, which accounts for their higher survival rate.

5   Most other men in the parish worked in agriculture, with their wives and daughters employed in seasonal farm work and/or domestic service. GB Historical GIS|University of Portsmouth|Ingatestone SubD through time|Industry Statistics|Occupation data classified into the 24 1881 'Orders', plus sex, *A Vision of Britain Through Time* http://www.visionofbritain.org.uk/unit/10538373/cube/OCC_ORDER1881; accessed 4 July 2013.

6   Very few London girls went into domestic service in houses of the wealthy (see Davin, *Growing up Poor*, p.151). All the Bankes children were born in their London house.

7   Snell, K.D.M., *Annals of the Labouring Poor* (Cambridge: Cambridge University Press, 1985, p.387).

8   Bankes, *A Kingston Lacy Childhood*, p.3.

9   Davidoff, *Thicker Than Water*, pp.112–23.

10 Lee, L., *Cider with Rosie* (Harmondsworth: Penguin, 1959; 1967, p.28).

11 Perrin, R., *Agriculture in Depression* (Cambridge: Cambridge University Press, 1995, p.22).

12 Light, *Virginia Woolf*, p. 20. In 1901 Annie's father was 69 and widowed; one of his daughters kept house for him.

13 See Maggs, C., *The Origins of General Nursing* (London: Croom Helm, 1983, pp.42–8).

14 Laois Education Centre, Emo Court Project, 'Servants at Emo Court'. See http://www.laoisedcentre.ie/Dreamemo/servants/; accessed 1 May 2013.

15 Bankes, *A Kingston Lacy Childhood*, p.10.

16 Lawrie, P., Glengyle House, built by Rob Roy MacGregor ©2004. See http://www.glendiscovery.com/glengyle-house.htm; accessed 1 May 2013.

17 1891 census entry for 5 Huntly Gardens, Kelvinside, Lanarkshire. See also Glasgow West End addresses and their occupants, 1844–1915. See http://www.glasgow-westaddress.co.uk/Huntly_Gardens/5_Huntly_Gardens.htm; accessed 1 May 2013.

18 See Testimonial Book for Una Sheriff McGregor held in NCA.

19 It may have been compulsorily purchased, as Loch Katrine was a reservoir.

20 A report in *The Times* in July 1915 stated that Sylvia was travelling on the boat alone and narrowly escaped being deported via Ellis Island, but does not mention that she had a nanny with her.

21 *Norland Quarterly*, Christmas 1933.

22 Personal communication from Sylvia's godson, Ian Hamilton.

23 Raymond, D., 'A Biography of Pamela Frankau', vol. 1, unpublished autobiography.

24 Zweiniger-Bargielowska, I., 'Housewifery', in Ina Zweiniger-Bargielowska (ed.), *Women in Twentieth-Century Britain* (London: Pearson Education, 2001, pp.159–60).

25 Plant, R., *Nanny and I* (London: William Kimber & Co, 1978, pp.34, 66).

26 Ibid., pp.201–2.

27 Ibid., pp.202–3.

28 Hardy, G., *Rise and Fall of the British Nanny*, pp.28–30.

29 Davenport-Hines, R., *Ettie* (London: Wiedenfeld & Nicolson, 2008, p.101).

30 Letters from Ivo Desborough to Harriet Plummer, HRO, DE/RvC1130/134140.

31 Davenport-Hines, *Ettie*, p.260.

32 See Cohen, D., *Family Secrets: Living with Shame from the Victorians to the Present Day* (London: Penguin Viking, 2013, Chapter 3).

33 Letters from Harriet Plummer to Lady Ettie Desborough, HRO DE/RvC2086/107144.

34 Hardy, *Rise and Fall of the British Nanny*, p.30.

35 Letter to Margaret Harland, 20/3/1974 (courtesy of Nicola Harland).

36 'Au pair girls', from a special correspondent, *The Times*, 31 October 1960, p.15.

37 *Nursery World*, 28 April 1926.

38 For legislation in this area see MacDonald, I. and Toal, R., *Macdonald's Immigration Law and Practice: First Supplement to the Seventh Edition* (London: Butterworth's Law, 2009).

39 McKibbin, R., *Classes and Cultures in England, 1918–1951* (Oxford: Oxford University Press, 1998, p.61).

40 Giles, J., *The Parlour and the Suburb: Domestic Identities, Class, Femininity and Modernity* (Oxford: Berg, 2004, p.75).

41 *Nursery World*, 17 February 1926.

42 Youth Department Correspondence, 'Phone message from Mr Griffiths', 29 May 1962, LMA. 'Overseas au pair girls 1961–1965', ACC/1888/026.

7 Imaginary Nannies in Fiction and Film

1   Schappell, E., 'The best laid plans', in Susan Davis and Gina Hyams (eds), *Searching for Mary Poppins: Women Write About the Intense Relationships Between Mothers and Nannies* (New York: Hudson Street Press, 2006, p.126).

2   These tales were a parody of cautionary tales popular in the nineteenth century. Belloc, H., 'Jim', *Cautionary Tales for Children* (London: Duckworth n.d. (1920s?)) pp.9–16

3   See the Wondering Minstrels. At http://wonderingminstrels.blogspot.co.uk/2001/06/jim-hilaire-belloc.html; accessed 1 May 2013.

4   Anon, *Little Willies* (Boston, MA: Carol Press, 1911). An earlier version appeared in Smith, N.G. Royde (comp.), *The Westminster Problems Book* (London: Methuen, 1908).

5   Nelson, C., *Boys Will Be Girls: The Feminine Ethic and British Children's Fiction, 1857–1917* (New Brunswick, NJ: Rutgers University Press, 1991, p.119).

6   See Hodgson Burnett, F., *The Secret Garden*, Chapter 1 (London: Heinemann, 1911).

7   The dog's innate qualities as a nurse can be traced to Barrie and his wife Mary's own dogs, the Saint Bernard Porthos and the Landseer Newfoundland Luath, who became substitutes for the children the couple never had. The dogs joined in Barrie's games with the five young boys for whom he originally wrote the play, and Luath once even played the part of Nana on stage. Barrie believed that Luath was naturally cut out for domesticity, and that he should have been a nurse or, above all, a mother. See Chaney, L., *Hide and Seek with the Angels: A Life of J.M. Barrie* (London: Hutchinson, 2005, p.193).

8   Chaney, *Hide and Seek with the Angels*, p.236.

9   This happens in the final act of the play, written as an afterthought.

10 This was probably rooted in Barrie's childhood efforts to get his mother to offer him the love she had lavished on a favourite elder brother who had died young.

11 This description comes in the book version of the story first published in 1911. *Peter Pan in Kensington Gardens, Peter and Wendy* (Oxford: Oxford University Press, World Classics, p.71).

12 In the nineteenth century, spinsters were commonly deemed 'redundant', and it was suggested that they be shipped out to the colonies to find husbands.

13 See Grenby, M.O., *Children's Literature* (Edinburgh: Edinburgh University Press, p.128).

14 The Edith Nesbit Society. See http://www.edithnesbit.co.uk/biography.php; accessed 1 May 2013.

15 Nesbit, E., *The Story of the Amulet* (Harmondsworth: Puffin Books, 1906; 1959, p.16).

16 Nesbit, E,. *Five Children and It* (Harmondsworth: Puffin Books, 1902; 1959, p.42).

17 Hardyment, *Dream Babies*, p.151.

18 The Bastables, the other main family in Nesbit's stories, have six children. *The Railway Children* is an exception, with only three children.

19 Milne, A.A., *When We Were Very Young* (London: Methuen, 1924); Milne, A.A., *Now We Are Six* (London: Methuen, 1927).

20 Milne, C., *The Enchanted Places* (Harmondsworth: Penguin, p.41).

21 Milne, *Now We Are Six*. My thanks to Grey Osterud for making this last point.

22 Milne, *The Enchanted Places*, p.45.

23 It left him clinging to his father for many years as a substitute for the loved one he had lost.

24 Bull, A., *Noel Streatfeild* (London: William Collins, 1984, pp.142–3).

25 Streatfeild, N., *Ballet Shoes* (1936) (Harmondsworth: Penguin, 1975, pp.12, 53).

26 Ibid., p.41.

27 'Her character is similar to that of several other nannies in Streatfeild novels. All were a tribute to the author's grandparents' much loved nanny, whose life story Streatfeild eventually fictionalised in a book of her own entitled *Gran-Nannie* (1975). In Bull, A., *Noel Streatfeild*, pp. 36, 240. Other books that contain nannies modelled on Gran-Nannie are *The Whicharts* (1931), *Parson's Nine* (1932), *White Boots* (1931), and *Wintle's Wonders* (1957).

28 Flanagan, C., 'Becoming Mary Poppins: P.L. Travers, Walt Disney, and the making of a myth', *New Yorker*, 19 December 2005. See http://www.newyorker.com/archive/2005/12/19/051219fa_fact1?currentPage=all; accessed 1 May 2013.

29 Di Ciacco, J.A., *The Colors of Grief: Understanding a Child's Journey Through Loss from Birth to Adulthood* (London: Jessica Kingsley Publishers, 2008, p.50).

30 Flanagan, 'Becoming Mary Poppins'.

31 Pamela Travers's biographer, Valerie Lawson, suggested that Mary Poppins was the fantasy mother that Pamela longed for during her Australian childhood. She grew up with a harassed, preoccupied mother who was unable to cope with her children, much like the fictional Mrs Banks. Mary Poppins also contained elements of Travers's Great-Aunt Ellie who often cared for her as a child, a dominating but fixed and reliable presence in her young life.

32 Travers, P.L., *Mary Poppins* (London: HarperCollins, 1934; 1995, p.25).

33 This term was coined by psychoanalyst Donald Winnicott in the 1960s.

34 Travers, *Mary Poppins*, p.24, p.211, p.219.

37 Travers, *Mary Poppins*, p.222.

38 O'Keefe, D., *Good Girl Messages: How Young Women were Misled by their Favourite Books* (London: Continuum, 2000, p.137).

39 Merkin, D., 'Nannie dearest', in Susan Davis and Gina Hyams (eds), *Searching for Mary Poppins: Women Write About the Intense Relationships Between Mothers and Nannies* (New York: Hudson Street Press, 2006, p.208).

40 Herbert, Sir A., *APH: His Life and Times* (London: William Heinemann Ltd, 1970, pp.4–5).

41 Herbert, A.P., *Ballads for Broadbrows* (London: Ernest Benn Ltd, 1930, pp.13–15).

42 Herbert, *APH*, p.110.

43 Holden, *The Shadow of Marriage*, pp.34–5.

44 Waugh, E., *Brideshead Revisited* (4th edn; London: Chapman & Hall, 1945, p.302).

45 Mitford, N., *The Pursuit of Love* (London: Penguin Books, 1949), p.204.

46 Gorer, G., 'Nanny transformed' (1952).

47 Davis, *Modern Motherhood*, p.131.

48 Brand, C., 'Nurse Matilda', in *The Collected Tales of Nurse Matilda* (London: Bloomsbury, 1964; 2007, p.383).

49 Davis, *Modern Motherhood*, p.131.

50 Brand, 'Nurse Matilda', p.10.

51 Ibid., p.128.

52 Flanagan, 'Becoming Mary Poppins'.

53 McLeer, A., 'Practical perfection? The nanny negotiates gender, class, and family contradictions in 1960s popular culture', *National Women's Studies Association Journal*, 14:2, Summer 2002, pp.80–101.

54 Szumsky, B.E., '"All that is solid melts into the air": the winds of change and other analogues of colonialism in Disney's Mary Poppins', *The Lion and the Unicorn*, 24:1, January 2000, pp.97–109.

55 McLeer, 'Practical perfection?'.

56 Ibid.

57 Piper, E., *The Nanny* (London: Secker and Warburg, 1964, p.165).

58 In the book, the characters suffered a much darker fate.

59 Frankau, P., *Sing For Your Supper* (London: William Heinemann Ltd, 1963).

60 Bates, H.E., *The Distant Horns of Summer* (1967) (Harmondsworth: Penguin, 1969, p.267). Patricia Highsmith's short story 'The Heroine', published at around the same time, tells a similar tale, depicting tragic consequences when an inexperienced unhappy girl is put in charge of children (in Patricia Highsmith, *Eleven* (Harmondsworth: Penguin, 1970)).

61 *Nanny*, BBC, Series 1 (1981) DVD. (Acorn media UK, 2008).

62 Delap, *Knowing Their Place*, Chapter 5; Cox, R., 'The au pair body: sex object, sister or student?', *European Journal of Women's Studies*, 14:3, August 2007, pp.281–96.

63 *London Opinion*, May 1939.

64 It was much loved by single mother Hannah as a 14-year-old, as her 1962 diary testified; *Stranger on the Shore* (1961). See http://www.televisionheaven.co.uk/sots. htm; accessed 1 May 2013. See also Cox, 'The au pair body'.

65 See YouTube for a trailer of *Au Pair Girls* (1972): http://www.youtube.com/watch?v=JH5_ZukBo3o; accessed 1 May 2013.

66 Princess Christian College Annual Report 1981, GMRO, M753 2006/33 Box 1.

67 BBC Nationwide Norland Nursery Training College 1981 – Norland Nannies. See http://www.youtube.com/watch?v=JcTrTk2vfQk; accessed 1 May 2013.

8 Epilogue: Nannies Today

1 This series was imitated in the United States under the title 'Nanny 911'. It was followed by the series 'Extreme Parental Guidance'. She has also written several books of advice for parents.

2 'Jo Frost: nanny state', *The Independent*, Saturday 8 September 2007.

3 Ibid.

4 Ibid.; Oddy, J., 'I'd adopt if it finally meant being a Mum', *Daily Express*, 4 July 2011.

5 Aitkenhead, D. 'You've been very, very naughty', *Guardian*, Saturday 22 July 2006.

6 Davis, *Modern Motherhood*, Chapter 5.

7 *Working Mums*, 31 March 2011, online magazine. See http://www.workingmums. co.uk/working-mums-magazine/all/2453966/number-of-fulltime-working-mums-increases.thtml; accessed 1 May 2013.

8 Gregson and Lowe, *Servicing the Middle Classes*.

9 Kline, B., *White House Nannies: True Tales from the* Other *Department of Homeland Security* (New York: Tarcher/Penguin Group, 2006, p.50).

10 Gibbs, M.A., *The Years of the Nannies* (London: Hutchinson and Co, 1960).

11 For example, Mayer, M., *The Nannies* (New York: Dellacoret, 2005); Giselle Renarde, *Nanny State, Lesbian Kink* (New York: EXcessica Publishing, 2012).

12 Mclaughlin, E., and Kraus, N., *The Nanny Diaries* (New York: St Martin's Press, 2002).

13 Lee, F.R., 'Nannies Still Draw a Keen Audience', *New York Times*, 13 July 2010.

14 Stockett, K., *The Help* (Penguin, 2009).

15 Kaylin, L., *The Perfect Stranger: The Truth about Mothers and Nannies* (New York: Bloomsbury, 2007); Auerbach, J., *and nanny makes three: Mothers and Nannies tell the truth about work, love, money and each other* (New York: St Martin's Press, 2007). See also Davies and Hyams (eds), *Searching for Mary Poppins*.

16 Macdonald, *Shadow Mothers*; Tamara Mose Brown, *Raising Brooklyn: Nannies, Childcare, and Caribbeans Creating Community* (New York: New York University Press, 2008).

17 Hochschild, A., 'The nanny chain', *American Prospect*, 19 December 2001.

18 Miller, D., 'Getting THINGS right: motherhood and material culture', *Studies in the Maternal*, 3:2, 2011. See www.mamsie.bbk.ac.uk; accessed 1 May 2013.

19 For an overview, see Howie, D., *Attachment Across the Life Course* (London: Palgrave, 2011).

20 Cox, R., 'Competitive mothering and delegated care: class relationships in nanny and au pair employment', *Studies in the Maternal*, 3:2, 2011. See www.mamsie.bbk.ac.uk; accessed 1 May 2013.

21 Ibid.

22 Ibid.

23 'Will we ever be a Manny state?' *The Times*, 19 September 2012, p.16; 'I'm a home Dad and I like it', *The Guardian*, Family Section, 26 January 2013; Búrliková and Miller, *Au Pair*.

ACKNOWLEDGEMENTS

One of the difficulties in making acknowledgements is knowing who to include. Ideas have been discussed with and leads given by so many people that it would be impossible to name them all. An added problem is the cloak of anonymity under which most of my interviewees told their stories, enabling them to speak more frankly than if they had been named. The oral testimony at the heart of this book was a gift freely offered and I am deeply grateful for it. I learned an enormous amount; without it my work on nannies would have been so much less interesting. Rather than listing names and acknowledging some but not all of them, I am therefore offering heartfelt collective thanks to everyone who recorded interviews with me. I am similarly grateful to those who offered insights, information and suggestions or commented on papers or talks that I gave. These include members of my family, friends, acquaintances, colleagues, librarians and archivists.

A few people's contributions to the project have been of particular importance or pivotal in certain respects. Lesley Hall, who attended one of the first papers I gave on this subject at the Oxford Women's History

Network conference in September 2009, led me to the Bowlby papers (which proved to be such a rich and important set of sources) and put me in touch with Tim D'Arch Smith, nephew of the novelist Pamela Frankau. As well as recording his memories of their nanny Agnes, Tim shared photographs, lent me an unpublished biography of Frankau, helped me with census searches and took me to his nanny's grave. I made a similar trip to meet Ian Armstrong, who showed me the grave shared by his godmother Sylvia Fletcher Moulton and her nanny. Sadly the photographs I took on both occasions were not of good enough quality to include in the book. The clear and accurate professional service of transcribing the interviews undertaken by Sue Rodman was worth its weight in gold. So also was the voluntary help of Kelly Mullins, who assisted me with picture research at the end of the project, a time when I was in desperate need of support. Norland College and Nursery World generously opened up their archives to me and gave me permission to publish many of the images in the book; thanks especially to Katy Morton. A grant from the British Academy was essential in enabling me to pursue the project as it paid my research expenses and transcription costs. The research leave granted by the history department and my former employers at the University of the West of England was equally valuable at the writing stage.

Finally the ongoing support of my friends Janet Fink, Megan Doolittle and Leonore Davidoff has been invaluable. They read and offered advice on successive drafts of most chapters and, in Megan and Janet's cases, commented on a draft of the whole book. I thank them for their persistence in the face of my doubts and their belief in me. I am also deeply grateful for the careful reading and editing of the final draft by Grey Osterud and the proof check by Tracey Loughran, both of whom saved me from many errors. As always, my friend Helen Kendall has been my most important support and critic, offering advice and help at every stage of the writing and in every other aspect of my life.

INDEX

If you enjoyed this book, you may also be interested in…

All in the Family: Parenting the 1950s Way
ELIZABETH LONGFORD

Elizabeth Longford proves the truth of the old saying that Mother knows best, a theory that is being treated with renewed respect by many of todays experts in child-rearing. She cites from her own experience as the mother of a large family, and quotes from letters which she received from other parents. Written in a witty and entertaining style, All in the Family contains an abundance of practical advice that no parent would want to miss.

978 0 7509 5066 4

Our Baby for Mother and Nurses
J. LANGTON HEWER

Before Miriam Stoppard, and even before Dr Spock, there were few books with advice for new mothers. In the late Victorian and early Edwardian era, there was Mrs J. Langton Hewer's *Our Baby for Mothers and Nurses*. Full of useful information on everything from what to dress baby in to finding a baby's nurse, and from diseases to feeding, It was a veritable bible for expectant and new mothers and is as useful today, with much information still valid to the modern mother, but is also as an interesting record of how families lived a century ago.

978 0 7524 4234 1

A 1950s Mother: Bringing up Baby in the 1950s
SHEILA HARDY

Embarking on motherhood was a very different affair in the 1950s to what it is today. From how to dress baby to how to administer feeds, the child-rearing methods of the 1950s are a fascinating insight into the lives of women in that decade. In The *1950s Mother* Sheila Hardy collects heart-warming personal anecdotes from those women who became mothers during this fascinating post-war period. The wisdom of mothers from the 1950s reverberates down the decades to young mothers of any generation and is a hilarious and, at times, poignant trip down memory lane for any mother or child of the 1950s.

978 0 7524 6990 4

Royal Babies
ANNIE BULLEN

The birth of HRH Prince George of Cambridge, our future king, has been greeted with joy by the British public. This celebratory and beautifully illustrated guide commemorates this Royal birth and looks at the history of children of the monarchy from Queen Elizabeth II to her great-grandchildren. Age-old customs, ceremonies, christenings, toys and pastimes, nannies, nurseries and the Royal line of succession are also explored, presenting an illuminating portrait of Royal children through the ages.

978 1 8416 5436 2

Visit our website and discover thousands of other History Press books.

www.thehistorypress.co.uk